OLD ASSUMPTIONS,
NEW REALITIES

The Russell Sage Foundation

The Russell Sage Foundation, one of the oldest of America's general purpose foundations, was established in 1907 by Mrs. Margaret Olivia Sage for "the improvement of social and living conditions in the United States." The Foundation seeks to fulfill this mandate by fostering the development and dissemination of knowledge about the country's political, social, and economic problems. While the Foundation endeavors to assure the accuracy and objectivity of each book it publishes, the conclusions and interpretations in Russell Sage Foundation publications are those of the authors and not of the Foundation, its Trustees, or its staff. Publication by Russell Sage, therefore, does not imply Foundation endorsement.

Library of Congress Cataloging-in-Publication Data

Old assumptions, new realities : economic security for working families in the 21st century / Robert D. Plotnick ... [et al.].
  p. cm.
  Includes bibliographical references and index.
  ISBN 978-0-87154-677-7 (alk. paper)
  1. Working poor—United States. 2. Social security—United States. 3. United States—Social policy—21st century. I. Plotnick, Robert D.
  HD4901.O56 2010
  331.5'4—dc22

2010025153

The paper used in this publication meets the minimum requirements of American National Standard for Information Sciences—Permanence of Paper for Printed Library Materials. ANSI Z39.48-1992.

Text design by Suzanne Nichols.

RUSSELL SAGE FOUNDATION
112 East 64th Street, New York, New York 10065
10 9 8 7 6 5 4 3 2 1

OLD ASSUMPTIONS, NEW REALITIES

ECONOMIC SECURITY FOR WORKING FAMILIES
IN THE 21ST CENTURY

ROBERT D. PLOTNICK
MARCIA K. MEYERS
JENNIFER ROMICH
STEVEN RATHGEB SMITH
EDITORS

A WEST COAST POVERTY CENTER VOLUME

RUSSELL SAGE FOUNDATION • NEW YORK

CONTENTS

Contributors

MARCIA K. MEYERS is professor of social work and public affairs and associate dean for academic affairs at the School of Social Work, University of Washington, and director of the university's West Coast Poverty Center.

ROBERT D. PLOTNICK is professor of public affairs at the Evans School of Public Affairs and affiliate of the West Coast Poverty Center at the University of Washington.

JENNIFER ROMICH is associate professor of social work and associate director of the West Coast Poverty Center at the University of Washington.

STEVEN RATHGEB SMITH is professor of public policy and the Waldemur A. Nielsen Chair in Philanthropy at the Georgetown University.

SCOTT W. ALLARD is associate professor at the School of Social Service Administration at the University of Chicago.

ALISON EARLE is principal research scientist at the Institute for Urban Health Research at Northeastern University and co-director of the Project on Global Working Families.

JACOB S. HACKER is Stanley B. Resor Professor of Political Science and resident fellow at Yale University's Institution for Social and Policy Studies.

JODY HEYMANN is founding director of the Institute for Health and Social Policy and the Project on Global Working Families and holds a Canada Research Chair in Global Health and Social Policy at McGill University.

PAUL OSTERMAN is professor of human resources and management at the Sloan School of Management at Massachusetts Institute of Technology.

JODI R. SANDFORT is associate professor and chair of the leadership and management area at the Hubert H. Humphrey School of Public Affairs at the University of Minnesota.

MICHAEL SHERRADEN is the Benjamin E. Youngdahl Professor of Social Development at the George Warren Brown School of Social Work at Washington University in St. Louis, and the founder and director of the Center for Social Development at Washington University.

MICHAEL A. STOLL is professor and chair of the Department of Public Policy in the School of Public Affairs at the University of California–Los Angeles.

ACKNOWLEDGMENTS

The chapters in *Old Assumptions, New Realities* were initially presented at a conference co-hosted by the West Coast Poverty Center and the Nancy Bell Evans Center on Nonprofits and Philanthropy at the University of Washington in September 2008. The authors have revised the chapters to reflect comments from conference participants, two anonymous reviewers, and the editors, as well as the economic and policy changes that have taken place since the fall of 2008.

The West Coast Poverty Center and the Office of the Assistant Secretary for Planning and Evaluation in the U.S. Department of Health and Human Services sponsored the conference, with additional support from the Russell Sage Foundation and the Seattle Foundation. We would like to acknowledge the support and sound advice of David Harrison, Michael Brown, and Caroline Maillard of the Seattle Foundation and Suzanne Nichols, director of publications, and Aixa Cintron-Velez, senior program officer of the Russell Sage Foundation. The West Coast Poverty Center's program director Rachel Lodge, program coordinator Denise Novotny, and research assistants Bethanne Barnes and Shannon Harper provided invaluable logistical support for the conference and subsequent preparation of this volume. Ms. Harper also developed the figures in chapter 1.

The views expressed in this book are those of the chapter authors and should not be construed as representing the official position or policy of any sponsoring institution, agency, or foundation.

PREFACE

In early 2007, as we began developing the conceptual framework that led to a conference and this volume, housing prices were starting to plunge and there was some foreshadowing of the economic downturn to come. But the economy overall was still growing, and key economic indicators such as employment, the unemployment rate, and stock prices gave little cause for concern. By the 2008 conference and into 2009, public debate had turned to whether the country was facing a recession or a worldwide depression paralleling that of the 1930s, the economic cataclysm that gave rise to the foundation of the U.S. welfare state, the Social Security Act of 1935.

As this book goes to press, economic recovery is slowly under way, although unemployment remains high and consumer confidence low relative to much of the past few decades. The federal bailout of General Motors focused attention on the remains and future of the American manufacturing sector, as unemployed autoworkers compete with other out-of-work Americans for scarce jobs. Consumer spending is still depressed, more Americans than ever before rely on federal assistance to buy food, and many families with jobless workers are struggling to get by. Millions are reeling as housing values have plummeted; many have lost their homes entirely. These circumstances highlight the extent to which citizens' well-being and the health of the economy as a whole are intertwined.

The United States' demographic, economic, social, and policy realities have changed enormously since Congress enacted the Social Security Act seventy-five years ago. Contemporary realities are often at odds with the old assumptions about economic and social arrangements that motivated passage of the act and subsequent expansions of the American welfare state. This gap between old assumptions and new realities may be a fundamental reason why current policies have not kept up with the changes in the economic and social structure and, as a result, are failing to assure the economic security of many working-age adults and their children.

Given these premises, contributors to this volume who attended the Old Assumptions, New Realities conference assessed contemporary challenges to ensuring the economic and social security of working-age adults and their families and recommended revised or new approaches that would more closely align public policies with contemporary realities. Authors especially focused on low-skilled workers and low-income families because public supports are particularly important for these persons' well-being and because their experiences of the welfare state are revealing indicators of the robustness of the system itself. The Great Recession of 2007 to 2009, and the inadequacy of existing federal and state policies to prevent or respond to the ensuing economic and social dislocations, give even greater urgency to these questions.

CHAPTER 1

OLD ASSUMPTIONS, NEW REALITIES

MARCIA K. MEYERS, ROBERT D. PLOTNICK,
AND JENNIFER ROMICH

In an era of rapid technological change and continuing globalization of labor, capital, and product markets, old economic notions of a trade-off between "efficiency" and "equality" have been replaced by a more nuanced understanding of the interdependence of economic and social development. Governments in all industrialized countries balance economic impera-tives to increase the size, efficiency, and productivity of their economies, with social imperatives to promote individuals' productivity, economic opportunity, economic security, and social inclusion in their communi-ties. Although governments are charged with achieving these social goals for all populations in their countries, it is particularly critical to assure the health and security of working age adults, who as workers are the engines of economic productivity and as parents are the means for social reproduction.

Governments manage economic imperatives through fiscal, monetary, trade, regulatory, and other policies aimed at growing the economy. They advance social goals by providing income support, health and other pro-grams that cushion temporary or permanent loss of market income, assure minimum levels of income and of essential goods and services, facilitate employment, improve the skills of the workforce, protect the health and

1

safety of workers, expand social and economic opportunities, and meet the special needs of particularly vulnerable populations.

Debates about whether the United States has a welfare state are long over; the U.S. has a large and complex array of social, health, family, and employment policies designed to address these social imperatives. The scholarly debate about whether the U.S. welfare state is big enough, or too big, is also winding down in the wake of new analyses that suggest that social and health spending is more similar than different across the mature welfare states (Garfinkel, Rainwater, and Smeeding 2010).

The current questions for scholars and policymakers are: Do U.S. income support, social, health, and employment policies meet the needs of the country and its residents? If not, why not? How could they be improved?

Events in the first decade of the twenty-first century suggest that the answer to the first question is no, particularly for working-age individuals and their families. Even before the Great Recession of 2008, the U.S. trailed other rich countries on many indicators of social and economic security for families and children, with higher poverty rates, greater economic inequality, worse school and health outcomes, more individuals lacking health care, and a larger share of the workforce in low wage jobs than in most other OECD (Organisation for Economic Co-Operation and Development) countries (OECD 2007). As the economy slid into recession in 2007 and 2008, rising unemployment compounded these and related social problems.

The response of U.S. policymakers to the economic downturn reinforces our pessimistic conclusion about the current capacity of the welfare state to support workers and their families. Response to the financial dimensions of the downturn was swift and dramatic. Response to social and economic dislocation was slow and hesitant. As record numbers of families lost their jobs, incomes, health care, homes, retirement savings, and other assets, the vast system of federal and state welfare and employment programs was able to do little to prevent dislocation. Nonprofit and charitable organizations that provide emergency assistance were overwhelmed. Policymakers at the federal level responded with short-term extensions of unemployment insurance and food assistance and temporary stimulus spending to jump-start recovery. State policymakers, forced to balance budgets devastated by declining income and sales tax revenues, cut back on essential social and health services even as demand for these services was growing. Debates about health-care reform, arguably the most important social legislation of the decade, swung wildly off topic even as rising unemployment put more families at risk, but ultimately culminated in the March 2010 passage of the Patient Protection and Affordable Care Act.

Many of the inadequacies in the nation's response to the social and economic dislocations of the Great Recession can be traced to structural features of the welfare state put in place more than seventy years earlier. This motivates us to address the second and third questions posed above. If the American welfare state is not meeting the needs of working adults and their families, why not? And what can we do differently as we recover from the current economic crisis and move forward into the twenty-first century?

The Big Bang of U.S. Social Policy

The U.S. welfare state is often described as having been created somewhat like the universe: out of nothing—or at least, very little in the way of national social policy. A "big bang" of policymaking during the Great Depression created the 1935 Social Security Act (SSA). The SSA has served as the foundation for major social and health policy in the U.S. ever since, with programs added piecemeal over, on and around this foundation. If adoption of the SSA was the big bang of the U.S. welfare state, welfare state expansions in the 1960s and 1970s and neoliberal reforms of the 1980s and 1990s were important but smaller cosmic events that modified the structures created by the SSA without fundamentally changing them.

Understanding the historical foundations of social policy is important because once policies are adopted, the structures of those policies themselves influence and constrain possibilities for reform for many years to come. As students of social institutions and policy feedback have taught us, major policy initiatives change the balance of political influence, create or derail the development of institutional capacity, and deeply inform citizen's understanding of their identities, their rights, their social responsibilities, and the role of the state in fostering social welfare. More than seventy-five years ago, the United States adopted the legislation that set these processes in play for the welfare state.

The SSA reflected the belief of policymakers in the early twentieth century that the populations most at risk in a capitalist economy were the aged, the temporarily jobless, and needy children, whose mothers were not expected to work. Soon thereafter, the amendments of 1939 added dependents' benefits for the spouse and minor children of a retired worker and survivors benefits for the family of a deceased worker. These extensions transformed Social Security from a retirement program for individuals into a family-based economic security program. Amendments in 1954 created

Disability Insurance, which provided working families with additional economic security. Yet this expanded economic security program was incomplete, for it largely ignored risks to the economic or social security of able-bodied working-age adults and their dependents.[1]

The 1935 and 1939 legislation reflected the organization of work and family life, the structure of employment, and the population characteristics of that era. It was informed by the assumptions of that time about the proper role of the state and the responsibilities of the public and private sectors and of families and individuals.

During the second major period of welfare state development, in the 1960s and 1970s, the focus shifted to the crises of race and extreme economic marginalization in U.S. cities and rural areas, to public funding of health care for the elderly and needy through Medicare and Medicaid, and to expanding social services for needy populations. Broader concerns about economic, health, and social security for working-age families received little attention. Welfare reform in the mid-1990s ratified the emerging consensus and economic reality that all parents—high- and low-earning, single, and partnered—would engage in paid employment while caring for children and other family dependents. But there was little expansion of services or other forms of support for working-age adults. Child-care assistance and tax credits available to the lowest-income families expanded but fell far short of assuring economic security.

Posing the Question

The chapters of *Old Assumptions, New Realities* began as papers for a conference that brought together leading scholars from economics, political science, social welfare, and public affairs to examine the challenges of ensuring the economic security of working-age adults and their children in the twenty-first century. Prominent policy practitioners joined the scholars in a two-day dialogue about the interconnected issues of social, health, and economic security. Two observations provided the intellectual impetus for the conference and resulting volume.

First, the context for the American welfare state—including labor markets, the organization of family life, the demographic characteristics of the population, and social norms and expectations—has changed enormously since the passage of the Social Security Act in 1935, the prosperity following World War II, and the expansion of social welfare programs in the 1960s and 1970s. The institutions of the welfare state have also changed, especially the sizes and roles of the public and nonprofit sectors.

Second, these new realities are at odds with many of the old assumptions about economic and social arrangements that motivated the initial structure of the SSA and its subsequent expansion. This gap between old assumptions and new realities may be a fundamental reason why current policies are failing to assure the economic security of working-age adults and their children.

The chapters in this volume consider the state of the social, health, family, and employment policies that support working-age individuals and their families in the United States. They describe major components of the U.S. welfare state at the beginning of the twenty-first century in the domains of income support, health care, employment and training, asset ownership, and family policy. They pay particular attention to the well-being of low-skilled workers and low-income families, both because public supports are particularly important for this population and because their experiences of the welfare state serve to indicate the robustness of the system itself. Two chapters consider major institutional issues in the modern welfare state: the structure of public services and the role of nonprofit organizations.

Each chapter takes up the volume's theme by discussing the implications of "old" assumptions that shaped the structure of the U.S. welfare state and the most relevant new demographic, economic, social, and policy realities. Authors assessed contemporary challenges of assuring the economic and social security of working-age adults and their families and recommended revised or new approaches that would more closely align policies with contemporary realities. Two experts, a scholar and a policy practitioner, reviewed each paper presented at the conference. The chapters in the volume incorporate these comments and critical perspectives.

OLD ASSUMPTIONS, NEW REALITIES

Before starting our examination of specific domains of the modern welfare state, it is worth pausing to consider how much the world has changed since the passage of the SSA in 1935, and how assumptions that informed the SSA and social policies of the following three decades may be at odds with contemporary realities. Consider these stylized facts that contrast the old assumptions with new realities.

One Male Breadwinner per Family

When the SSA was passed, families functioned as economic and home production units in which a male breadwinner earned a "family wage" sufficient to support himself and his dependents, and a female homemaker provided full-time, uncompensated carework in the home.

FIGURE 1.1   Labor-Force Participation Rate for Men and Women, Age 25 to 54, and Mothers, 1948 to 2005

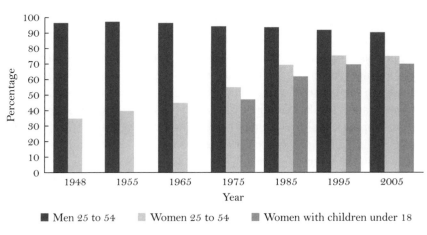

Source: Authors' compilation based on data from Mosisa and Hipple (2006, table 1).

When the SSA passed, it seemed reasonable to expect that the employment earnings and benefits of a male breadwinner would support a family and the household labor of wives, and mothers would support full-time workers. But even in the 1930s this assumption did not hold for all families.

The economics and organization of work and family life have changed dramatically since the 1930s. Low-skill adults, whether male or female, find it difficult to earn enough to support a family. Labor-force participation by prime-working-age women (from twenty-five to fifty-four) more than doubled between 1948 and 1995 before leveling off, while the participation rate for prime-working-age men has gradually declined (figure 1.1). Most women, including those raising children, now work, and their earnings have slowly converged with men's (figures 1.1 and 1.2). As women have shifted their labor from the home to the market, families have scrambled to replace lost hours of caregiving and domestic labor (see Heymann and Earle, chapter 6, this volume). Care of dependent family members is increasingly outsourced from the nuclear family to other providers of child care, afterschool care, and elder care.

Changing Family Patterns

When the SSA was passed, most nuclear families remained together and were able to pool income and share caregiving across the lifecycle.

FIGURE 1.2   Women's Median Annual Earnings as a Percentage of
Men's (Full-Time and Full-Year), 1951 to 2007

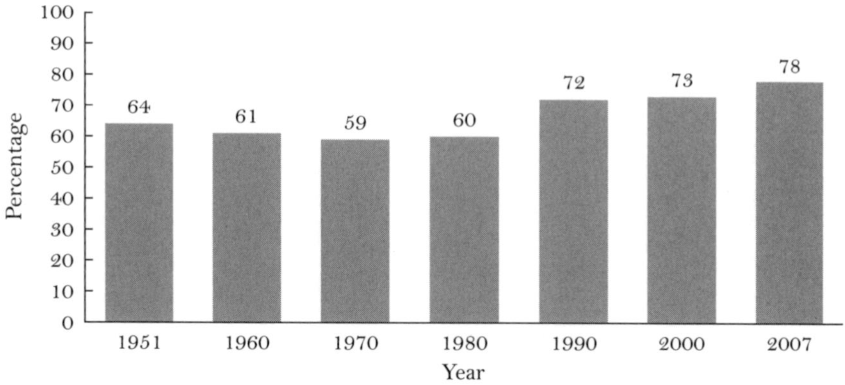

Source: Authors' compilation based on National Committee on Pay Equity (2009).

Patterns of family formation have changed substantially over the decades, with significant consequences for the ability of nuclear and extended families to ensure the economic security of all members. The marriage rate has fallen (figure 1.3). The divorce rate tripled between 1930 and 1980. It has since declined, but about half of all marriages now end in divorce. Since 1950 the rate of nonmarital childbearing has more than tripled and the percentage of all births by unmarried women has risen tenfold, to almost 40 percent of all births. These changes have greatly increased economic risk for the one half of children born today who can expect to spend at least part of their childhood with a single parent (figures 1.4 and 1.5). Remarriage, cohabitation, and having children with multiple partners are far more common than in the thirties, a circumstance that has created new, more complex living, parenting, and economic arrangements.

Young adults spend more years preparing for their careers, and marry and have children at much later ages (Furstenberg 2010). One consequence is that the economic burden of supporting children has risen for more and more parents. Older adults, enjoying much higher incomes than their counterparts in the mid-twentieth century, are more likely to live apart from their adult children. Their greater independence has meant they provide less caregiving labor within the family—and they receive less caregiving from the family.

FIGURE 1.3   Marriage and Divorce Rates per Thousand Population, 1930 to 2007

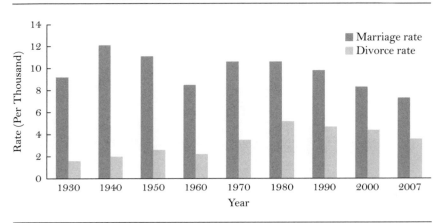

Source: Authors' compilation based on U.S. Census Bureau (N.d.; 1950, table 64; 1970, table 75; 2000, table 144, and 2010, table 126).
Note: Rates for men and women age fifteen and older show similar trends, but are only available through 1993.

FIGURE 1.4   Nonmarital Birth Rate and Nonmarital Birth Ratio, 1940 to 2006

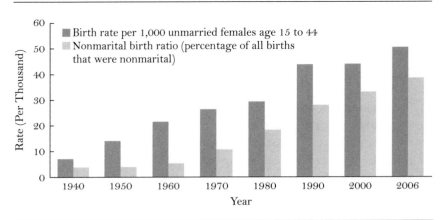

Source: Authors' compilation based on Ventura and Bachrach (2000) (data for 1940 to 1990) and Hamilton, Martin, and Ventura (2007) (data for 2000 to 2006).

FIGURE 1.5   Children Under Eighteen Years Living with
             One Parent, 1960 to 2009

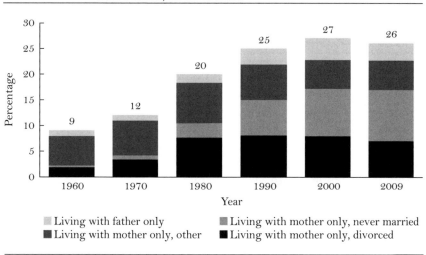

Source: Authors' figure based on U.S. Census Bureau (2010a).

Changing Employment Patterns

When the SSA was passed, individuals expected to have stable and continuous employment throughout their working years.

The original SSA programs were designed to provide insurance against specific lifecycle risks to earnings—old age, widowhood, and, later, disability—for adults who were otherwise stably employed, often with a single employer throughout their working years. The economy of the twenty-first century provides new opportunities and creates forms of risk that would have been impossible to foresee seventy-five years ago. In recent decades, although we have seen historically high employment rates, voluntary and involuntary employment transitions have grown, job tenure has substantially fallen (Farber 2007) and family incomes have become increasingly volatile (Hacker 2008; Hacker, chapter 2, this volume). As the share of workers in nontraditional job arrangements—including contingent and temporary positions—has grown, the likelihood of disruptions in employment and earnings has grown as well.

Who Pays for Retirement and Health Insurance?

When SSA was passed, employment was expected to be the primary mechanism for securing health and retirement benefits.

Beginning with the industrial welfare movements of the Progressive Era, employers and organized labor in the U.S. promoted workplace benefits as an alternative to state provisions. During and after World War II, unions' success in bargaining for health and retirement benefits solidified assumptions that employers would provide these and other benefits. The extent to which the U.S. relies on employer-provided benefits, and deeply subsidizes these arrangements by exempting the costs of benefits from income and payroll taxes (Adema and Ladaique 2005), remains exceptional compared to the practice of other rich industrialized countries.

Employment-based benefits never reached all workers. Currently, only about 60 percent of all companies provide health benefits for their workers, and about half offer retirement benefits (U.S. Department of Labor 2009). Provision of health insurance by private employers has declined steadily in recent years and dropped sharply after the 2007 recession. The share of workers with access to a private pension or retirement savings plan has also fallen since the early 1980s. As with wages, employment-based benefits have become more unequal in recent years as coverage has eroded most for workers in the lowest-earning groups.

Who Has Enjoyed Most of the Gains from Economic Growth?

After the Great Depression and World War II, economic expansion was expected to absorb new workers with the returns from increasing prosperity shared broadly across all income levels.

The failure to recognize risks to the incomes of working-age individuals and their dependents resulted in part from the postwar optimism that an expanding economy would provide economic security for all, into the foreseeable future. Belief that a rising tide of prosperity would "lift all boats" was largely confirmed for many decades, as the U.S. economy grew steadily, and apart from short recessions, per capita income increased and poverty and income inequality deceased. But the equalizing and poverty-reducing effects of economic growth ground nearly to a halt in the 1970s. For the past thirty years, the U.S. economy has indeed grown in both absolute and per capita terms, but the benefits have increasingly flowed to those in the highest income brackets. Though work effort is substantial in the United States, it has not been enough to assure economic security for all families, even during periods of robust economic performance (Mishel, Bernstein, and Allegretto 2007; U.S. Department of Labor 2008).

Real earnings have stagnated for most men; median earnings actually fell between 1991 and 2008 for men with some high school or a high school degree (see figure 1.6). Earnings have grown modestly for women, largely

FIGURE 1.6   Real Median Earnings of Male Workers (A) and
Real Median Earnings of Female Workers (B),
1967 to 2008 (2008 Dollars)

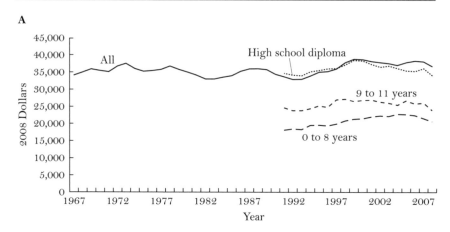

A

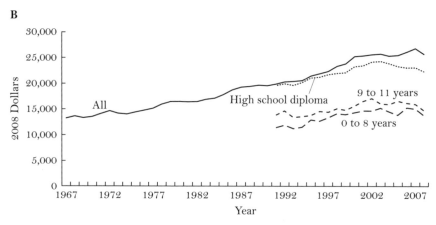

B

Source: Authors' calculations based on U.S. Census Bureau (2010b).

because of increases in their hours of employment; less-educated women have gained the least (Blank, Danziger, and Schoeni 2006). Figure 1.7 portrays the increase in income inequality. The share of income received by families in the lowest 20 percent of the income distribution has fallen in comparison to 1947 and, especially, to the 1970s. Conversely the income shares of the highest 20 percent and top 5 percent are well above their levels from 1947 through the mid-1980s. Wealth (as opposed to income) inequality has also increased.

FIGURE 1.7   Share of Aggregate Income of High- and Low-Income
Families Compared to 1947[a]

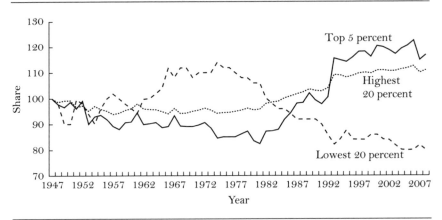

Source: Authors' calculations based on U.S. Census Bureau (2010b).
[a] The income share of each group is set to 100 in 1947. The value for year T is the ratio of the income share in T to the share in 1947, multiplied by 100.

In the mid-twentieth century, unions' success in securing greater job security, higher wages, and employer-provided benefits for working-class and middle-class families helped create high expectations for work and economic security, and also played a key role in meeting them. To the extent that those expectations were predicated on the continuing strength of unions, labor-market realities gradually but steadily undercut them. Union membership declined from about 35 percent of private-sector wage and salary workers in the period from 1940 to 1959, to less than 8 percent in 2010 (see figure 1.8).

Changing Demographics

When the SSA was passed, the U.S. population was distributed in an age pyramid with a small dependency ratio: a large working-age population was available to support a small elderly population.

Dramatic increases in life expectancy that were impossible to foresee in the 1930s, coupled with declines in fertility, have steadily increased the share of population age sixty-five and over; at 6.8 percent in 1940, in 2000 it was 12.4 percent.[2] The U.S. Census Bureau (2005) projects the share to exceed 16 percent by 2020. Such growth, particularly among the "oldest old" who are in frail and declining health, is rapidly increasing the demand

FIGURE 1.8   Percentage of Private Wage and Salary Workers in Unions, 1929 to 2006

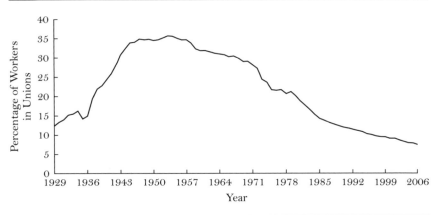

Source: Authors' compilation based on Hirsch (2008, data appendix).

for health and caregiving services both within and beyond the family. The increase in demand for long-term care, currently provided for most seniors by family members or through privately financed nursing home arrangements, is creating heavy burdens on many working-age families' time and economic resources.

The rising proportion of elders in the population is placing ever greater financial demands on Social Security and Medicare. Burgeoning costs of these two core welfare state programs, coupled with large federal deficits, pose fiscal threats to the expansion of publicly supported child care, family leave, workforce development programs, asset building programs, and other programs that enhance economic security for working-age families. The crucial exception is the comprehensive health-care reform of 2010, which seeks to expand health coverage available to working-age families. It also seeks to rein in Medicare costs, which would free up funds for other social programs and for debt reduction. Whether the reform accomplishes either or both of these goals remains to be seen.

Unforeseen Groups at Risk for Poverty

When the SSA was passed, economic insecurity among the working-age population was expected to wither away, and long-term poverty among the aged was seen as the major poverty problem.

FIGURE 1.9   U.S. Poverty Rate by Age, 1959 to 2008

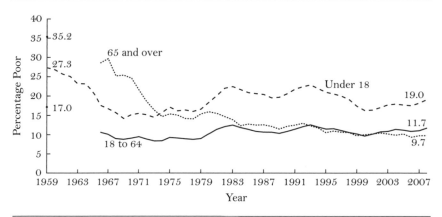

Source: Authors' calculations based on U.S. Census Bureau (2009b, table B-2.)

The legislation approved in 1935 and 1939 focused on risks to elders' income from retirement and widowhood. Over time, provisions were made for other forms of risk, including permanent disability and health care for the elderly and very poor. These incremental changes built directly on the 1935 legislation and produced a rapid decline in poverty among the elderly.[3] They did little to affect the factors that place working-age individuals and their children at risk of poverty, including long-term joblessness, low wages, divorce, and single parenthood. Social policy reforms in the 1960s and 1990s focused attention on the effects of family poverty, but did not substantially reduce it.

Since 1974 the official poverty rate for the elderly has dropped well below that of children, and poverty among both children and working-age adults remains stubbornly high (figure 1.9). The poverty and economic insecurity created by low earnings is compounded by the structure and paucity of America's public income support, health, employment, and other social benefits for working-age adults and their children, as compared to support structures in most comparably rich countries (Rainwater and Smeeding 2003).

Increased Diversity of Population Receiving Benefits

When the SSA was passed, restrictive policies limited the diversity of claimants for social benefits.

Through policy design and administrative practices, the initial benefits of the Social Security Act flowed disproportionately to U.S.-born citizens of European ancestry. Following earlier practices that excluded many African Americans from private charity benefits and Mothers' Pensions, the SSA specifically restricted access for African Americans by excluding most agricultural and domestic workers from coverage. African Americans' and Hispanics' exclusion from the conventional labor market and financial system historically has limited their opportunities to achieve economic security through work and asset accumulation (Sherraden, chapter 5, this volume; Stoll, chapter 3, this volume). The civil rights movement of the mid-twentieth century expanded the rights of African Americans to claim social benefits, but U.S. social policy remained highly racialized. The insurance-based benefits of the SSA and state unemployment insurance programs continued to flow disproportionately to white, male, and regularly employed citizens. As opposed to this source of benefits were means-tested programs such as food stamps and housing assistance. By design, means-tested programs benefit the poor. After the expansions of the Great Society and War on Poverty in the sixties and early seventies, these means-tested programs became even more concentrated on inner-city, economically marginalized, and nonwhite populations. Although most poor and welfare-recipient families in the United States are white, race continues to play an outsized and divisive role in public, media, and policy discussions of social policy.

In recent years, changes in immigration law and in immigrants' origins have increased the size and diversity of the immigrant and minority populations, creating new social cleavages along racial and ethnic lines. In the 1930s the American population was about 10 percent African American and 90 percent white European. In 2008, racial and ethnic minorities accounted for 35 percent of the total population and fully 43 percent of persons under age twenty (U.S. Census Bureau 2006, 2008a; Johnson and Lichter 2010). Hispanics are now the largest minority (15 percent), followed by African Americans (12 percent), Asians and Pacific Islanders and others (5 percent), and persons identifying themselves as multiracial (2 percent). Foreign-born residents currently make up 12 percent of the population, the highest level since 1930 (U.S. Census Bureau 2006, 2008b) and double the share from 1950 to 1980. Citizenship status, once a relatively minor issue for U.S. social policy, has become more salient as the composition of immigrant populations has changed. Length-of-residency tests for recently arrived immigrants, and specific exclusion of undocumented immigrants, have limited and complicated the delivery of social, health, and other services to first- and even second-generation immigrant families.

Changing Role of Government in Social Policy

When the SSA was passed, the government, particularly at the federal level, played a limited role in social and health policy.

With some notable exceptions such as Civil War Veterans' Benefits, before the Great Depression, state and local governments were largely responsible for health and social welfare programs. The SSA was the first legislation to create a significant public and federal responsibility for social welfare. As the SSA social insurance programs have matured, their costs have grown both in absolute dollars and as a share of public expenditures. Income support, health, workforce development and social service programs enacted in the 1960s and 1970s further raised social welfare expenditures that are funded by general tax revenues rather than the Social Security trust funds. Congress also expanded tax expenditures (in the form of tax credits and deductions and thus uncollected tax) for retirement savings, employer-provided health insurance, and other private means of enhancing economic security (Howard 1997). Seventy-five years after the passage of the SSA, the United States can no longer be characterized as a nation with a small public social welfare system. But the decentralized "system" has grown haphazardly over the years. The result has left gaps in some areas of provision and redundancies in others, large regional variations, and a mix of social insurance, public assistance, social services, and tax benefits that varies sharply with income and is of dizzying complexity for needy families to understand and access.

Changing Mix of Private and Public Social Services Providers

When the SSA was passed, and well into the 1960s, government and private charities played distinct roles in social welfare and health provision.

Before the "big bang" of the SSA legislation in 1935, churches and private charities financed and provided much of the social welfare and health assistance outside of workplace benefits; they continued to do so well into the 1960s. Between 1935 and the 1960s, government efforts to foster economic security focused largely on income support, while private secular and faith-based organizations continued to provide most social services. Public spending for social services began expanding in the 1960s. As expansion of the public sector has continued since the sixties, the boundary between the public and private sectors has grown much fuzzier. An increasingly diverse sector of private nonprofit, private for-profit, quasi-public, secular, and faith-based organizations has obtained contracts to deliver a significant share of publicly funded social services (Allard 2009; Allard, chapter 7, this volume; Smith and Lipsky 1993). The separate public and nonprofit domains of an earlier era have given way to a complex, growing interdependency between the two sectors.

Because government is now the largest source of funding for many private nonprofit social service providers, new governance and accountability requirements have arisen (Sandfort, chapter 8, this volume). Within personal social services, demands for greater individual choice and self-advocacy and the emergence of extensive networks of nonprofit and public service providers are challenging the traditional organization of the "labor" and "management" roles in human services. The government's role is moving away from old administrative assumptions of rule-bound authority toward a focus on governance, coordination, and oversight.

OVERVIEW OF THIS BOOK

As we have just outlined, the world and the United States have changed in many ways since the passage of the SSA. The questions posed to the authors at the Old Assumptions, New Realities conference were: Are the social, economic, employment, and health policies that have over the years been built on to the foundation of the 1935 SSA congruent with new social, economic, and political realities? If not, what can be done to revise or replace these policies as we enter the twenty-first century? The deep, lasting recession in the first decade of the new century and the inadequacy of existing federal and state policies to prevent or respond to major economic and social dislocations gives these questions greater urgency.

Suppose the nation were starting from scratch to create a social welfare system consistent with the realities of the twenty-first century. The resulting set of policies and organizational structures surely would differ considerably from the array of programs that have grown incrementally from the Social Security Act of 1935. But starting over is not an option. The task, rather, is to identify politically and administratively feasible reforms that build on but improve current programs and organizational structures.

Policy reform can take two broad approaches: change the programs, or change the new realities themselves. With the first approach, one tries to bring the assumptions undergirding social policies into better line with the realities of the twenty-first century. For example, expanding child-care choices, improving its quality, and increasing its affordability are policy directions that enhance economic security by recognizing and adapting to the reality of mothers' long-term commitment to the workforce. Another would be to incentivize more flex-time arrangements for all parents.

The second approach to improving the alignment between current needs of populations and the programs that should serve them is to enhance economic security by adopting policies that change some of the new realities. Labor law reforms that are more supportive of unionization and stronger enforcement of wage and hours laws are two examples.

The broad divergences between old social and economic assumptions and new realities described in the previous section underlie the many challenges facing today's social welfare state, but that accounting is hardly exhaustive. Each chapter elaborates on this theme by identifying important tensions between earlier assumptions and current conditions in a specific policy arena or organizational sphere, then drawing out the implications for the safety net in the twenty-first century.

Economic Security

To provide economic security to workers and their families the United States relies on workplace benefits to a far greater extent than other rich capitalist countries. This employment-based approach to economic security was never fully inclusive for working-aged adults. Jacob Hacker observes in chapter 2 that it has become less inclusive since the late 1970s, as employers have reduced the coverage and extent of their health, pension, and other benefits. This contraction, coupled with declining employment security and increasing income volatility, has increased economic risk for workers and their families. As private risk has increased, public programs have failed to expand commensurately, thereby amplifying rather than reducing private risk.

The "great risk shift" (Hacker 2008) from employers and the public sector to workers and their families has occurred in major areas of working families' finances: jobs, provision for retirement, health care, home financing, savings, and strategies for balancing work and family. Passage of health-care reform in 2010 was a major breakthrough that will shift some risk back and profoundly affect the delivery and financing of health care. Nevertheless, Hacker argues, the new legislation falls well short of other wealthy countries' efforts to provide universal coverage and control medical costs. Hacker contends that government and employers can make several changes to better support workers and their families and close gaps in the current social safety net.

Hacker contends that government and employers can change the current social safety net to create a stronger foundation of economic security that would allow middle-class Americans to look toward the future with optimism, rather than anxiety, and seize the economic opportunities before them. He suggests revisions to the recent health-care reform that would strengthen it as well as reforms of unemployment insurance that would improve its coverage and effectiveness. Hacker also recommends "wage insurance" to help workers facing permanent job loss find work and a universal 401(k) account that would follow workers across jobs.

More far-reaching, Hacker proposes a Universal Insurance program that would provide all workers and their families with protection against large and sudden income declines. He argues that such a program, while costly, would reduce wasteful spending and inefficiencies in the current safety net.

Low-Skill Labor Markets

When the SSA was passed, economists and public policy experts shared the optimistic assumption that the fruits of economic growth would be shared across all income classes. A growing economy would absorb new workers, providing them with stable employment. The returns from increasing productivity would flow to both investors and the workers who made that increase possible. Government had a role in the provision of universal primary and secondary education. Policymakers and employers assumed that this education, along with employer-provided on-the-job training, would provide the skills to secure and retain employment and wages needed to support workers and their dependents.

Since the 1970s the benefits from economic growth have increasingly flowed to those in the highest income brackets. In chapter 3, Michael Stoll argues that as manufacturing jobs declined in significance, employers began to demand workers with higher-level job skills who can acquire new skills during their worklife. But public workforce development programs, both in and out of school, have been limited in scale and funding and are often isolated from the private sector.

Shifts in demand for labor and weak enforcement of labor standards and other labor-market regulations have eroded the economic bargaining power of workers. Earnings have stagnated and declined for less-skilled male workers and have grown only modestly for less-skilled women. Contingent, temporary, and contract work is more prevalent, the job market in general has become more volatile, and job losers are increasingly unlikely to return to their old employers when they find work.

In chapters 3 and 4, Michael Stoll and Paul Osterman speak to the disjuncture between the old assumptions about the labor market and the new realities that govern it, and what we can do to improve labor-market outcomes in the future. Stoll addresses the supply side of the labor market. He argues that existing workforce policies have been unable to prevent less educated men's wages from stagnating or falling in the face of declining unionization, reduced enforcement of anti-discrimination laws, technological changes that shifted demand away from low-skill workers, and the movement of low-skill jobs from cities into suburbs.

Notwithstanding these changes, Stoll sees opportunities for education and workforce development programs that teach specific problem-solving and advanced skills that meet modern employers' needs. Within schools, he recommends expansion of Career Academies, which integrate college-preparatory career training with relevant work experience in partnership with local employers. Outside schools, workforce development programs should create and maintain stronger relationships with employers and tailor their training to match employer and employee needs.

Stoll also examines three sources of friction in labor markets that disadvantage low-skill workers: spatial mismatch between low-skill workers' place of residence and the location of low-skill jobs, racial discrimination in housing and labor markets, and offender status. He suggests that cooperation among regional workforce development agencies would help mitigate existing spatial frictions and minimize future ones. To address discrimination among employers based on their belief that many minority job applicants have criminal backgrounds, Stoll argues that better relationships between employers and job training programs will encourage employers to hire program participants regardless of their race. He also calls for increased reliance on criminal background checks and tougher enforcement of anti-discrimination laws.

In chapter 4, Paul Osterman examines the demand side of the labor market. He notes that many of the jobs that companies offer to low-skill adults are inadequate on many dimensions, including wages, benefits, training opportunities, and job security. There is evidence that companies, under intense competitive pressure and in an environment of decreased regulation, are degrading low-skilled employment even further, which they get away with by evading laws relating to wages and number of hours worked. Unemployment Insurance eligibility and benefit policies have not kept pace with changes in the nature of employment.

Like Stoll, Osterman argues that skill acquisition remains central. However, Osterman's main interest is influencing the demand side of the market. He calls for better enforcement of labor standards to improve working conditions. Increasing unionization of low-wage labor markets by reforming labor law to speed up elections and reduce unfair labor practices would be an important component of any strategy. He favors expansion of Community Benefit Agreements, in which a coalition of community groups identifies a large development project that requires city approval and then negotiates with the developer regarding hiring, wage standards, and other topics such as affordable housing and recreation.

Building and Protecting Assets

In chapter 5, Michael Sherraden explores the disjuncture between older assumptions about wealth, asset accumulation, and education and the realities of the twenty-first century. He argues that in the early and middle years of the twentieth century it was widely assumed that assets, especially owning both a home and shares of stock, were only for the rich, who could afford to take market risks. The new reality is that home ownership and stock market equity have reached more than half the population as a result of changes in housing and mortgage markets, personal and employer investment practices, and tax laws. The risks associated with investments in stock, housing, and other assets are now widespread as well.

College, graduate, and professional educations were likewise once considered the domain of the privileged. This assumption is far out of date for contemporary globalized and technologically advanced economies, where a middle class lifestyle increasingly requires post-secondary education. Even with public and private financial aid, access to postsecondary education depends to an important degree on family wealth and is out of reach (or believed to be out of reach) for many poor adolescents.

A third critical assumption of the twentieth century was that working-age people can support their families on current income and retirees can primarily rely on Social Security. While this model worked well for many decades, working-age people are now increasingly obliged to build private assets over the life course to both cushion short-term income losses and provide retirement income. Yet many middle- and low-income families lack pensions and have little or no wealth outside of housing equity. These workers face the reality that Social Security benefits will not be sufficient to maintain their standard of living in retirement without additional private savings and pensions.

Sherraden advances several policy recommendations to close the gap between old assumptions about assets and new realities for working families. The federal government should reform current tax policy so that it subsidizes accumulation for the entire population, including the poor. Individual Development Accounts (IDAs), universal and progressive 401(k)s, and similar savings vehicles can all be part of a strategy to help the whole population build lifelong assets. He calls for greater regulation of financial services to reduce investor risks and curtail predatory financial practices.

Sherraden also advocates for Child Development Accounts, a wealth-building mechanism in which parents save for their children's future in tax-sheltered accounts and public funds subsidize low-income parents' savings. Such accounts could be based on the existing platform of state college savings (529) plans. Inclusive asset-based programs can supplement the traditional income support programs of the social safety net and enhance financial security for all American families.

Balancing Work and Family Life

Enacted in an era when most women with young children either did not work or worked part-time, the SSA did not provide or subsidize paid sick leave, maternity leave, family leave, child care, or preschool education. Nor did it create child or family allowances, like those that in much of Europe help offset the costs of raising children. The drafters of the SSA did not anticipate far-reaching changes in work and family life, including dramatic increases in women's paid employment and in single-parent families in the late twentieth century. Despite recent federal and state legislation that has begun to address these issues, Jody Heymann and Alison Earle document in chapter 6 that current policies fall well short of enabling adults to thrive economically while adequately caring for family members, given the realities of work and family life in the twenty-first century.

Drawing on the experiences of the many countries with far more extensive work-family policies than the United States, Heymann and Earle lay out a broad policy agenda that would increase families' economic security and reconcile the demands of working and caring in the context of a competitive globalized economy. The elements of their agenda include universal paid sick leave, medical leave, and family leave (both for new parents and to care for ailing family members) and mandated breastfeeding breaks, expanded early childhood care and education, quality after-school programs, a longer school year, and visiting care providers to help elders meet basic needs. Notwithstanding weak political support for such initiatives in the past, Heymann and Earle suggest that the Great Recession of 2007 to 2009 (like the Great Depression) and new electronic forms of political organization may give impetus to major legislation to expand social protections and economic security.

Nonprofit Organizations and Economic Security

The public and private organizations that provide a safety net for the poor in the United States have undergone a significant but often overlooked transformation in the past several decades. Scott Allard in chapter 7 points out that the traditional assumption that cash assistance is the dominant approach to assisting the poor no longer holds. In the twenty-first century, social service programs have become the primary mode for delivering assistance to families near and below the poverty line. Public spending for these programs now exceeds spending on cash assistance by tens of billions of dollars annually. While attention often focuses on social policy at the national or state level, today much of the important action shaping whether working poor families have access to safety net assistance happens at the local level.

Allard explores a new landscape for delivering services characterized by a complex web of relationships between government and private entities that makes it difficult to coordinate activity and target resources efficiently. Providing help to low-income populations is yet more daunting amidst a volatile funding environment that contracts when need rises. Allard also finds that low income people's access to services varies spatially and racially because local governmental and nonprofit agencies are more likely to locate in certain areas than others.

Allard observes that volatility in funding and difficulties in accessing services destabilize the agencies and organizations that make up the safety net and make assistance less available to the needy. If we are to improve the effectiveness and reliability of social services for the working poor, federal agencies, states, and communities need to maintain stable funding for widely accessible programs. Policymakers also need to take account of how changes in other social policy areas affect the health and efficacy of the nonprofit service sector.

A growing understanding of successful new nonprofit organizational forms, joint public-private ventures, and social enterprise may help local actors adopt solutions that aid the working poor, and do so with more diversified and sustainable revenue streams than is currently the case. Allard and other contributors to this volume provide examples of innovative ways to organize and deliver employment and social services that American communities are currently implementing.

Reforming Delivery Systems of the Safety Net

The SSA focused on economic risks of the unemployed, single mothers, the elderly, the disabled, and their survivors. Provisions to improve economic security for other populations, particularly low-earning families, followed piecemeal over the years through a variety of federal, state, and local programs. Jodi Sandfort argues in chapter 8 that the set of programs that has been cobbled together over since 1935 has not produced a coherent safety net. Instead, each policy initiative—cash assistance, tax credits, employment services, health care, and others—tended to develop its own institutional structure to implement its programs without necessarily considering how that structure interacted with other programs. Today's fragmented delivery systems for social programs fail to provide convenient, accessible services to clients, especially those who are employed, and place extra burdens in particular on low-income families. For example, means-tested programs such as Food Stamps and Child Nutrition Assistance often require separate applications with differing eligibility requirements and in-person eligibility interviews.

Working from the perspective of the client and frontline workers, Sandfort imagines what types of reforms would provide more efficient service delivery while ensuring fair determination of eligibility, accessible services, appropriate matching of services to particular family circumstances, and reliable information to aid policy-making, and suggests that these reforms would be most likely to occur at the state level. While recognizing that states will make different choices about the programs to include in system redesign and the specific institutions that operate a reconstituted safety net, Sandfort expects that direct service providers, intermediaries, and public governance would be key actors in any restructured system.

Direct service providers would need access to information that would help them lead clients sequentially through appropriate services. Intermediaries, such as associations of service professionals or think tanks, could increase direct service providers' capacities by building administrative capacity and networks, providing budget analyses and access to new sources of funding, and cultivating policy knowledge. The government's role would need to evolve from old assumptions of bureaucratic, rule-bound authority to a more streamlined role of *governance* involving systemwide design, oversight, and collaborative management of partnerships and assuring accountability of partners. Together, Sandfort argues, the reforms she envisions would help the social safety net better support working and low-income families.

CONCLUDING THOUGHTS

The chapters in this volume document that America's demographic, economic, and social realities have changed enormously since Congress enacted the Social Security Act. Indeed, many have significantly changed since the expansion of social welfare programs in the 1960s and 1970s. The chapters contain convincing arguments that the new realities are at odds with most of the old assumptions about economic and social arrangements that motivated the legislation that created the Social Security Administration and its programs, the landmark law that has had enduring effects on the structure of the American welfare state. The gap between old assumptions and new realities may be a fundamental reason why current social, health, income support, employment, asset building, and family policies often fail to ensure the economic security of working-age adults and their children.

To meet the twenty-first century's challenges of ensuring economic security for working-age families, the nation needs either to better align the assumptions that undergird specific social policies with today's realities or, alternatively, to adopt policies that change the new realities in ways that enhance economic security. The Great Recession of 2007 to 2009 and the inadequacy of existing policies to prevent or respond to major economic and social dislocations give even greater urgency to addressing these challenges.

The authors of this book offer promising reforms or new approaches to help meet these challenges. They especially attend to policies and institutional designs for fostering the well-being of low-skilled workers and low-income families, both because public supports are particularly important for these persons and because their experiences of the welfare state serve as telling indicators of the robustness of the system itself. The ideas put forward by the volume's authors give testimony to the nation's capacity to close the gap between old assumptions and new realities if it has the political will to do so.

NOTES

1. Policymakers expected the need for the income-tested benefits of Aid to Dependent Children (the forerunner of Aid to Families with Dependent Children and Temporary Assistance for Needy Families) to decline as more and more families qualified for Survivors Insurance.
2. Life expectancy was 62.9 in 1940 and 77.7 in 2006 (U.S. Centers for Disease Control 2009).
3. A large gap between the poverty of children and the elderly remains (that is, the proportion of children living in poverty is far greater than the proportion of the elderly living in poverty), after adjusting the poverty statistics for in-kind benefits, taxes, the Earned Income Tax Credit, and other types of income omitted from the official measure (U.S. Census Bureau 2009a).

REFERENCES

Adema, William, and Maxime Ladaique. 2005. *Net Social Expenditure, 2005 Edition: More Comprehensive Measures of Social Support.* OECD Social, Employment and Migration working papers no. 29. Paris: Organisation for Economic Co-operation and Development.

Allard, Scott. 2009. *Out of Reach: Place, Poverty, and the New American Welfare State.* New Haven, Conn.: Yale University Press.

Blank, Rebecca M., Sheldon H. Danziger, and Robert F. Schoeni, eds. 2006. *Working and Poor: How Economic and Policy Changes Are Affecting Low Wage Workers.* New York: Russell Sage Foundation.

Farber, Henry. 2007. "Is the Company Man an Anachronism? Trends in Long Term Employment in the U.S., 1973–2006." Working Paper Series, no. 518. Princeton: Princeton University, Industrial Relations Section.

Furstenberg, Frank. 2010. "On a New Schedule: Transitions to Adulthood and Family Change." *The Future of Children* 20(1): 67–88.

Garfinkel, Irwin, Lee Rainwater, and Timothy Smeeding. 2010. *Wealth and Welfare States: Is American a Laggard or Leader?* New York: Oxford University Press.

Hacker, Jacob S. 2008. *The Great Risk Shift: The New Economic Insecurity and the Decline of the American Dream.* New York: Oxford University Press.

Hamilton, Brady, Joyce Martin, and Stephanie Ventura. 2007. "Births: Preliminary Data for 2006." *National Vital Statistics Reports* 56(7): 11.

Hirsch, Barry. 2008. "Sluggish Institutions in a Dynamic World: Can Unions and Industrial Competition Coexist?" *Journal of Economic Perspectives* 22(1): 153–76. Data appendix available at: www2.gsu.edu/~ecobth/Current_Papers. htm; accessed July 12, 2010.

Howard, Christopher. 1997. *The Hidden Welfare State: Tax Expenditures and Social Policy in the United States.* Princeton, N.J.: Princeton University Press.

Johnson, Kenneth, and Daniel Lichter. 2010. "Growing Diversity Among America's Children and Youth: Spatial and Temporal Dimensions." *Population and Development Review* 36(1): 151–76.

Mishel, Lawrence, Jared Bernstein, and Sylvia Allegretto. 2007. *The State of Working America 2006–2007.* Washington, D.C.: Economic Policy Institute.

Mosisa, Abraham, and Steven Hipple. 2006. "Trends in Labor Force Participation in the United States." *Monthly Labor Review* 129(10): 35–57.

National Committee on Pay Equity. 2009. "The Wage Gap Over Time: In Real Dollars, Women See a Continuing Gap." Available at: www.pay-equity.org/info-time.html; accessed July 12, 2010.

Organisation for Economic Co-operation and Development (OECD). 2007. *Employment Outlook, Statistical Annex.* Paris: OECD.

Rainwater, Lee, and Timothy Smeeding. 2003. *Poor Kids in a Rich Country: America's Children in Comparative Perspective.* New York: Russell Sage Foundation.

Smith, Steven Rathgeb, and Michael Lipsky. 1993. *Nonprofits for Hire.* Cambridge, Mass.: Harvard University Press.

U.S. Census Bureau. 2005. "65+ in the United States: 2005." Current Population Reports. Publication no. p23–209. Available at: www.census.gov/prod/2006 pubs/p23-209.pdf; accessed July 7, 2010.

———. 2006. "Historical Census Statistics on the Foreign-Born Population of the United States: 1850 to 2000." Population Division working paper no. 81. Available at: www.census.gov/population/www/documentation/twps0081/ twps0081.html; accessed July 7, 2010.

———. 2008a. "American Community Survey, ACS Demographic and Housing Estimates: 2006–2008." American FactFinder. Online database. Available at: http://factfinder.census.gov/servlet/ADPTable?qr_name=ACS_2008_1YR_ G00_DP5&geo_id=01000US&ds_name=ACS_2008_1YR_G00_&gc_url= null&_lang=en; accessed July 7, 2010.

———. 2008b. "Foreign-Born Population of the United States: Current Population Survey—March 2008, Detailed Tables; Table 1.1. Population by Sex, Age, Nativity, and U.S. Citizenship Status: 2008." Available at: www.census.gov/ population/www/socdemo/foreign/cps2008.html; accessed July 7, 2010.

———. 2009a. "Table 2. Percent of persons in poverty, by definition of income and selected characteristics: 2007 CPI-U-RS." Current Population Survey, Annual Social and Economic (ASEC) supplement. Available at: www.census. gov/hhes/www/macro/032008/rdcall/2RS_000.htm; accessed July 7, 2010.

———. 2009b. Current Population Survey. "Poverty Status of People, by Age, Race, and Hispanic Origin: 1959 to 2008," Table B-2. Available at: www.census. gov/prod/2009pubs/p60–236.pdf; accessed July 13, 2010.

———. 2010a. Current Population Survey. "Table CH-5: Children Under 18 Years Living with Mother Only, by Marital Status of the Mother, 1960 to the Present." Available at: www.census.gov/population/socdemo/hh-fam/ch5.xls; accessed May 24, 2010.

———. 2010b. Current Population Survey, Annual Social and Economic (ASEC) supplement. Table F-2 for all races. Available online at: www.census.gov/ hhes/www/income/data/historical/families/index.html; accessed July 27, 2010.

———. N.d. "Statistical Abstracts." Available at: www.census.gov/prod/www/ abs/statab.html (accessed May 25, 2010).

U.S. Centers for Disease Control. 2009. "Deaths: Final Data for 2006." *National Vital Statistics Reports* 57(14): 27. Available at: www.cdc.gov/nchs/data/nvsr/ nvsr57/nvsr57_14.pdf; accessed July 7, 2010.

U.S. Department of Labor, Bureau of Labor Statistics. 2008. "A Profile of the Working Poor 2006." Report no. 1006. Available at: www.bls.gov/cps/ cpswp2006.pdf; accessed July 7, 2010.

U.S. Department of Labor, Bureau of Labor Statistics. 2009. "National Compensation Survey: Employee Benefits in the United States, March 2009." U.S. Bureau of Labor Statistics Bulletin 2731: 161. Available at: www.bls.gov/ncs/ebs/benefits/2009/ebbl0044.pdf; accessed July 6, 2010.

Ventura, Stephanie J., and Christine A. Bachrach. 2000. "Nonmarital Childbearing in the United States: 1940–1999." *National Vital Statistics Reports* 48(16): 17.

PART I

POLICIES TO INCREASE ECONOMIC SECURITY IN THE 21ST CENTURY

CHAPTER 2

WORKING FAMILIES AT RISK: UNDERSTANDING AND CONFRONTING THE NEW ECONOMIC INSECURITY

JACOB S. HACKER

Arnold Dorsett was an American success story. An air conditioner repairman, he earned more than his father ever did: almost $70,000 a year, thanks to a relentless schedule of eighty- to ninety-hour workweeks. He owned a good home in the suburbs. His wife, Sharon, training to be a nurse when they met and hoping to return to school soon, stayed home to care for their three kids. Arnold was driven, a striver. He was also, it turned out, the father of a young boy who was sick and getting sicker.

Zachary had been unhealthy since birth—one reason why Sharon had never received that nursing degree and Arnold was working so hard to pay the bills. But it was not until Zachary was eight that he was diagnosed with an immune system disorder that promised even bigger medical costs down the road. By then, the bills had crushed the family's finances. Despite having health insurance and refinancing their home, the Dorsetts had run up nearly thirty thousand dollars in outstanding credit-card balances and could no longer make their car or mortgage payments. In March 2005, they succumbed to the inevitable and filed for bankruptcy, becoming one of the roughly two million households filing that year. The choice was not easy. "I make good money, and I work hard for it," Arnold Dorsett said. "When I filed for bankruptcy, I felt I failed" (John Leland, "When Even Health Insurance Is No Safeguard," *New York Times*, October 23, 2005, A1).

Crises like Arnold Dorsett's rarely make the headlines as they did in this case. The health woes of everyday families have simply become too familiar. Every fifteen seconds, someone files a bankruptcy claim that is due in part to medical costs and crises (Himmelstein et al. 2009). In 2007, more than three fifths of the nation's personal bankruptcy filings (and probably a similar proportion of mortgage foreclosures (Robertson, Egelhof, and Hoke 2008)) were related to medical costs and lost income due to illness or injury—a 60 percent increase since 2002 (Himmelstein et al. 2009). Most who end up facing these economic calamities have health insurance. Most are working. But insurance and work are not always enough.

In the twelve months prior to May 2007, for example, around three in ten nonelderly adults who had health insurance lacked adequate coverage, according to a survey by *Consumer Reports* (Gopoian 2007). The median family income of these "underinsured" Americans is nearly $60,000— almost exactly the same as the median income of those with adequate coverage. The underinsured are as likely to be white as the well-insured, nearly as well-educated, and as likely to work full-time and in large or medium-sized companies. The only consistent way in which they differ from those who are better protected is that they are at grave economic risk.

Of course, the underinsured *have* coverage, however inadequate. Millions more lack even this basic protection. Everyone has heard the numbers: 46 million Americans without health insurance (compared with fewer than 30 million in 1980), the vast majority of them in working families (DeNavas-Walt, Proctor, and Smith 2009). But the uninsured are a constantly shifting group that includes many more people than that. In the two years beginning in 2007, nearly 87 million people—one out of three nonelderly Americans—went without health insurance at some point (Families USA 2009). Almost two thirds were uninsured for at least half a year; more than half were uninsured for at least nine months. Even those whose spells without insurance are short may find themselves facing an unexpected disaster and end up not just with huge bills but also facing future coverage denials for "preexisting conditions."

This is not simply a matter of dollars and cents. It is a matter of life and death. Researchers at Harvard University estimate that 45,000 working-age Americans die each year because of the lack of universal health insurance in the United States (Wilper et al. 2009). According to a recent study, the United States ranks nineteenth out of nineteen rich nations in the rate of "amenable mortality"—deaths before age seventy-five that could have been prevented with the provision of timely and effective care (Nolte and McKee 2008). A decade ago, we were five places higher on the list. But we are nowhere near the nations with the best rates, all of which provide affordable quality care to all their citizens. If, for example, the United States had the same rate of amenable mortality as the three nations with the lowest rates of preventable death, more than 100,000 fewer people would die in the United States each year (Nolte and McKee 2008). These are risks that all Americans face because of the costly, fragmented, and inadequate American framework of medical financing.

For years, these ordinary Americans at extraordinary risk have remained off the American political agenda, a problem seen as insoluble in our polarized partisan climate. In 2010, however, the U.S. Congress passed and President Barack Obama signed the Affordable Care Act. A remarkable policy breakthrough, the Affordable Care Act's price tag of roughly $1 trillion in federal spending over ten years (funded through tax increases and spending reductions) gives only a partial sense of its scope. The bill involves extensive new regulation of private health insurance, the public creation of new insurance-purchasing organizations called exchanges, the reorganization and expansion of Medicaid for the poor, and major reduction in spending growth within, as well as substantial changes to, the Medicare program for the aged and disabled. Given all this, the more revealing numbers concern not federal spending, but the predicted effects: more than 30 million more Americans will be covered by 2019, and there will be a substantial reduction in the cost of insurance for those who buy it through the exchanges, thanks to large new federal subsidies for coverage, greater economies of scale in administration, and new insurance rules that prohibit price discrimination against higher-risk patients (Congressional Budget Office 2010).

To be sure, the Affordable Care Act falls well short of the international health policy standard of universal coverage and robust efforts to restrain medical costs. The affluent democracy closest to us in terms of the structure and history of health insurance, Switzerland, has featured subsidized universal insurance since the mid-1990s and its per capita spending is roughly 60 percent of ours (OECD 2009). But in light of the long history of reform's defeat, the Affordable Care Act represents a decisive departure from the past politics and policy of American health care. It also grows out of a major ongoing debate about how to update the American social contract. In the wake of the steepest economic downturn since the Great Depression, anxious conversations in corporate boardrooms and around kitchen tables have grown into a grand struggle over the role of government in the twenty-first century.

This chapter is about that grand struggle—its roots, its implications, and its future. The policy battles of 2009 and 2010 did not emerge fully formed out of the recent economic downturn. Rather, they were rooted in a deeper transformation of the American economy and American politics. Over the last generation, economic risk has increasingly shifted from the broad shoulders of government and corporations onto the backs of American workers and their families. This sea change has occurred not just in health care, but in nearly every area of Americans' finances: their jobs, their retirement pensions, their homes and savings, their strategies for balancing work and family. But until the economic collapse that began at the end of 2007, the extent of this shift was largely missed and its causes largely unexplored.

Even now, the focus remains on the immediate economic crisis and the major financial players who are deemed "too big to fail." But the economic crisis facing working families emerged well before the market crash, and tracing *its* roots is at least as crucial as examining the meltdown at the top of the economic pyramid. For it is at the heart of American family finances that we find the clearest evidence of what I have called the "Great Risk Shift," the massive downward transfer of economic risk and responsibility that has reshaped the financial lives of so many Americans. The erosion of American health insurance was only one aspect of this transformation, and the recently passed reform bill is only a partial solution to this aspect.

This chapter begins, therefore, by tracing the rise and fall of America's distinctive framework of economic security, which differs from other nations less in total size than in the form that social protections take. Responsibilities that in other nations were handled by government (perhaps with the cooperation of nonprofit mutual insurers) fell to employers and for-profit providers instead. Encouraged by a complex array of subsidies and regulations, this uniquely "divided welfare state" (Hacker 2002) has crumbled over the last generation in the face of growing economic pressures on employers, as well as increasing political resistance to the ideal of economic security itself.

The chapter then considers the political roots of this transformation, including the rise of a conservative counterattack on government in the 1970s, the growing polarization of Americans politics, and the pressures on both parties to cater to narrow economic interests rather than respond to the broad strains facing working families. Only by understanding the political forces that have abetted growing economic insecurity—why, that is, middle- and working-class Americans have been, until recently at least, "too small to save"—can we effectively forge a new set of assumptions for our new realities.

Finally, I turn to the question of what can be done. The health-care bill represents a major step forward. Even after its passage, however, the United States still badly needs a twenty-first-century social contract that protects families against the most severe risks they face, without clamping down on the potentially beneficial processes of change and adjustment that produce some of these risks. This will require not just building on the steps taken in the health-care bill, but also moving beyond health care to recognize the more fundamental source of American economic insecurity: the deep mismatch between today's economic realities and the American framework for providing economic security. It will also require recognizing that economic security and economic opportunity are not antithetical; they go hand in hand. Just as investors and entrepreneurs need basic protections to encourage them to take economic risks, so ordinary workers and their families require a foundation of economic security to confidently invest in their futures and seize the risky opportunities before them.

AMERICA'S UNIQUE—AND ENDANGERED—FRAMEWORK OF ECONOMIC SECURITY

We often assume that the United States does little to provide economic security compared with other rich capitalist democracies. This is only partly true. The United States does spend less on government benefits as a share of its economy, but it also relies more—far more—on private workplace benefits, such as health-care and retirement pensions. Indeed, when these private benefits are factored into the mix, the U.S. framework of economic security is not smaller than the average system in other rich democracies; it is actually slightly larger (Hacker 2002). With the help of hundreds of billions in tax breaks, American employers serve as the first line of defense for millions of workers buffeted by the winds of economic change.

The problem is that this unique employment-based system is coming undone, and in the process, risk is shifting back onto workers and their families. Employers want out of the social contract forged in the more stable economy of past, and they are largely getting what they want. Meanwhile, America's framework of government support is also strained. Social Security, for example, is declining in generosity, even as guaranteed private pensions evaporate. Medicare, while ever more costly, has not kept pace with skyrocketing health expenses and changing medical practice. And even as unemployment has shifted from cyclical job losses to permanent job displacements, unemployment insurance has eroded as a source of support and recovery for Americans out of work.

The history of American health insurance tells the story in miniature. After the passage of Medicare and Medicaid in 1965, health coverage peaked at roughly 90 percent of the population, with approximately 80 percent of Americans covered by private insurance (Hacker 2002). Since the late 1970s, however, employers and insurers have steadily retreated from broad risk pooling. The number of Americans who lack health coverage has increased with little interruption. Private health coverage now reaches just over 160 million Americans, or slightly more than half the American population.

Employment-based health insurance has not been the only casualty. Companies have also raced away from the promise of guaranteed retirement benefits. Twenty-five years ago, 83 percent of medium and large firms offered traditional "defined-benefit" pensions that provided a fixed benefit for life. Today, the share is below a third (Langbein 2006). Instead, companies that provide pensions—and roughly half the workforce continues to lack a pension at their current job—mostly offer "defined-contribution" plans such as the 401(k), in which returns are neither predictable nor assured.

Defined-contribution plans are not properly seen as pensions, at least as that term has been traditionally understood. They are essentially private investment accounts sponsored by employers that can be used for building up a tax-free estate as well as for retirement savings. As a result, they greatly increase the degree of risk and responsibility placed on individual workers for retirement planning. Traditional defined-benefit plans are generally mandatory and paid for largely by employers (in lieu of cash wages). They thus represent a form of forced savings. Defined-benefit plans are also insured by the federal government and heavily regulated to protect participants against mismanagement. Perhaps most important, their fixed benefits protect workers against the risk of stock market downturns and the possibility of living longer than expected.

None of this is true of defined-contribution plans. Participation is voluntary, and owing to the lack of generous employer contributions, many workers choose not to participate or contribute inadequate sums (Munnell and Sundén 2006). Plans are not adequately regulated to protect against poor asset allocations or corporate or personal mismanagement. The federal government does not insure defined-contribution plans. And defined-contribution accounts provide no inherent protection against asset or longevity risks. Indeed, some features of defined-contribution plans— namely, the ability to borrow against their assets, and the distribution of their accumulated savings as lump-sum payments that must be rolled over into new accounts when workers change jobs—exacerbate the risk that workers will prematurely use retirement savings, leaving inadequate income upon retirement. Perversely, this risk falls most heavily on younger and less highly paid workers, the very workers most in need of secure retirement protection.

We do not yet know how severely the market crisis that began in 2008 will reduce private pension wealth, but the signs are deeply worrisome. Just between mid-2007 and October 2008, an estimated $2 trillion in retirement wealth in 401(k)s and individual retirement accounts was lost (Orszag 2008). A 2009 survey found that two thirds of adults aged fifty to sixty-four lost money in mutual funds, individual stocks, or 401(k) accounts, and the vast majority of these lost more than 20 percent of their investments (Pew Research Center 2009).

Although we cannot yet know how sustained these losses will be, we do know they come after a generation of decline in the retirement-preparedness of Americans. According to researchers at Boston College, the share of working-age households that are at risk of being financially unprepared for retirement at age sixty-five rose from 31 percent in 1983 to 43 percent in 2004 and a projected 51 percent in 2009 (Munnell, Webb, and Golub-Sass 2009). Younger Americans are far more likely to be at risk than older Americans: roughly half of those born from the mid-1960s through the early 1970s are at risk of being financially unprepared, compared with 35 percent of those born in the decade after World War II. The least financially prepared are low-income Americans in every age group.

In sum, as private and public support has eroded, workers and their families have been forced to bear a greater burden. This is the essence of the Great Risk Shift. Rather than enjoying the protections of insurance that pools risk broadly, Americans are increasingly facing economic risks on their own, and often at their peril. In the new world of work and family, the buffers that once cushioned Americans against economic risk have become fewer and harder.

THE NEW WORLD OF WORK AND FAMILY

The erosion of America's distinctive framework of economic protection might be less worrisome if work and family themselves were stable sources of security. Unfortunately, they are not. The job market has grown more uncertain and risky, especially for those who were once best protected from its vagaries. Workers and their families now invest more in education to earn a middle-class living, and yet in today's postindustrial economy, these costly investments are no guarantee of a high, stable, or upward-sloping path. For displaced workers, the prospect of gaining new jobs with relatively similar pay and benefits has fallen, and the ranks of the long-term unemployed and "shadow unemployed" (workers who have given up looking for jobs altogether) have grown. These are not just problems faced by workers at the bottom. In the 2001 downturn, the most educated workers actually experienced the worst effects when losing a full-time job, and older and professional workers were hit hardest by long-term unemployment (see, for example, Stettner and Allegretto 2005).

Meanwhile, the family—once a refuge from economic risk—is creating new risks of its own. At first, this seems counterintuitive. Families are much more likely to have two earners than in the past—a basic form of private risk sharing. To most families, however, a second income is not a luxury but a necessity in a context in which wages are relatively flat and the mains costs of raising a family (health care, education, housing) are high and rising. According to calculations by Jared Bernstein and Karen Kornbluh (2005), more than three quarters of the modest 24 percent rise in real income experienced by families in the middle of the income spectrum between 1979 and 2000 was due to increased work hours rather than rising wages. (Some of this overall gain has been reduced by recent family income declines.) In time-use surveys (for example, Jacobs and Gerson 2004), both men and women who work long hours indicate they would like to work fewer hours and spend more time with their families—which strongly suggests they are not able to choose the exact mix of work and family they would prefer.

With families needing two earners to maintain a middle-class standard of living, their economic calculus has changed in ways that accentuate many of the risks they face. Precisely because it takes more work and more income to maintain a middle-class standard of living, the questions that face families when financially threatening events occur are suddenly more stark. What happens when women leave the workforce to have children, when a child is chronically ill, when one spouse loses his or her job, when an older parent needs assistance? In short, events within two-earner families that require the care and time of family members produce special demands and strains that traditional one-earner families generally did not face.

The new world of work and family has ushered in a new crop of highly leveraged investors—middle-class families. Consider just a few of the alarming facts:

Volatility of Family Income

The instability of family incomes has risen substantially over the last three decades. Although the precise magnitude of the increase depends on the approach to measuring income variance that is used, my own research using the Panel Study of Income Dynamics (PSID) suggests that short-term variance in family income essentially doubled from 1969 to 2004 (Hacker and Jacobs 2008). Much of the rise in income volatility occurred prior to 1985, and volatility dropped substantially in the late 1990s. But it has risen in recent years to exceed its 1980s peak. The proportion of working-age individuals experiencing a 50 percent or greater drop in their family income has climbed from less than 4 percent in the early 1970s to nearly 10 percent in the early 2000s. And while less-educated and poorer Americans have less stable family incomes than their better-educated and wealthier peers, the increase in family income volatility affects all major demographic and economic groups. Indeed, Americans with at least four years of college experienced a larger increase in family income instability than those with only a high-school education over the past generation, with most of the rise occurring in the last fifteen years.

Increase in Family Economic Security

Family income instability is only one aspect of Americans' growing economic insecurity. Along with a team of researchers (and with funding from the Rockefeller Foundation), I have developed the "Economic Security Index," or ESI. The ESI provides a simple measure of the joint occurrence of three major risks to economic well-being:

1. Experiencing a major loss in income

2. Incurring large out-of-pocket medical expenses

3. Lacking adequate financial wealth to buffer the first two risks

In a nutshell, the ESI represents the share of Americans who experience at least a 25 percent decline in their inflation-adjusted "available household income" from one year to the next and who lack an adequate financial safety net to replace this lost income until it has returned to its original level. "Available household income" is income that is reduced by nondiscretionary spending, including, most substantially, the amount of a household's out-of-pocket medical spending. Thus, Americans may experience income losses of 25 percent or greater due to a decline in income or an increase in medical

FIGURE 2.1   Percentage of Americans Who Are Insecure,
1985 to 2007 (With 2008 to 2009 Projections)[a]

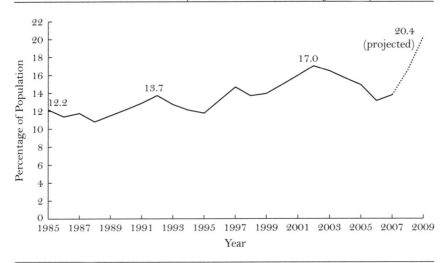

Source: Author's compilation based on Hacker et al. (2010).
[a] The "insecure" are those whose available household income declines by at least
25 percent from one year to the next (after adjusting for inflation), as a result of a
decline in household income or an increase in out-of-pocket medical spending, and who
lack an adequate financial safety net. Thus an individual is considered insecure if the
sum of the increase in medical expenditures and lost annual income totals at least
25 percent of his or her previous year's available income. Household income includes all
private and government sources of income, including the estimated income value of
defined-contribution retirement accounts, such as 401(k)s, for households with heads
age sixty or older. Household income is adjusted to reflect the economies of scale of
pooling household resources and expenses. Household income is also reduced by the
amount needed to pay off liquid financial debts when net financial wealth is negative.
Individuals with adequate holdings of liquid financial wealth are not treated as insecure
even when they experience 25 percent or higher income losses. We define "adequate" as
enough liquid financial wealth to compensate for the lost income until typical recovery
to pre-drop income or for six years, whatever comes first. Those entering retirement
are also excluded from the count of the insecure, even if available household income
declines by 25 percent or more concurrent with retirement; once retired, however, they
are counted as insecure when they experience such declines.

spending or a combination of the two. The ESI, available from 1985 through
2007 (with projections for 2008 and 2009) shows that economic insecurity
has increased substantially over the last quarter century (see figure 2.1). In
1985, 12 percent of Americans experienced a major economic loss sufficient
to classify them as insecure in the ESI. During the recession of the early
2000s, this had risen to 17 percent, and projections suggest that in 2009 the
level of economic insecurity experienced by Americans was greater than at

any other time over the past quarter century, with approximately one in five (20.4 percent) Americans experiencing a decline in available household income of 25 percent or greater.

Increased Incidence of Personal Bankruptcy

Personal bankruptcy has gone from a rare occurrence to a relatively common one, with the number of households filing for bankruptcy rising from less than 300,000 in 1980 to more than 2 million in 2005.[1] Over that period, the financial characteristics of the bankrupt have grown worse and worse, contrary to the claim that bankruptcy is increasingly being used by people with only mild financial difficulties. Strikingly, married couples with children are much more likely to file for bankruptcy than are couples without children or single individuals (Warren and Tyagi 2003). Otherwise, before they file the bankrupt are pretty much like other Americans: slightly better educated than average, roughly as likely to have had a good job, and modestly less likely to own a home. They are not the persistently poor, the downtrodden looking for relief; they are refugees of the middle class, frequently wondering how they fell so far so fast (Warren 2003a).

Incidence of Home Loss on the Rise

Americans are also losing their homes at record rates. Even before the housing market collapsed in 2008, there had been a fivefold increase since the 1970s in the share of households that fall into foreclosure (calculated from Elmer and Seelig 1998)—a process that begins when homeowners default on their mortgages and can end with homes being auctioned to the highest bidder in local courthouses. The run-up of housing prices before the economic downturn had much less of a positive effect on Americans' net worth than might be supposed, because even as home prices rose, Americans held less and less equity in their home. As recently as the early 1980s, equity was around 70 percent of home values on average; in 2007, it was 43 percent—the lowest level on record (Weller and Lynch 2009). In the recent downturn, approximately 20 percent of homeowners owe more on their home than it is worth (Simon and Hagerty 2009). For scores of ordinary homeowners—roughly one in twenty-five mortgage-owning households in the past few years—the American Dream has mutated into the American nightmare.

Increase in Americans' Debt

American families are drowning in debt. Since the early 1970s, the personal savings rate has plummeted from around a tenth of disposable income to essentially zero (U.S. Department of Commerce 2009). Meanwhile, the total debt held by Americans has ballooned, especially for families with children. As a share of income in 2004, total debt—including mortgages, credit cards, car loans, and other liabilities—was more than 125 percent of income for the median married couple with children, or more than three times the level of debt held by married families without children, and more than nine times the level of debt held by childless adults (Hacker 2008b). According to a recent analysis of families with incomes between two and six times the federal poverty level and headed by working-age adults, more than half of middle-class families have no net financial assets (excluding home equity), and nearly four in five middle-class families do not have sufficient assets to cover three quarters of essential living expenses for even three months should their income disappear (Wheary, Shapiro, and Draut 2007). Of course, the recent economic crisis has only exacerbated the problem, causing a loss of $15 trillion—yes, trillion—in private family assets and wealth between June 2007 and December 2008 (Weller and Lynch 2009).

As these examples suggest, economic insecurity is not just a problem of the poor and uneducated, as is frequently assumed. It affects even educated, middle-class Americans—men and women who thought that by staying in school, by buying a home, by investing in their 401(k)s, they had bought the ticket to upward mobility and economic stability. Insecurity today reaches across the income spectrum, across the racial divide, across lines of geography and gender. Increasingly, all Americans are riding the economic roller coaster once reserved for the working poor. This means that, increasingly, all Americans are at risk of losing the secure financial foundation they need to reach for and achieve the American Dream.

Economic security matters deeply to people. When most of us contemplate the financial risks in our lives, we do not concern ourselves all that much with the upside risks—the chance we will receive an unexpected bonus, for example. We worry about the downside risks, and worry about them intensely. In the 1970s, the psychologists Daniel Kahneman and Amos Tversky (1979) gave a name to this bias: "loss aversion." Most people, it turns out, are not just highly risk-averse—they prefer a bird in the hand to even a very good chance of two in the bush. They are also far more cautious when it comes to bad outcomes than when it comes to good outcomes of exactly the same magnitude. The search for economic security is, in large part, a reflection of a basic human desire for protection against losing what one already has.

This desire is surprisingly strong. Americans are famously opportunity-loving, but when asked in 2005 whether they were "more concerned with the opportunity to make money in the future, or the stability of knowing that your present sources of income are protected," 62 percent favored stability and just 29 percent favored opportunity (Lake Snell Perry and Associates and Tarrance Group 2005).

It should not be surprising, therefore, that recent polling shows extremely high levels of economic anxiety among all but the richest Americans. In April 2009, for example, two in three adults said "today's economy presents [me] with more risks" than my parents confronted—six times as many who said they faced fewer risks (Brownstein 2009). A poll that I helped design, fielded as part of the American National Election Studies, shows that in 2009, more than half of Americans reported being "very" or "fairly" worried about their economic security. As table 2.1 shows, across a range of economic risks, more than half—and often more than two thirds—of Americans report having some worries about their economic security. (The one exception is "keeping up housing payments," which was "not at all" a worry of 55 percent of homeowners.) The greatest worries concern retirement income adequacy (54 percent of respondents reported they were "very" or "fairly" worried), out-of-pocket medical costs and health insurance premiums (more than 40 percent), keeping or finding a job (39 percent), getting out of debt (39 percent), and losing one's spouse or partner due to death or family separation (39 percent).

Even before the recent economic crisis, however, Americans overwhelmingly declared that the economy had become less secure in the last decade (65 percent, according to a February 2007 survey), instead of more secure (19 percent), and the strongest sense of rising insecurity was felt among those with family incomes between $36,000 and $92,000 (67 percent of those in this income range said things have grown less secure, versus 17 percent who said they had not; see Rockefeller Foundation 2007). In the same 2007 poll, a majority of Americans also expected things to become less secure over the next 20 years.

It would be one thing if all this risk came with great rewards for the middle class, but it has not. The Congressional Budget Office has put together a comprehensive measure of the distribution of income, based on actual tax records as well as reported income in surveys (see figure 2.2). Taking into account all government taxes and benefits, as well as private workplace health insurance and pensions, the middle quintile of households (that is, the 20 percent of households above the bottom 40 percent and below the top 40 percent) saw their inflation-adjusted incomes rise

TABLE 2.1   Prevalence of Reported Worry About Economic Risks, Spring 2009

Domains of Risk	Reported Prevalence, by Intensity of Worry			
	Very Worried	Fairly Worried	Slightly Worried	Not At All Worried
Overall economic security	24.3%	28.5%	35.7%	11.5%
Employment				
Keeping or finding a job	19.2	19.7	30.7	30.5
Wealth and housing				
Keeping up with housing payments	12.4	11.6	25.0	55.0
Getting out of debt	20.6	18.6	25.4	35.4
Adequate retirement income	30.1	24.1	25.7	20.0
Nursing home costs in retirement	11.5	15.5	32.5	40.5
Medical insurance				
Out-of-pocket medical costs	19.0	22.1	34.6	24.3
Losing health insurance	17.3	16.7	31.1	35.0
Cost of insurance premiums	19.9	22.4	35.8	21.9
Familial responsibilities				
Helping out family financially	11.6	20.0	38.4	30.0
Losing one's spouse or partner	21.8	17.7	27.2	33.3

Source: Author's compilation based on American National Election Studies (2008–2009).
Note: 2008 to 2009 Panel Study, wave 15, comprising U.S. citizens in the general population age eighteen or older as of November 2008, fielded between March 11 and April 9, 2009.

from $41,900 to $52,100 between 1979 and 2006—a gain of 21 percent (Congressional Budget Office 2009). The average after-tax incomes of the richest 1 percent of households rose from just over $337,100 a year to more than $1.2 million over the same period—an increase of more than 250 percent. Put another way, more than a third (36 percent) of total economic gains over the 1979-to-2006 period accrued to the richest 1 percent of households. By contrast, only 8 percent were received by the middle fifth. And recall that most of the income gains of middle-class families are due to the fact that family members are working more hours, not to higher pay. The risk-reward trade-off looks more like a risk-reward rip-off.

FIGURE 2.2   Change in Average Household After-Tax Annual
Income, Including Public and Private Benefits
Between 1979 and 2006[a]

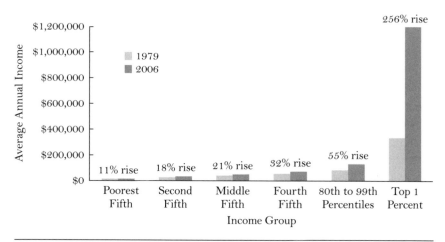

Source: Author's calculations based on data in Congressional Budget Office (2009 table at www.cbo.gov/publications/collections/tax/2009/average_after-tax_income.xls; accessed on January 1, 2010).
[a] Income includes wages, salaries, self-employment income, rents, taxable and non-taxable interest, dividends, realized capital gains, cash transfer payments, and cash retirement benefits, as well as all in-kind benefits, such as Medicare, Medicaid, employer-paid health insurance premiums, food stamps, school lunches and breakfasts, housing assistance, and energy assistance. Federal taxes are subtracted from income and account for not just income and payroll taxes paid directly by individuals and households, but also taxes paid by businesses (corporate income taxes and the employer's share of Social Security, Medicare, and federal unemployment insurance payroll taxes).

THE POLITICAL CHALLENGE

Growing economic insecurity is often viewed as an issue independent of politics. Yet it is deeply related to a series of fundamental changes in the American political system over the last generation that have pushed toward the restriction of government efforts to deal with growing inequality and increasing risk of economic loss (Hacker and Pierson 2010). The most fundamental of these shifts is the one that we most frequently take for granted: the rise of an aggressive, well-organized, and politically powerful conservative movement. The Republican Party suffered such serious losses at the polls (and in opinion polls) in 2006 and 2008 that it is difficult to remember just how powerful they became during the thirty years in which economic insecurity and inequality rose, or how pervasively they reshaped U.S. economic and social policy over this era. But it is important to understand the sources and the effects of the more hard-edged conservative critique of U.S. social and economic policy that has come to characterize the contemporary GOP—not least because, as of this writing (May 2010) the Republican Party is poised to make major gains in the fall midterm election by capitalizing on widespread voter discontent with the economy and the bailout of the financial sector.

Conservatism was on the defensive in the 1960s and early 1970s, as was vividly confirmed by Barry Goldwater's crushing defeat by Lyndon Johnson in 1964. In the wake of the repudiation of Goldwater, however, conservatives regrouped and refashioned their strategies. Mixing a libertarian emphasis on free markets and limited government with the more authoritarian prescriptions of America's emerging social conservative movement, the Republican Party and its grassroots backers roared back in the late 1970s—particularly in the South, where the national Democratic Party's support for civil rights had caused its once-dominant one-party regime to implode. With voting patterns forged during the New Deal finally loosened, Republicans crafted a new electoral and governing coalition that was able to capture the White House in every election but two from 1980 on, and that finally took Congress in 1994.

The success of conservatism in American politics was not felt only in electoral victories. Arguably, in fact, conservatives' greatest success came in their ability to leverage often-slim electoral margins into mandates to make fundamental changes in the tenor and direction of American policy debates (Hacker and Pierson 2005). Conservative political elites sought to privatize existing programs so as to increase personal responsibility and personal exposure to risk. They emphasized greater control over individual behavior as an alternative to expanded redistribution or insurance. They argued for a shift away from progressive taxation and toward a so-called consumption tax that would reduce taxes on the wealthy and raise them on the middle class.

Many of these ambitious goals have proved politically infeasible, but that does not mean they have not been pursued in more incremental, subterranean fashion. Such strategies of stealth took three main forms (Hacker 2004):

1. Efforts to "convert" existing policies by changing the way they are carried out on the ground

2. Efforts to "layer" new policies on top of old ones so as to change the operation of the old

3. Efforts to abet the "drift" of policies away from their original pur-
    poses by blocking attempts to update existing policies to new social
    circumstances

During the 1980s and 1990s, for example, conservatives advocated
the expansion of tax-favored retirement accounts such as 401(k)s in part
to create a "parallel system" of retirement savings that could compete
directly with Social Security and ultimately become a basis for a shift
away from the public pension program (Butler and Germanis 1983). They
also expanded the role of private health plans within Medicare, arguing
that the program should shift away from a guaranteed-benefit model to
a system of government-regulated competition in which seniors would
have a fixed amount with which to purchase private health plans (Hacker
2004, 2006).

Moreover, in an environment of new or worsening social risks, conservatives did not have to enact major policy reforms to move policy toward
their favored ends. Merely by delegitimizing and blocking compensatory
interventions designed to ameliorate intensified risks, they were able to
gradually transform the orientation of existing programs, allowing these
programs to "drift" away from their original mission.

In their campaign to prevent policies from being updated, conservatives
were greatly aided by the fragmented character of American government,
with its multiple "veto points" where action could be blocked, as well as by
the growing "polarization" of members of Congress, which made it harder to
reach agreement on policy measures to update the eroding social contract.
Gridlock was much better for the conservative project than it was for the
cause of maintaining American social protection in the face of economic and
social changes.

Perhaps the most important institutional source of stalemate in the
1990s and 2000s was the rising prominence of the Senate filibuster. The
filibuster—the tradition of unlimited debate in the Senate that requires
sixty Senate votes to overcome—has metastasized from a procedure that
was used rarely by intense minorities in the Senate into a normalized tool
of minority obstruction. Cloture motions to end filibusters tell part—but
only part—of the story. Since the 66th Congress of 1919 to 1920, more
than 1,200 motions have been filed to invoke cloture.[2] More than 80 percent of them were filed since the 97th Congress of 1981 to 1982, and
more than 60 percent just since the 103d Congress of 1993 to 1994.
Although the filibuster surely displaced other, less formal forms of Senate
obstruction, these activities were simply nothing like the hard-and-fast

"rule of sixty" that now reigns. Controversial laws were routinely passed with majorities well short of the cloture threshold (which was higher before the 1970s). As David Mayhew (2008, 274), the dean of congressional scholars, has put it, "Never before has the Senate possessed any anti-majoritarian barrier as concrete, as decisive, or as consequential."

The filibuster matters in part because of how skewed the Senate already is in favor of less populated and generally more conservative states, thanks to the "great compromise" of two senators per state. This skew is actually greater now than it was in earlier eras, when the filibuster was less commonly used. Compared with the population-based apportionment of the House of Representatives, disproportionately Senate constituencies are more rural, more Republican, and whiter. This affects the apportionment of funds, the representation of minority groups, and the outcome of big legislative fights (Lee and Oppenheimer 1999; Griffin 2006). Even when a filibuster is unsuccessful in preventing legislation from coming to a vote, it shifts the center of political gravity substantially away from the center.

The filibuster would matter much less, however, if the two parties in government had not become increasingly ideologically cohesive and distinct. Much contemporary commentary centers on the "polarization" of American politics, but the term is misleading, inasmuch as it implies that both parties have moved away from the center of American politics at equal speed. In fact, the Republican Part has moved substantially farther to the right of the political spectrum than Democrats have moved to the left (Hacker and Pierson 2005, 2010). The reasons for the shift also differ: Republicans have moved right because nearly all Republican politicians are more conservative than Republicans of a generation ago. Most of the Democratic Party's shift to the left, by contrast, has occurred because conservative Southern Democrats in the South have lost office to conservative Republicans, thus affecting the aggregate profile of elected officials in that party. In short, the growing difficulty of reaching agreement in American politics is not an equal opportunity affair—equally attributable to each party. It has been driven by the shift of the right to the extreme right. Its effect has been to encourage the drift of American economic and social policy away from providing a basic foundation of economic security for workers and their families.

The inference most analysts take from the rightward shift of the Republican Party is that American voters as a whole have grown more conservative. Certainly, popular concerns did spur GOP political gains in the late 1970s. But according to the weight of the evidence, middle-of-the-road Americans have not grown more conservative since the early 1980s, and may even have become slightly more liberal. James Stimson has developed a comprehensive measure of public mood that shows that Americans are substantially more liberal today than they were in the early 1980s.[3] Given the difficulty of coming up with consistent measures of public opinion that are comparable over time (and not simply reactive to present circumstances), Stimson's results should be viewed with considerable caution, but they do strongly suggest that the shift of the Republican Party to the right over the course of an era in which the GOP has become the dominant force in American politics is not driven by a general shift to the right by the American public.

Nor does the rise of a more conservative American political establishment seem to reflect an elevation of "moral issues" above economic concerns, which might be thought to explain why in an era of rising insecurity and inequality, voters have not turned against the Republican Party with its low-tax, limited-redistribution messages. Instead, voting has become more class-stratified—with low-income voters tending to vote Democrat, and high-income voters tending to vote Republican—than it was immediately after World War II (McCarty, Poole, and Rosenthal 2006; Bartels 2008). At the same time, economic issues appear to have become more important in motivating voter choice, and have become a more prominent element of both parties' platforms (Bartels 2008; Smith 2007). Whatever the reason for the conservative ascendance, it certainly does not signal that economic issues have faded in importance as a source of conflict between the parties or as motivators of voter choice.

Indeed, many of the most important changes in American politics have occurred at the level of political organization, rather than at the level of voter opinions or roll-call votes in Congress. The decline of organizations that once represented middle- and working-class voters on economic issues, such as unions and fraternal societies, has been accompanied by the rise of a well-networked and politically savvy conservative movement, organized at the grassroots level through churches and local business organizations and at the national level through think tanks, expanded business lobbies, and GOP-affiliated political action committees (Skocpol 2003).

Perhaps most important, as the cost of campaigns has skyrocketed, money has become markedly more important as a political resource. And money has always been the most unequally distributed of political resources: In 2000, an eighth of American households had incomes greater than $100,000; these fortunate households made up 95 percent of those who gave a thousand dollars or more to a campaign that year (American Political Science Association, Task Force on Inequality and American Democracy

2004). The parties now contact between a quarter (Democratic Party) and a third (Republican Party) of the wealthiest of Americans directly during campaign seasons, up from less than 15 percent of these high-income voters in the 1950s (Campbell 2007). Recent studies of representation suggest that lower-income Americans have little or no influence over the voting or policy choices of their elected representatives, while the most affluent have the greatest sway (Gilens 2005; Bartels 2008).

Tallying up the effects of these organizational shifts is not easy. For example, while business groups have been gaining ground, so have new "public-interest" organizations, organized around the environment and other single-issue causes. But these public-interest groups have not coordinated their activities as effectively as conservative organizations have, nor have they focused their attention on the economic issues that continue to motivate voters and drive party conflict. Overall, therefore, the changes in American political organization just described have clearly weakened the political voice of the less advantaged on economic issues—which, of course, was never all that loud to begin with. With the exception of organizations representing the elderly and a greatly weakened labor movement, few groups representing middle- and lower-income Americans are now major players in America's fierce debates over economic issues.

POLICY PRESCRIPTIONS FOR A NEW SOCIAL CONTRACT

Despite the force of the factors just described, the Great Risk Shift is not a financial hurricane beyond human control. True, sweeping changes in the global and domestic economy have helped propel it, but America's leaders could have responded to these forces by reinforcing the floodwalls that protect families from economic risk. Instead, lacking strong political pressure to address new and newly intensified risks and shore up dwindling protections, those leaders have acted in ways that have further eroded the floodwalls that protect families. Proponents of these changes speak of a nirvana of individual economic management—an "ownership society" in which Americans are free to choose. What they are helping to create, however, is very different: a world of economic insecurity in which far too many Americans are free to lose.

We cannot turn back the clock on many of the changes that have swept through the American economy and American society in the past thirty years, nor would we always want to. Accepting our new economic and social realities does not, however, mean accepting the new economic insecurity, much less accepting the assumptions that lie behind the current assault on the ideal of security. Americans will need to do much to secure themselves in the new world of work and family, but they should be protected by an improved safety net that fills the most glaring gaps in present protections, providing all Americans with the basic security they need to reach for the future as workers, as parents, and as citizens.

The first priority for restoring security should be the Hippocratic Oath: "Do no harm." Undoing what risk pooling remains in the private sector without putting something better in place does harm. Piling tax break upon tax break to allow wealthy and healthy Americans to opt out of our tattered institutions of social insurance does harm. And though simplifying our tax code makes eminent sense, making it markedly less progressive through a flat tax or national sales tax would also do harm. A progressive income tax, after all, is effectively a form of insurance, reducing our contribution to public goods when income falls and raising it when income rises.

Yet while we should work to preserve the best elements of existing policies, we should also recognize that the nature and causes of insecurity, as well as our understanding about how to best address it, have evolved considerably. During the New Deal, economic insecurity was largely seen as a problem of drops or interruptions in males' earnings, whether due to unemployment, retirement, or other costly events. Even as working women became the norm, our programs failed to respond to the special economic strains faced by two-earner families. They also failed to take account of the distinctive unemployment patterns that became increasingly prevalent as industrial employment gave way to service work—for example, the rising prevalence of long-term unemployment and the shift of workers from one economic sector to another that often leads to large cuts in pay and the need for specialized retraining. (In 2010, it took on average more than twenty weeks to find a new job—double the time it took in the recession of 1982 and 1983 [Scherer 2010].)

Flaws in existing policies of risk protection have also become apparent. Our framework of social protection overwhelmingly focuses on the aged, even though young adults and families with children face the greatest economic strains. It is geared to helping with short-term exits from the workforce, even though long-term job losses and the displacement and obsolescence of skills have become bigger problems. It embodies, in places, the antiquated notion that family strains can be dealt with by the exit of a second earner, usually a woman, from the workforce. Above all, it is based on the idea that job-based private insurance can easily fill the gaps left by public programs, even though it is becoming ever clearer that this is not the case.

These shortcomings suggest that an improved safety net should emphasize portable insurance to help families deal with major interruptions to income and big blows to wealth. They also mean that these promises should be mostly separate from work for a particular employer; benefits must move with the individual from job to job. If this sometimes means corporations are off the hook for insurance, so be it. In time, they will pay their workers more to compensate for fewer benefits, and there are plenty of ways to encourage corporate entities to contributes their fair share to society without giving them the power to decide who gets benefits and who does not.

By the same token, we should not force massive social risks onto institutions incapable of effectively carrying them. Bankruptcy should not be a backdoor social insurance system. Private charity care should not be our main medical safety net. Credit cards should not be the main way that families get by when times are tight. To be sure, when nothing better is possible, the principle of "do no harm" may dictate protecting even incomplete and inadequate safety nets. The ultimate goal, however, should be a new framework of social insurance that revitalizes the best elements of the present system, while replacing those parts that work less effectively with stronger alternatives geared toward today's economy and society.

In doing all this, we should not be seduced but the false belief that a strong safety net only helps those who have had bad fortune or have fallen on hard times. Providing economic security has far broader benefits for our economy and our society. Corporate law has long recognized the need to limit the downside of economic risk-taking as a way of encouraging entrepreneurs and investors to make the risky investments necessary to advance in a capitalist economy. The law of bankruptcy and the principle of limited liability—the notion that those who run a firm are not personally liable if the firm fails—allow entrepreneurs to innovate with the security of knowing they will not be financially destroyed if their risky bets fail (Moss 2002).

Just as basic protections are needed for entrepreneurs in order to foster their risk taking, families also need a basic foundation of financial security if they are to feel confident in making the investments needed to advance in a dynamic economy. All of the major wellsprings of economic opportunity in the United States—from assets to workplace skills to education to investments in children—are costly and risky for families to cultivate. Providing security can encourage families to make these investments, aiding not just their own advancement but the economy as a whole.

Providing economic security appears even more beneficial when considered against some of the leading alternatives that insecure citizens may otherwise back. Heavy-handed regulation of the economy, strict limits on cross-border trade and financial flows, and other intrusive measures may gain widespread support from workers buffeted by economic turbulence, and yet these measures are likely to reduce economic growth.

The challenge, then, is to construct a twenty-first-century social contract that protects families against the most severe risks they face, without clamping down on the potentially beneficial processes of change and adjustment that produce some of these risks. Three areas of economic risk in particular cry out for attention: employment risks, retirement income risks, and health-care risks. But it would be a mistake to only design economic protections narrowly around specific economic concerns. Another priority is to create new and flexible policies for dealing with economic risks of all kinds. I propose one such policy, "Universal Insurance," at the end of this section.

Blunting Risks to Workers

Nowhere is the need for both restoration and reform more transparent than in our need to upgrade protections for the unemployed, after decades of drift and neglect of these protections. Unemployment insurance has eroded dramatically in the last generation (see, for example, Graetz and Mashaw 1999). True, important reforms were passed in 2009 as part of the American Recovery and Reinvestment Act of 2009 (the so-called stimulus package), but they were much less sweeping than needed. Moreover, their success remains dependent on state policy decisions and state financing of unemployment insurance trust funds, both of which have limited their impact to date and could be subject to future reversals. Broad ideas for restoring unemployment insurance through comprehensive, national action are not hard to find, and the cost would be comparatively modest (see, for example, Kletzer and Rosen 2006).

Restoring strong national standards that require states to cover workers who have worked for a minimum time would go a long way toward filling the gaps in the present program. An automatic trigger that extends benefits beyond their usual six-month cutoff on a progressively less generous basis would deal with increases in long-term unemployment while also encouraging workers to find new jobs. Long-term unemployment benefits could also be provided in the form of retraining vouchers to use for the purchase of private educational services. (See Stoll, this volume, chapter 3, for a discussion of education and training programs.)

Unemployment insurance is not, however, designed to deal with the most serious risk of losing a job: long-term declines, rather than temporary

interruptions, in earning power and standard of living. Long-term joblessness has grown much more severe in the post-2007 downturn, though the
problem of permanent job displacement predates the recent recession. There
is increasing agreement among economists that some form of wage insurance is needed for workers displaced by the effects of globalization trade or
reengineering—technical changes that they are unprepared for—who are
unable to find a new job with comparable pay or benefits (see, for example, Kletzer 2001). Different wage insurance proposals differ in their details,
but all would provide a supplement to wages to encourage workers to take
new jobs even if they pay less than old jobs. To encourage workers to continue to search aggressively for higher-paying jobs, such assistance should
cover only a portion of the wage loss that follows a job switch, and should
decline gradually over time.

These proposals are vastly superior to restrictions on company hiring
and firing, which can lead to labor-market inflexibility. It is for this reason
that even some of the most ardent free-marketeers support wage insurance.

However, such policies should not be limited to workers displaced by
trade, as is true of most existing government help for displaced workers.
The experience of losing a job is just as devastating if your job disappears
forever as it is if your job heads off to a country where labor costs are lower.[4]

Unemployment insurance could also be the platform for dealing with the
most serious work-family conflict faced by many Americans today: the difficulty of taking time off when children enter our families. Encouraging
states to provide several weeks of paid leave to care for newborns, newly
adopted children, and newly placed foster children would, in a stroke,
greatly reduce the strain that working Americans face when they decide to
start a family. (See Heymann and Earle, this volume, chapter 6, for discussion of family leave and related work-family policies.)

Securing Retirement

If young workers need assurances and backup to raise the next generation
of Americans, they also need assurances and backup to plan for their own
future. The incentives for higher-income Americans to save have ballooned
with the expansion of tax-favored investment vehicles. Yet most Americans
receive relatively modest benefits from these costly tax breaks. In the words
of one knowledgeable commentator, our incentives for saving are "upside
down," delivering most of their benefits to people who have substantial
income and assets and virtually nothing to the vast majority of Americans
who most need to save (Orszag 2004).

What Americans need is support and incentives for asset building that is both broad and progressive. Replacing the current welter of tax breaks for nonretirement savings with a single Universal Savings Account that is most generous for Americans of ordinary means would go a long way toward restoring the balance. (See Sherraden, this volume, chapter 5, for further discussion of asset-building policies.)

Yet when it comes to personal savings, the biggest challenge today is preserving a system of guaranteed retirement pensions, including Social Security. Defined-benefit pensions are a thing of the past for most current workers, and defined-contribution plans such as 401(k)s are failing miserably to provide a secure foundation for workers' retirement. Securing our one system of guaranteed benefits, Social Security, is thus all the more essential. The future financial threats to Social Security are well known, if often exaggerated. But dealing with them does not require abandoning the core elements of the program: guaranteed lifetime benefits paid on retirement, provided as a right, and linked to lifetime earnings. The funding shortfall within the program (due to become an issue in the next decade) can be relatively easily closed by increasing revenues into the program by raising the portion of high-income Americans' wages and salaries that are subject to payment into the Social Security Trust Fund and by levying a Social Security tax on capital as well as labor income. Further measures could include making Social Security benefits very modestly more progressive (that is, more generous for low- and middle-income workers) and tying benefits to future longevity so that fortunate generations that live longer than the last receive slightly less from the program than is currently promised. (For a proposal along these lines—one that in my view relies more on benefit cuts than necessary—see Diamond and Orszag 2005).

Even with these changes, however, today's workers will need additional sources of income in retirement. One of the most popular sources of additional retirement funds is the 401(k) account. As they are presently constituted, however, 401(k)s are not the solution to providing adequate additional retirement income. Too few workers have access to them, enroll in them, put enough money in them, or roll the amounts in their accounts into other tax-favored retirement accounts when they leave a job (see, for example, Munnell and Sundén 2006). Instead, we should create a universal 401(k) that is available to all workers, whether or not their employer offers a traditional retirement plan. Employers would be encouraged to match employee contributions to these plans, and the government could provide special tax breaks to employers that offered better matches to lower-wage workers.

Since all workers would have access to universal 401(k)s, there would no longer be the possibility that lump-sum payments would be spent instead of saved for retirement when workers lose or change jobs. All benefits would remain in the same account throughout a worker's life. As with today's 401(k)s, workers could withdraw this money before retirement only with a steep penalty. Unlike in the present system, the same rules that now protect traditional pension plans against excessive investment in company stock would govern 401(k)s. What is more, the default investment option under 401(k)s should be a low-cost index fund with a mix of stocks and bonds that automatically shifts over time as workers age, to limit the market risk as they approach retirement. Finally, and no less important, there should be serious consideration of the idea of requiring that 401(k) accounts be transformed into a lifetime guaranteed income at age sixty-five, unless workers specifically request otherwise and can show they have sufficient assets to weather market risk. Moreover, to help workers plan ahead, 401(k) balances should be reported to account holders not simply as a cash sum, but also as a monthly benefit amount that workers would receive when they retired if they had an average life expectancy, just as Social Security benefits are reported.

Providing Health Care for Americans

Health care is at the epicenter of economic insecurity in the United States today for two interwoven reasons: health-care costs have exploded and coverage has dwindled. The only way to solve these twin problems is to solve them simultaneously: broadening coverage in a way that fosters effective control over costs.

This is the double-barreled goal of the Affordable Care Act of 2010. The act is a major step forward in providing health security, but it is incomplete in several key respects and will require major updating over time. In addition, its passage by no means signals the end of the fierce political conflict that preceded its enactment.

The Affordable Care Act rests on three policy pillars:

1. A requirement that all Americans purchase insurance (with hardship waivers for those with very high premium costs as a share of income)

2. A framework for obtaining insurance outside of employment (state insurance exchanges) along with new regulations on insurers

3. Large new federal subsidies to defray the cost of coverage for low- and middle-income families who obtain coverage through the exchanges, coupled with expansion of Medicaid for the near-poor

Although the Congressional Budget Office projects that the act will cover more than 30 million people by 2019 and more than pay for itself, it is important to recognize that these projections are only that—projections. Much depends on the implementation of the law and the resolution of political battles currently surrounding it. Indeed, the main features of the law do not take effect until 2014.

The Affordable Care Act has two notable weaknesses that must be addressed to ensure broader health security is achieved and maintained. First, it relies heavily on the cooperative behavior of three sets of actors with their own distinct policy goals: states, employers, and insurers. The first are charged with creating the exchanges and expanding the Medicaid program, as well as carrying out the regulations of insurers. Although there is federal authority to intervene if states fail to set up exchanges, the law is more ambiguous when it comes to partial compliance, and very vigilant oversight at the federal level will be required to ensure that states carry out the mandate of the law. Moreover, the law creates a parallel set of national health plans for those without insurance, run by the Office of Personnel Management (OPM), the federal agency that handles the Federal Employees Health Benefit Program. This part of the law creates opportunities as well as risks, too.

Employers' and insurers' cooperation is required as well. Employers that now provide insurance may decide to drop it so their workers can receive coverage through the exchanges (which will entail paying a penalty, but could nonetheless be attractive to many employers). If this occurs on a broad scale, the effects of the law will be much more sweeping and potentially destabilizing than projected. As for insurers, they are certain to work hard to undermine the reach of the insurance regulations—and in many states they may have the upper hand politically.

The second notable weakness of the Affordable Care Act concerns cost containment. Put bluntly, the cost controls in the act are weak. Mostly for political reasons, the act relies heavily on innovations in payments in Medicare, which, it is hoped, will diffuse into the private sector. Enhanced insurance market competition is a second, more speculative source of savings. The evidence that such measures will substantially slow the rate of increase in U.S. health spending is weak to nonexistent, and indeed the CBO did not project large premium savings. Most of the savings achieved by families will occur because of the direct federal subsidies and expansion of Medicaid (Congressional Budget Office 2010). But without serious restraint on costs going forward, the aims of the legislation—broader coverage, more affordable insurance, and thus greater health security—will not be achieved.

Worse, the budgetary pressure on the federal government may well lead to cutbacks in the subsidies for coverage, reversing some of the gains made by the law. It may also lead to calls for slashing Medicare by, for example, converting it into a defined-contribution plan that provides a fixed voucher for private coverage for Medicare enrollees. This would push more risk onto Americans, rather than push back against the Great Risk Shift.

Many commentators suggest that cost control is beyond the capacity of the federal government. This is false: In fact, since payment controls were first introduced into the Medicare program in the early 1980s, Medicare's costs per patient have risen slower, on average, than private health insurance spending per patient, and the gap has been particularly pronounced in recent years. Between 1997 and 2006, for example, health spending per enrollee (for comparable benefits) grew at 4.6 percent a year under Medicare, compared with 7.3 percent a year under private health insurance, even as Medicare maintained high levels of provider participation and patient access to care (Hacker 2008a).

Certainly, Medicare faces serious strains. Yet the common critique of Medicare, that it is overly generous, is without basis. Medicare coverage is substantially less generous than the norm in the private sector. If we decide as a nation that we cannot "afford" Medicare, then we are deciding that we cannot afford to provide even relatively basic health care to the aged. Few Americans, I am certain, are ready to accept this dismal conclusion, and rightly so. Almost every other advanced industrial country provides insurance not just to the aged, but to all citizens, while spending much less on a per-person basis than the incomplete system of the United States (Woolhandler and Himmelstein 2002). Furthermore, many of these nations have older populations than we do, have citizenries that go to the doctor more often, and have better basic health outcomes. Yet their overall health spending remains far below ours and in many countries has also been growing more slowly (Anderson et al. 2000).

In the end, the main problem with Medicare has nothing to do with its effectiveness but rather with its limitation to the aged and disabled. This limitation hobbles the public sector's ability to control costs because the program's reach is so restricted. It also means that paying for Medicare inevitably pits the needs of younger Americans against the needs of older Americans. Rather than take away the security of Medicare because younger Americans lack comparable protections, we need to build on the Medicare model while shoring up employment-based coverage where it works well. The key to doing this is the creation of a "public option" that would ensure that all Americans without secure workplace coverage have access to a new public health insurance plan as well as regulated private options.

How can this be done? By building on the new law in two key areas. First, we should broaden the requirement on employers so that, rather than relying on a penalty system sanctioning employers that don't cover their workers, all employers would instead be given an affordable choice: They could provide insurance at least as generous as provided by the new national plans overseen by OPM, or they could pay a modest amount to help finance coverage for their workers, who would then be enrolled automatically in either these plans or the state exchanges. (Over time, I would argue for moving toward a national exchange.) People enrolled through these non-employment-based means would pay subsidized, affordable premiums based on their income and family size. More important, they should be able to choose a new Medicare-like public plan as an alternative to private insurance plans, a second major amendment to the 2009 law that needs to be made.

Those who followed the 2009 debate will recognize this last idea as the public option that I first developed in the early 2000s and which was nearly included in the legislation (Hacker 2001, 2007, 2008a, 2009; Lewin Group 2008). Critics of the public option argued that it would wipe out private health insurance, but this is false on two counts. First, employment-based coverage may well decline under the current law, because employers will choose to pay a penalty rather than provide insurance. But this is true regardless of whether or not there is a public option. Under the approach I recommend, however, employers would instead be given a choice that ensures their workers were covered, while requiring that they make at least a minimal commitment to financing coverage for their workers. In higher-wage firms and unionized industries, it would still be in the best interest of companies to provide broad coverage. Unlike the present reform law, then, the refined framework I am proposing would ensure that everyone who works has secure health insurance, that many more workers can choose their plan (including a plan with free choice of doctors and specialists), and that companies that now struggle to provide health benefits, or cannot provide them at all, have an attractive, low-cost option for doing so.

Second, the new public option would coexist alongside private plans, competing with them on a level playing field. This would foster competitive pressures on private plans to hold down costs, creating greater savings and health security for all Americans. The goal is a system that encourages private insurance and public insurance to compete in a regulated market that rewards plans that deliver better value and health to their enrollees. Public insurance can be a benchmark for private plans and a source of stability for enrollees, especially those with substantial health needs. Private plans can provide an alternative for those who feel that public insurance does not serve their needs and a source of continuing pressure for innovation in benefit design and care management. And both should have a chance to prove their strengths and improve their weaknesses in a competitive partnership.

Over time, the program I have just described could evolve in different directions, depending on how employers, on the one hand, and the public option and regulated private plans, on the other, fared in controlling costs. If employers came under greater financial strain in their management of health costs, they would have the option of contributing to the cost of coverage through the exchanges rather than providing coverage directly. If, however, they improved their ability to control costs, they would be more inclined to provide coverage on their own. Thus, this system would create a constructive public-private dynamic that would ensure the largest number of patients were enrolled in the sector best able to provide affordable, high-quality health care—without holding the health security of ordinary Americans hostage.

Universal Insurance

I have left for last the most inclusive and novel idea for dealing with the rising economic risks facing Americans: a new program I call "Universal Insurance." Universal Insurance would protect workers and their families against catastrophic drops in their incomes and budget-busting expenses.

The guiding principle behind Universal Insurance is that working families should have access to more than the highly segmented programs that now characterize American social protection. Instead, we should work to create a framework of insurance that covers all working Americans, that moves seamlessly with the individual from job to job and state to state, and that deals with the most severe risks to family finances, even when these risks do not fit neatly into existing program categories.

The name "Universal Insurance" is meant to connote two key features of the program. First, Universal Insurance would cover almost every citizen with any direct or family tie to the labor force, providing at least some direct benefits to virtually all families that experience covered risks. Second, Universal Insurance would cover a wide range of risks to family income. Universal Insurance is not a health program, a disability program, or an unemployment program. It is an income security program.[5]

Under Universal Insurance, all workers and their families would be automatically enrolled through their place of employment, paying premiums in the form of a small income-related contribution (preferably including capital gains as well as labor income). In return, workers would receive coverage for four potential shocks to family labor income that are large, serious, primarily beyond individual control, and incompletely protected against by present policies: unemployment, disability, illness and maternity, and the death of a family earner. In addition, Universal Insurance would provide coverage against catastrophic health costs, which are a leading source of economic strain and personal bankruptcies. It could also be expanded to include paid family leave when workers need to take time off to have or raise children or care for family members in need of assistance. This coverage would apply to all families whose income was below a relatively high threshold (the ninety-fifth percentile of family income in their state of residence), and it would be available to families with assets as well as those without assets.[6]

Although nearly all families would be protected, Universal Insurance would be especially generous for lower-income Americans, who are most likely to experience large financial shocks and to be most in need of help when they do. Figure 2.3 shows that the Economic Security Index is higher (more insecurity) for less affluent families than for more affluent ones. Lower-income families generally have little or no wealth to protect their standard of living when income declines, and they are least likely to have access to workplace health or disability insurance. Not surprisingly, therefore, unemployment has a much greater effect on the consumption patterns of lower-income families than it has on those of higher-income families.

Universal Insurance coverage would aim to fill the gaps left by existing social insurance programs rather than replace these programs. It would thus be similar to private stop-loss insurance purchased by corporations to limit their exposure to catastrophic economic risks. By providing limited protection against large and sudden income declines, Universal Insurance would provide a much more secure backstop against catastrophic economic loss than Americans now enjoy. Moreover, Universal Insurance would provide this backdrop through the popular and successful method of inclusive social insurance, which pools risks broadly across all working families.

All these changes, of course, will not come without costs, and they certainly will not come without political struggle. Yet against the cost one must balance the savings. Billions in hidden taxes are currently imposed by laws that facilitate bankruptcy, mandate emergency-room care, and bail out the politically sympathetic when things go bad. The elimination of

FIGURE 2.3   Share of Americans Who Are Insecure, 1985 to 1995
and 1997 to 2007, by Income Quintile[a]

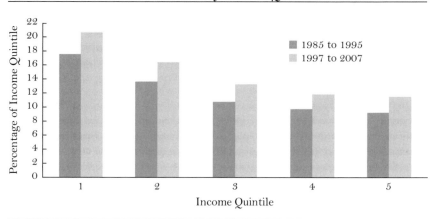

Source: Author's compilation based on Hacker et al. (2010).
[a] The "insecure" are those whose available household income declines by at least
25 percent from one year to the next (after adjusting for inflation), as a result of a
decline in household income or an increase in out-of-pocket medical spending, and
who lack an adequate financial safety net. Thus an individual is considered insecure if
the sum of the increase in medical expenditures and lost annual income total at least
25 percent of his or her previous year's available income. Household income includes all
private and government sources of income, including the estimated income value of
defined-contribution retirement accounts, such as 401(k)s, for households with heads
age sixty or older. Household income is adjusted to reflect the economies of scale of
pooling household resources and expenses. Household income is also reduced by the
amount needed to pay off liquid financial debts when net financial wealth is negative.
(All income is adjusted for inflation and expressed in 2009 dollars.) Individuals with
adequate holdings of liquid financial wealth are not treated as insecure even when they
experience 25 percent or higher income losses. We define "adequate" as enough liquid
financial wealth to compensate for the lost income until typical recovery to pre-drop
income or for six years, whatever comes first. Those entering retirement are also
excluded from the count of the insecure, even if available household income declines by
25 percent or more concurrent with retirement; once retired, however, they are counted
as insecure when they experience such declines.

these expenses must be accounted for when tallying up the bill for new policies, as should the huge drain that our current system imposes when people do not change jobs, do not have kids, do not invest in new skills because
they fear the downside risks. And we should not forget that the United
States already spends as much as many European nations on social benefits; we just do so in a way that is enormously wasteful, inefficient, and incapable of providing economic security to those who most need it.

NEW ASSUMPTIONS FOR NEW REALITIES

When it comes to economic risk, for almost a century Americans have seen a basic foundation of economic security as essential to the nation's economic prosperity and social health. The Great Depression of the 1930s—which left "a third of the nation," in FDR's famous telling, "ill-housed, ill-clothed, ill-nourished"—was widely seen as a natural disaster beyond the control or responsibility of the Americans it struck. In its wake, and especially after World War II, political and business leaders put in place new institutions designed to spread broadly the burden of key economic risks. These public and private institutions were never open to everyone. They required work, ongoing contributions, and proof of eligibility. But they were based on the notion that certain risks can only be effectively dealt with through inclusive institutions that spread costs across rich and poor, healthy and sick, able-bodied and disabled, young and old.

Today, however, this public-private framework is coming undone just when new economic risks are increasingly buffeting American families. Over the last generation we have witnessed a major transfer of economic risk from broad structures of insurance onto the balance sheets of American families. This transformation has reworked Americans' relationship to their government, their employers, and each other, with consequences for American politics and society that grow more worrisome with each passing day.

In extreme form, American developments provide a window into transformations taking place in many affluent democracies, as fiscally constrained welfare states confront new and newly intensified social risks. The eminent sociologist Gosta Esping-Andersen (1997) has argued that the rise of new or newly intensified risks has strained the capacity of existing social welfare frameworks. In the "postindustrial" world of economic and family risks, the welfare state has had to run to avoid falling behind—to do more merely to secure past gains.

In other affluent countries, this growing gap between risks and benefits is mostly a result of exogenous shocks to stable welfare states. In the United States, however, the Great Risk Shift has occurred as a result of active efforts to cut back benefits, driven in part by concerted political attacks on the ideal of economic security itself. Although public social programs have largely resisted the political and economic onslaught of recent decades, efforts to update them to make them more responsive to changing social risks have failed; their ground-level operation has shifted in directions at odds with their initial goals; and new policies that subvert or

threaten them have been put in place. The result has been a significant erosion of American social protection, despite the absence of many dramatic
instances of policy reform. This helps explain why the United States stands
out in cross-national comparisons of economic security; only the United
Kingdom and a few other nations appear to be following a similar trajec-
tory of declining security—though in these countries the symptoms are
still markedly less dire than in the United States.

Old assumptions are clearly no longer up to new realities. But the failure to revisit these assumptions and to face these new realities is not simply the result of outmoded thinking. It is the result of a profound political
bias against effective responses to the new economic insecurity, grounded
in major changes in American politics over the last generation. These
include the rise of the filibuster as a barrier to active efforts to update our
social policies, the increased sway of money and organized interests in
American politics, and the rise of a powerful, organized conservative movement. To reclaim the ideal of economic security, therefore, requires not just
new policy ideas but also an initiative to build public support and political
momentum for a new social contract.

Today, America's public-private framework of risk protection is under
strain, and most of that strain is coming from the erosion of private workplace benefits. It was once argued that government was not needed to provide basic risk protection—that private insurers could take care of health
care; that private employers would ensure that everyone had a good pension.
No one can confidently hold that view today. The only question is whether
government should step in to assume the growing risks of America's flexible, dynamic, and, yes, uncertain economy, or whether Americans should be
left to cope with these risks largely on their own.

The argument for having government pool these risks is powerful: it
could provide all Americans with the financial security they need to survive
and thrive in a highly uncertain economy, and encourage workers to accept
the downs as well as the ups of the free market. Social insurance programs
such as Medicare and Social Security feature low administrative costs and
broad public acceptance and popularity. And because of the public sector's
formidable bargaining power and unmatched standard-setting capacity,
public health insurance programs are also arguably better placed than private-sector benefits to control spending on health services and encourage
cost-effective medical utilization in the future. Certainly families like the
Dorsetts—thrust into the dark realities of medical bankruptcy by lack of
adequate coverage—could expect greater health security if they had coverage under a broad public plan with guaranteed benefits and strict limits on

out-of-pocket spending. That is why I have argued for expanding the Affordable Care Act to ensure a more seamless means of covering people either through employment-based insurance or regulated insurance markets with a public option.

But arguments like these are hardly universally accepted. For those who believe that risk protection interferes with the free play of competitive forces, for those who believe that government insurance merely coddles people who make the wrong choices, the only solution is to shift even more risk onto Americans' shoulders. The great debate of the twenty-first century will be whether the privatization of risk should be halted or hurried. And the outcome may well determine not just the future of U.S. social policy, but of the American model of capitalism as well.

NOTES

1. The year 2005 was unusual because of the rush of filings before the 2005 bankruptcy bill took effect. The number in 2004, however, still exceeded 1.56 million, and it has been climbing back to pre-reform levels since 2006, despite the more stringent requirements that filers must now meet. In 2009 there were more than 1.4 million filings for personal bankruptcy.
2. Data are available at "Senate Action on Cloture Motions," www.senate.gov/pagelayout/reference/cloture_motions/clotureCounts.htm; accessed July 6, 2010.
3. See Stimson's graph, "Public Policy Mood: 1952 to 2009," at www.unc.edu/~jstimson. See also Stimson (2004).
4. Complementing the income security policies discussed here are policies that encourage employers to provide more stable employment (see Osterman, this volume, chapter 4).
5. Because Universal Insurance is an income-protection program, it would not take into account so-called in-kind benefits, such as Medicaid and subsidized child care. Under the proposal, Universal Insurance benefits would also not count against eligibility for antipoverty programs (although they would be treated as taxable income for all beneficiaries at the end of the year). Universal Insurance would, however, prevent many Americans from falling into poverty and would thus reduce the need for antipoverty benefits.
6. Families with very extensive assets would not be covered.

REFERENCES

American Political Science Association, Task Force on Inequality and American Democracy. 2004. "American Democracy in an Age of Rising Inequality." Available at: www.apsanet.org/imgtest/taskforcereport.pdf; accessed July 8, 2010.

American National Election Studies. 2008–2009. 2008-2009 Panel Study. Available at: http://www.electionstudies.org/studypages/2008_2009 panel/anes2008_2009panel.htm (accessed October 4, 2010).

Anderson, Gerard F., Jeremy Hurst, Peter Sotir Hussey, and Melissa Jee-Hughes. 2000. "Health Spending and Outcomes: Trends in OECD Countries, 1960–1998." *Health Affairs* 19: 150–57. Available at: http://content.healthaffairs.org/cgi/reprint/19/3/150.pdf; accessed July 8, 2010.

Bartels, Larry M. 2008. *Unequal Democracy: The Political Economy of the New Gilded Age.* Princeton, N.J.: Princeton University Press.

Bernstein, Jared, and Karen Kornbluh. 2005. *Running Faster to Stay in Place: The Growth of Family Work Hours and Incomes.* Briefing paper. Washington, D.C.: New America Foundation Work & Family Program. Available at: www.newamerica.net/publications/policy/running_faster_to_stay_in_place; accessed July 8, 2010.

Brownstein, Ronald. 2009. "Financial Risk Cuts Deeper, Poll Finds." *National Journal*, April 25. Available at: www.nationaljournal.com/njmagazine/cs_20090425_8127.php; accessed July 8, 2010.

Butler, Stuart, and Peter Germanis. 1983. "Achieving a 'Leninist' Strategy." *Cato Journal* 3(2): 548. Available at: http://zfacts.com/metaPage/lib/Cato-Heritage-1983-Lenin-Plan.pdf; accessed July 8, 2010.

Campbell, Andrea Louise. 2007. "Parties, Electoral Participation, and Shifting Voting Blocs." In *The Transformation of American Politics: Activist Government and the Rise of Conservatism,* edited by Paul Pierson and Theda Skocpol. Princeton, N.J.: Princeton University Press.

Congressional Budget Office. 2009. *Historical Effective Federal Tax Rates: 1979–2006.* Washington: Congressional Budget Office.

———. 2010. *Manager's Amendment Reconciliation Proposal.* Available at: www.cbo.gov/ftpdocs/113xx/doc11379/AmendReconProp.pdf; accessed July 8, 2010.

DeNavas-Walt, Carmen, Bernadette D. Proctor, and Jessica C. Smith. 2009. *Income, Poverty, and Health Insurance Coverage in the United States: 2008.* Current Population Reports, P60-235. Washington: U.S. Bureau of the Census.

Diamond, Peter A., and Peter R. Orszag. 2005. "Reforming Social Security: A Balanced Plan." Brookings Institution policy brief no. 126. Washington, D.C.: Brookings Institution. Available at: www.brookings.edu/papers/2003/12saving_orszag.aspx; accessed July 8, 2010.

Elmer, Peter J., and Steen A. Seelig. 1998. "The Rising Long-Term Trend of Single-Family Mortgage Foreclosure Rates." FDIC working paper 98-2. Washington, D.C.: Federal Deposit Insurance Corporation, Division of Research and Statistics.

Esping-Anderson, Gosta. 1997. "Welfare States at the End of the Century: The Impact of Labour Market, Family, and Demographic Change." In *Beyond 2000: The New Social Policy Agenda.* Paris: OECD.

Families USA. 2009. "Americans at Risk: One in Three Uninsured." Report. Washington, D.C.: Families USA. Available at: www.familiesusa.org/assets/pdfs/americans-at-risk.pdf; accessed July 8, 2010.

Gilens, Martin. 2005. "Inequality and Democratic Responsiveness." *Public Opinion Quarterly* 69(5): 778–96. Available at: http://poq.oxfordjournals.org/cgi/reprint/69/5/778.pdf; accessed July 8, 2010.

Gopoian, David. 2007. *Health Care Experiences of the American Public: May 2007 Survey.* Washington, D.C.: Consumer Reports National Research Center.

Graetz, Michael J., and Jerry L. Mashaw. 1999. *True Security: Rethinking American Social Insurance.* New Haven, Conn.: Yale University Press.

Griffin, John D. 2006. "Senate Apportionment as a Source of Political Inequality." *Legislative Studies Quarterly* 31(3): 405–32.

Hacker, Jacob S. 2001. "Medicare Plus." In *Covering America: Real Remedies for the Uninsured,* vol. 1. Washington, D.C. Economic and Social Research Institute.

———. 2002. *The Divided Welfare State: The Battle over Public and Private Social Benefits in the United States.* New York: Cambridge University Press.

———. 2004. "Privatizing Risk Without Privatizing the Welfare State: The Hidden Politics of U.S. Social Policy Retrenchment." *American Political Science Review* 98 (2): 243–60.

———. 2006. *The Great Risk Shift: The Assault on American Jobs, Families, Health Care, and Retirement.* New York: Oxford University Press.

———. 2007. "Health Care for America." EPI briefing paper no. 180. Washington, D.C.: Economic Policy Institute. Available at: www.sharedprosperity.org/bp180.html; accessed July 8, 2010.

———. 2008a. "The Case for Public Plan Choice in National Health Reform: Key to Cost Control and Quality Coverage." Brief. University of California, School of Law, Institute for America's Future. Available at: http://institute.ourfuture.org/files/Jacob_Hacker_Public_Plan_Choice.pdf; accessed July 8, 2010.

———. 2008b. *The Great Risk Shift: The New Economic Insecurity and the Decline of the American Dream.* Revised and Expanded. New York: Oxford University Press.

———. 2009. "Healthy Competition: How to Structure Public Health Insurance Plan Choice to Ensure Risk-Sharing, Cost Control, and Quality Improvement." Policy brief. Washington, D.C.: Institute for Our Future. Available at: www.ourfuture.org/files/Hacker_Healthy_Competition_FINAL.pdf; accessed July 18, 2010.

Hacker, Jacob S., Gregory Huber, Philipp Rehm, Mark Schlesinger, and Rob Valletta. 2010. *Economic Security at Risk: Findings from the Rockefeller Economic Security Index.* New York: Rockefeller Foundation.

Hacker, Jacob S., and Elisabeth Jacobs. 2008. *The Rising Instability of American Family Incomes, 1969–2004: Evidence from the Panel Study of Income Dynamics.* EPI briefing paper no. 213. Washington, D.C.: Economic Policy Institute.

Hacker, Jacob S., and Paul Pierson. 2005. *Off Center: The Republican Revolution and the Erosion of American Democracy.* New Haven, Conn.: Yale University Press.

————. 2010. *Winner-Take-All Politics: How Washington Made the Rich Richer— And Turned Its Back on the Middle Class.* New York: Simon & Schuster.

Himmelstein, David U., Elizabeth Warren, Deborah Thorne, and Steffie Woolhandler. 2005. "Illness and Injury as Contributors to Bankruptcy." *Health Affairs* 63(1; February 2). Web exclusive. Available at: http://content.health affairs.org/cgi/reprint/hlthaff.w5.63v1.pdf; accessed July 8, 2010.

Himmelstein, David U., Elizabeth Warren, Deborah Thorne, and Steffie Woolhandler. 2009. "Medical Bankruptcy in the United States, 2007: Results of a National Study." *American Journal of Medicine* 122(8): 741–46. Available at: www.washingtonpost.com/wp-srv/politics/documents/ american_journal_of_medicine_09.pdf; accessed July 8, 2010.

Jacobs, Jerry, and Kathleen Gerson. 2004. *The Time Divide: Work, Family, and Gender Inequality.* Cambridge, Mass.: Harvard University Press.

Kahneman, Daniel, and Amos Tversky. 1979. "Prospect Theory: An Analysis of Decisions Under Risk." *Econometrica* 47(2): 263–91.

Kletzer, Lori G. 2001. *Job Loss from Imports: Measuring the Costs.* Washington, D.C.: Institute for International Economics.

Kletzer, Lori G., and Howard F. Rosen, 2006. *Reforming Unemployment Insurance for a Twenty-First-Century Workforce.* Discussion paper no. 2006-06. Washington, D.C.: Brookings Institution. Available at: www1.hamiltonproject.org/views/ papers/200609kletzer-rosen.pdf; accessed July 8, 2010.

Lake Snell Perry and Associates and Tarrance Group. 2005. "George Washington University Battleground 2004 Poll." March 9. Available at: www.lakeresearch. com/polls/BG101004.htm; accessed July 8, 2010.

Langbein, John H. 2006. "Understanding the Death of the Private Pension Plan in the United States." Unpublished manuscript. Yale Law School, New Haven.

Lee, Frances E., and Brue I. Oppenheimer. 1999. *Sizing Up the Senate: The Unequal Consequences of Equal Representation.* Chicago: University of Chicago Press.

Lewin Group. 2008. "Cost Impact Analysis for the 'Health Care for America' Proposal." Final report. Prepared for the Economic Policy Institute. Available at: http://www.sharedprosperity.org/hcfa/lewin.pdf; accessed July 6, 2010

Mayhew, David R. 2008. "Supermajority Rule in the Senate." In *Parties and Policies: How the American Government Works.* New Haven, Conn.: Yale University Press.

McCarty, Poole, and Rosenthal 2006. *Polarized America: The Dance Between Ideology and Unequal Networks.* Cambridge, Mass.: MIT Press.

Moss, David. 2002. *When All Else Fails: Government as the Ultimate Risk Manager.* Cambridge, Mass.: Harvard University Press.

Munnell, Alicia H., and Annika Sundén. 2006. "401(k) Plans Are Still Coming Up Short." Issue brief no. 43b. Boston: Boston College, Center for Retirement

Research. Available at: http://papers.ssrn.com/sol3/papers.cfm?abstract_id=
908264; accessed July 8, 2010.

Munnell, Alicia H., Anthony Webb, and Francesca Golub-Sass. 2009. "The
National Retirement Risk Index: After the Crash." Issue brief no. 9-22. Boston:
Boston College, Center for Retirement Research. Available at: http://crr.bc.
edu/images/stories/Briefs/ib_9-22.pdf; accessed July 8, 2010.

Nolte, Ellen, and C. Martin McKee. 2008. "Measuring the Health of Nations:
Updating an Earlier Analysis." *Health Affairs* 27(1): 58–71.

Organisation for Economic Co-Operation and Development (OECD), Directorate
for Employment, Labour and Social Affairs. 2009. "OECD Health Data 2009:
Statistics and Indicators." Available at: www.oecd.org/document/30/0,
3343,en_2649_33929_12968734_1_1_1_1,00.html; accessed July 9, 2010.

Orszag, Peter. 2004. "Statement of Peter R. Orszag, Joseph A. Pechman, Senior
Fellow, The Brookings Institution, Washington, DC." In "Strengthening
Pension Security for All Americans: Are Workers Prepared for a Safe and
Secure Retirement?" Statement Prepared for Hearing before the House
Committee on Education and the Workforce, 108th Congress. Available at:
www.gpo.gov/fdsys/pkg/CHRG-108hhrg10892176/html/CHRG-108
hhrg10892176.htm; accessed July 8, 2010.

———. 2008. "CBO Testimony, Statement of Peter R. Orszag, director; The
Effects of Recent Turmoil in Financial Markets on Retirement Security."
Testimony Before the Committee on Education and Labor, U.S. House of
Representatives, October 8, 2008. Prepared comments available at:
www.cbo.gov/ftpdocs/98xx/doc9864/10-07-RetirementSecurity_
Testimony.1.1.shtml; accessed July 9, 2010.

Pew Research Center. 2009 "Not Your Grandfather's Recession—Literally:
Different Ages, Different Downturns." Available at: http://pewresearch.org/
pubs/1223/not-your-grandfathers-recessionliterally; accessed
September 30, 2010.

Robertson, Christopher T., Richard Egelhof, and Michael Hoke. 2008. "Get Sick,
Get Out: The Medical Causes of Home Foreclosures." *Health Matrix* 18(65):
65–105. Available at: http://works.bepress.com/christopher_robertson/2/;
accessed July 8, 2010.

Rockefeller Foundation. 2007. *American Worker Survey: Complete Results.* New
York: Rockefeller Foundation. Available at: www.rockefellerfoundation.
org/uploads/files/1f190413-0800-4046-9200-084d05d5ea71-american.pdf;
accessed July 8, 2010.

Scherer, Ron. 2010. "Number of Long-Term Unemployed Hits Highest Rate
Since 1948." *Christian Science Monitor,* January 8.

Simon, Ruth, and James R. Hagerty. 2009. "House-Price Drops Leave More
Underwater." *Wall Street Journal,* May 6.

Skocpol, Theda. 2003. *Diminished Democracy: From Membership to Management in
American Civic Life.* Norman: University of Oklahoma Press.

Smith, Mark A. 2007. *The Right Talk: How Conservatives Transformed the Great Society into the Economic Society.* Princeton, N.J.: Princeton University Press.

Stettner, Andrew, and Sylvia A. Allegretto. 2005. "The Rising Stakes of Job Loss: Stubborn Long-Term Joblessness Amid Falling Unemployment Rates." EPI and NELP briefing paper no. 162. Washington, D.C.: Economic Policy Institute and National Employment Law Project. Available at: www.epi.org/publications/entry/bp162/; accessed July 8, 2010.

Stimson, James A. 2004. *Tides of Consent: How Public Opinion Shapes American Politics.* Cambridge: Cambridge University Press.

U.S. Department of Commerce, Bureau of Economic Analysis. 2009. "National Income and Product Accounts Table; Table 2.1: Personal Income and Its Disposition." Available at: www.bea.gov/national/nipaweb/TableView.asp?SelectedTable=58&Freq=Qtr&FirstYear=2008&LastYear=2010; accessed July 8, 2010.

Warren, Elizabeth. 2003. "Financial Collapse and Class Status: Who Goes Bankrupt?" *Osgoode Hall Law Journal* 41(1): 115–47.

Warren, Elizabeth, and Amelia Warren Tyagi. 2003. *The Two-Income Trap: Why Middle-Class Mothers and Fathers are Going Broke.* New York: Basic Books.

Weller, Christian E., and Jessica Lynch. 2009. *Household Wealth in Freefall.* Washington, D.C.: Center for American Progress.

Wheary, Jennifer, Thomas A. Shapiro, and Tamara Draut. 2007. *By a Thread: The New Experience of American Families.* Waltham, Mass.: Institute on Assets and Social Policy. Available at: http://iasp.brandeis.edu/pdfs/byathread_web.pdf; accessed July 8, 2010.

Wilper, Andrew P., Steffie Woolhandler, Karen E. Lasser, Danny McCormick, and David H. Bor. 2009. "Health Insurance and Mortality in US Adults." *American Journal of Public Health* 99(12): 2289–95.

Woolhandler, Steffie, and David U. Himmelstein. 2002. "Paying for National Health Insurance—And Not Getting It." *Health Affairs* 21 (July–August): 88–98. Available at: http://content.healthaffairs.org/cgi/reprint/21/4/88.pdf; accessed July 8, 2010.

CHAPTER 3

WORKFORCE DEVELOPMENT AND PUBLIC POLICY: ADDRESSING NEW REALITIES IN LOW-SKILL LABOR MARKETS

MICHAEL A. STOLL

O ver the four decades since 1970, significant economic and social transformations have changed the economic opportunities of and rewards
from work for those with limited education, especially if they live in poor,
urban, or minority communities. Over this period, good jobs that required
only a basic education began to disappear, leaving many unable to find
work and form strong labor-market attachment, thus raising the economic
cost of having a limited education. Many of these jobs have been replaced
by ones that require different sets of skills, and their geographic locations
have shifted as well. More often than not, these changing job-skill requirements demand more, not less, investment in schooling and training, and
require better job-matching assistance to lessen new frictions in labor
markets that limit job access and skill accumulation. Are current assumptions about problems in the labor market or policy approaches to the
challenges of less-educated workers appropriate for the new realities of
the changing labor market? What is required in education and job training
to keep up with these new realities of differing and potentially increasing

skill demands as well as additional frictions in labor markets that limit this access?

These and other related questions provide the backdrop for this chapter. More directly, these labor-market trends imply the need to scrutinize policy approaches aimed at enhancing the employment and earnings of those with limited education both in and out of school. The need to do so is more important than ever because of the severe economic recession that has driven unemployment rates to thirty-year highs, particularly in minority communities. The ability of the growing ranks of jobless to secure work in this period of high unemployment will partly depend on their ability to gain new or additional skills and credentials that maximize employment opportunities.

Many believe past workforce development efforts have not been up to the challenge of enhancing outcomes, given new realities of the labor market. Although not all the critics are right in this respect, certainly such programs can be improved either by improving program design or by taking into account the variety of the challenges faced by less-educated workers in the labor market. In particular, new realities in job requirements call for more general problem-solving skills that can be applied to a variety of different job and skill settings. This approach begs for the integration of work-based knowledge into education and training curriculums with active learning in an applied setting. Shifts in the location of employment away from concentrations of less-educated workers, as well as persistent discrimination on the basis of such characteristics as race or ex-offender status, imply the need for training programs that not only advance skills but also integrate regional approaches to employment and counteract the effects of discrimination in low-skill markets.

A major approach the United States has taken to address the potential skill deficits or mismatches of less-educated workers is through workforce development. Of course, there are many other approaches, such as increasing college-going, that can accomplish these goals as well and perhaps more effectively, but we do not focus on these approaches here. Policy efforts focusing on the demand side of the labor market such as through minimum-wage legislation, wage subsidies, or employer tax credits could also improve the employment and wages of less-educated workers. These, too, are beyond the scope of this chapter, but Paul Osterman (this volume, chapter 4) explores these questions in greater detail. This chapter focuses on workforce development efforts that use supply-side approaches to improve the labor-market performance of low-skill workers in and out of high school, especially racial and ethnic minorities.

To accomplish this, the chapter first considers employment and wage trends for less-educated workers, understood here as those with a high school diploma or less. Then, it revisits past in-school and out-of-school workforce development approaches to enhance skills and link workers to jobs by focusing on vocational education and more general employment and training programs. The limited success of these efforts can be attributed to a number of factors, but lack of relevance of the training and detachment from employers are chief concerns. Next, the chapter examines current programs and practices in employment and training both in and out of school that show great promise in revitalizing workforce development as an effective approach in raising employment and wages. The chapter closes with a discussion of three labor-market frictions that disadvantage low-skill workers and presents policy options that could help overcome them: spatial mismatch between low-skill workers' homes and low-skill jobs, racial discrimination in housing and labor markets, and offender status.

The term "workforce development" is used here to describe public policies and programs, such as the federal government's Job Training and Partnership Act (JTPA) and now the Workforce Investment Act (WIA), and other residential or transportation mobility programs that aim to improve the skills or employment of disadvantaged workers in the United States. Historically, much of the coordination of workforce development has emanated from federal government efforts, but increasingly, state and local governments, local secondary schools, and private foundations, among others, are helping to shape workforce development. The design and implementation of many of these are increasingly being done by nonprofit institutions, such as community-based organizations, other not-for-profits, and community colleges.

THE CHANGING ECONOMIC FORTUNES OF LESS-EDUCATED WORKERS

The economic fortunes of those with a high school diploma or less have changed markedly since 1980, with differing trends for men and women. From the early 1900s through the 1960s, the real earnings of less-educated (male) workers grew markedly (Mishel, Bernstein, and Schmitt 2003). Increased productivity, relative shortages of less-educated workers, expanding unionization, and federal minimum-wage legislation bolstered the economic fortunes of less-educated male workers in the United States. As a result, during this period a high school diploma or less education had few negative consequences for a worker's economic well-being.

This trend began to shift in the 1970s and 1980s. Especially after the oil embargo and recession of 1973, less-educated men earned less in absolute terms, as well as relative to the earnings of more-educated (that is, college-educated) workers. These declines accelerated during the 1980s, especially for young males with a high school diploma or less (Blackburn, Bloom, and Freeman 1990). This shift was all the more socially important since less-educated workers became more reliant on jobs and earnings, especially in the 1990s and 2000s, than they had been in earlier decades, partly as a result of shifts in federal and state social policies that greatly reduced or limited access to programs providing cash assistance.

Recent work on employment and earnings trends confirms these findings. Employment declined dramatically among less-educated men between 1979 and 2006, with most of this decline occurring between 1979 and 1995. As for earnings, the fifteen years following 1979 were a period of substantial wage loss for these men. Male workers without a high school diploma saw their average weekly wages decline from $548 in 1979 to $388 in 1994. Those with a high school diploma saw their weekly wages fall from $675 in 1979 to a low of $558 in 1991. Only among those with some post–high school training did wages rise during this period.

Since the early 1990s the labor market has looked somewhat better for all groups of men. Wages rose at all educational attainment levels, especially during the late 1990s. By 2006, average wages were $426 for high school dropouts, $607 for high school graduates, and $900 for those with more than a high school diploma. For the two less-educated groups, however, these 2006 wage levels were still well below where they had been in 1979 (Blank 2008; all figures are in 2008 dollars).

These trends were especially pronounced for certain demographic groups, especially young black men. Not only did the earnings and employment of young, less-skilled men decline generally over the late 1970s and 1980s, but young, less-skilled black men's outcomes fell dramatically relative to those of less-skilled whites (Bound and Freeman 1992; Holzer, Raphael, and Stoll 2006). This pattern reversed trends from about the 1940s to the 1970s, when a decade-by-decade convergence of black and white earnings had been observed (Jaynes and Williams 1989).

These trends are quite different for women. In general, all groups of women have increased their labor-force involvement over the past several decades. In contrast to less-educated men, comparable women experienced little decline in wages and earnings over these periods. Women with a high school diploma saw significant wage increases, while wages grew much less among those with less than a high school diploma. For example, women without a high school diploma reported average weekly wages of between $300 and $322 from 1979 through 2000, which rose slightly to $334 in 2006. Over the 1979 to 2006 period women with a high school diploma saw their wages grow from $385 to $455 (Blank 2008).

Many explanations have been offered for this reversal in the economic fortunes of less-educated men. Falling unionization rates and declining levels in the real value of the minimum wage are considered prime suspects (Osterman, this volume, chapter 4; Blackburn, Bloom, and Freeman 1990; Card 1996; Lee 1999). Others note that female workers were particularly affected by these factors, since a disproportionately large number of women work in minimum-wage jobs (DiNardo, Fortin, and Lemieux 1996). Yet in contrast to less-educated men, employment and earnings remained flat or increased over the 1980s and 1990s, when the minimum wage went unchanged or declined in real value. The declines in minimum wages in the 1980s may have been partially made up by later minimum-wage increases and by increases in the Earned Income Tax Credit (EITC) in the 1990s that allowed a growing share of low-wage workers to receive tax refunds, even if they owed no taxes.

Others point to "skill-biased technological change" (SBTC) and international trade as factors that might have affected less-educated men's employment and earnings (Autor, Levy, and Murnane 2003; Autor, Katz and Kearney 2008). SBTC refers to changes in technology that increase labor demand for workers at a particular skill level. The argument is that technological changes in the 1980s led to SBTC, with increased computer use for job tasks, from robotics to just-in-time inventory systems. This created increases in the demand for more skilled workers that outstripped supply increases, driving up wages for highly educated workers, and at the same time lowering demand and therefore employment and wages for less-educated workers.

Computerization could lead to both down-skilling and up-skilling of work, depending on how the technology is used and introduced at the workplace and for what management reasons (Cappelli 1996). For example, down-skilling might occur if computers substituted for certain skilled clerks and required only basic data input. Up-skilling could result from increased demand for software programmers, network administrators and consultants, and computer design makers. Although much of the research suggests that computerization could result in both of these outcomes, on balance, up-skilling appears to be raising skill requirements more than down-skilling lowers them (Autor, Levy, and Murnane 2003).

Labor-market trends specific to black men, such as weakened enforcement of antidiscrimination polices and restricted affirmative action programs, have probably contributed to their disadvantage (Jaynes and Williams 1989). Changes in the industrial-manufacturing sectors and declines in the economic vitality of central cities have undoubtedly played a role as well (Bound and Freeman 1992). For example, in 1950 about one in three metropolitan residents worked in manufacturing, mostly in central city plants. By 1990, only about one in five worked in manufacturing, and most were employed in suburban plants (Danziger, Farley, and Holzer 2000). Jobs in central cities were increasingly replaced with service jobs that on average required more skills and educational credentials (Kasarda 1995), while low-skill jobs raced to the suburbs (Stoll, Holzer, and Ihlanfeldt 2000; Wilson 1996). The combination of these factors has led to compound labor-market disadvantage for less-educated minority men.

Thus, over the past two decades, significant economic and social transformations have changed the availability of and rewards from work for those with limited education, especially for those living in poor communities. Increased investments in schooling could have attenuated these harmful labor-market trends by providing skills and credentials to access the broader metropolitan labor market. Generally, however, urban schools have not received this investment. Lack of investment came at great cost as schooling became increasingly important in order to thrive in the modern labor market and economy.

WORKFORCE DEVELOPMENT TO ENHANCE SKILLS AND EMPLOYMENT: OLD ASSUMPTIONS AND NEW REALITIES

The employment and wage trends for less-educated workers, especially for men, indicate a clear need for intervention. The United States' major approaches to enhance employment and earnings of disadvantaged workers have been, and continue to be, workforce development policies and programs. A myriad of employment and training programs could fall under the rubric of "workforce development." I focus on broad approaches to workforce development both within school and outside school that will likely be effective given the new realities in the labor market.

Before delving into this discussion, it is important to observe that older models of workforce development, such as vocational education and "work first" strategies (described in a later section), will no longer be effective because the old assumptions of the labor market and of training practices that drove these models are inconsistent with current realities. Vocational education, for example, which provides hands-on learning and career preparation, assumes that general skills and vaguely relevant specific skills will be consistently rewarded in the labor market. However, rapid shifts in employers' demands for skills and the inability of these programs to adapt quickly to these shifts have meant that these programs increasingly lacked relevant skills training, and resulted in a disconnect between them and employers' needs. Many employers viewed these programs as antipoverty efforts rather than more general training programs, were skeptical of the skills and productivity of program graduates, and therefore viewed them as irrelevant to their labor needs (Harrison and Weiss 1998; Blank 1997; Manski and Garfinkel 1992).[1]

Following the passage of the Family Support Act in 1988 (which included implementation of the Job Opportunities and Basic Skills program) and welfare reform in 1996, the dominant training model began to shift from basic education and training to job-search assistance, work experience, and other employment-related services. This approach, known as the "work-first" model, focused on rapid entry into the labor market by providing short-term training in employment-enhancing activities and direct job-search assistance, such as help with finding work, résumé writing, and interview training. The evaluation evidence on "work-first" training programs indicates that initial (two years) increases in employment and earnings quickly disappear in subsequent years and that the increases were driven by more hours worked rather than by higher wages (Friedlander and Burtless 1995; Kempel and Haimson 1994). These disappointing results have called into question the accuracy of the work-first model's main assumption that quick entry into employment is important for obtaining on-the-job experience that could translate to better employment and pay down the road. New realities of the labor market—including the disappearance of vertical job ladders across industries, which limits mobility out of low-skill jobs—mean that the old assumptions behind "work first" may no longer be valid, and may in fact harm labor-market performance over the long haul, since clients gain few additional skills.[2]

The Workforce Investment Act (WIA) of 1998 is now the primary vehicle for federal funding for job training and employment services. It altered the employment and training system in the United States by consolidating several federally funded employment and training programs, and further centralized authority over them to states and other local entities. More significantly, WIA introduced greater competition to improve the employment and training system through individual training accounts, performance and customer satisfaction measures, and certification of training providers.

It also changed the system from a focus on the "disadvantaged" to one of universal access for a range of worker skills through innovative "one stop" centers that provide a range of services for the differing employment and training needs of "clients" (Buck 2002).[3]

There are now three categories of employment services for adults under WIA: core, intensive, and training. Core services primarily involve self-directed use of the Employment Service and other local employment listings as well as staff-assisted job searches. Intensive services mostly consist of assessments of job skills and counseling. Individuals must access each of these two services before they can receive any training, and many are diverted into the workforce without receiving any training. Thus, WIA also reflects the "work-first" philosophy of moving participants as quickly as possible into jobs, despite concerns about the validity of the "work-first" model.

Evaluations (and their interpretations) of WIA will be difficult since WIA cannot even be considered a "program." It is simply a set of funding streams that are locally dispersed in many different ways. We have little knowledge of which of these efforts and training practices are relatively more or less cost-effective for the disadvantaged population. Given that many of those who do not receive WIA-funded services might be obtaining other services and programs (leading to "contamination" effects on the data), it might be difficult to interpret any results obtained from an evaluation of WIA for low-income youths or adults. Even if results from such evaluations were positive, it will be extremely difficult to identify the mechanisms and particular training practices that generate these results and whether and how that success could be reproduced.

NEW REALITIES IN LABOR MARKETS: CHALLENGES TO WORKFORCE DEVELOPMENT

Surely changes in the functioning of low-skill markets could and should affect the performance of workforce development programs. What are these new labor-market realities that may blunt the effectiveness of these programs and approaches if they do not adapt in timely ways?[4]

One new reality is changing employer requirements in the low and semiskilled job markets. An examination of the current literature notes the presence (and perhaps growing presence), rather than the absence, of work and job skill requirements in these markets. Several generalizations can be made about employer hiring behavior in entry-level labor markets (Holzer, Raphael, and Stoll 2002):

- Virtually all employers seek basic "work readiness" in prospective employees. Many also seek additional "hard" and "soft" skills, even in low-wage markets.

- Since most skills are not directly observable at the time of hiring, employers generally seek applicants with certain credentials that signal employability and skill, and tend to avoid those with certain stigmas, such as ex-offenders.

- Employers vary in the amounts of resources they can apply to hiring and compensation decisions, as well as in their information and expertise on these matters.

- Recruiting and screening choices (as well as compensation, promotion, and retention decisions) are often made informally, and can reflect varying degrees of employer prejudices, perceptions, and experiences.

- Employer access to a reliable and steady pool of applicants is also affected by their physical proximity to various neighborhoods and groups, their employee networks, as well as the tightness of the labor market locally and nationally.

These basic work-readiness requirements are now expected by virtually all employers. Most seek personal qualities such as honesty and reliability, an inclination to arrive at work on time every day, a positive attitude toward work, and so forth. Avoidance of problems that might be associated with high absenteeism and poor work performance, such as drug abuse or physical or mental health difficulties, is often viewed as critical (Holzer 1996; Moss and Tilly 2001).

In addition, as Frank Levy and Richard Murnane (1996) note in their influential book, *Teaching the New Basic Skills*, the new job skill realities needed to function in the new economy and earn a middle-class income include:

- Hard skills: basic mathematics, problem solving, and reading abilities at least at the high school level

- Soft skills: the ability to work in groups and to make effective oral and written presentations

- The ability to use computers to do simple tasks.

Even low-wage jobs require basic cognitive skills such as reading, writing, simple numeracy (such as the ability to make change), and rudimentary use of a computer, among other basic skills. The relevant "soft" skills very frequently include the ability to interact positively with customers and coworkers. Employers use credentials such as attainment of a high school diploma, previous work experience, and references to gain information on applicants' qualities and skills that they cannot observe directly. Skill tests are rare. Many employers make inferences regarding basic skills on the basis of educational attainment, the quality of writing on the application, and the interview, though these judgments are notoriously unreliable.

There is evidence that jobs in central cities are likely to have higher skill requirements than those in the suburbs, even though central cities may account for a smaller fraction of the metropolitan area's jobs as a result of decentralization (Stoll 2005). To the extent that this is true, the employment challenges of less-skilled central city minority youth are compounded by the skill requirements of jobs there (Ong and Terriquez 2008). John D. Kasarda (1995) shows that from 1970 to 1990, in most large metropolitan areas, the percentage of jobs in the central city that require a college degree was much higher than the share of residents with a college degree. He documents that such jobs in the central city rose dramatically from 1970 to 1990, and rose much faster than central city residents' attainment of a college degree over this period.

The new labor-market realities cry out for the redesign of job-training programs to include the creation and expansion of environments and curriculums that encourage participants to learn how to learn and gain problem-solving skills. Competence in basic skills is necessary, but training and knowledge in advanced specific skills will help, too. As many of these specific skills are best learned in a real-life setting, improving the workforce development system requires training efforts that are more relevant to employers' needs.

IN-SCHOOL APPROACHES TO WORKFORCE DEVELOPMENT: CAREER ACADEMIES

Career academies are a prime example of school-to-work approaches that are promising alternative responses to these new skill realities. Career academies are schools within schools that link students with peers, teachers, and community partners such as employers to foster skill development and academic success. This is accomplished through small learning communities and a college-preparatory curriculum with a career theme, combined with partnerships with local employers (Stern and Stearns 2009). In career academies, groups of students typically take the same classes together in each grade and stay with the same group of teachers for at least two years (Stern et al. 2007). Career academies can be thought of as a relatively intensive version of school-to-work programs, taking more seriously both integration with the workplace and work-based learning, as compared with intermittent programs in comprehensive schools.

A recent evaluation by MDRC shows some promising results (Kemple and Snipes 2000; Kemple 2001, 2005, 2008). The experimental evidence shows that career academies raise earnings by 12 percent relative to the control group. Importantly, these impacts persist for at least four years after students graduate from high school. Furthermore, they are stronger for disadvantaged young men than for other groups of young men, and stronger for young men than women—a finding which rarely appears in this literature (Kemple 2005). Positive impacts were observed on wages as well as employment rates.[5]

Margaret Terry Orr and her colleagues (2007) show promising academic and job-related results from a sample of career academy participants and a comparison group of non-academy students from the same schools. The results indicate that academy seniors were much more likely to have paid internships connected to school, school-based work experience, college-level courses (especially in computer technology), and career-related activities and classes (such as job interview training).

Notwithstanding popular concerns as to whether career education "tracks" minority or low-income youth into noncollege trajectories, the Career Academy participants received postsecondary education at the same rate as those in the control groups, and suffered no loss (nor gain) in academic achievement (Reller, 1984; Dayton, Weisberg, and Stern 1989; for additional sources see Stern, Raby, and Dayton 1992; Raby 1995). These studies and others (Neumark and Rothstein 2006; Cellini 2006; Lerman 2007) suggest that Career Academies help disadvantaged students finish both high school and college, and do not do so by lowering academic standards.

Though there is little direct empirical evidence, student tracking issues could still be a concern. For instance, students in the most advanced classes might gravitate to career academies, creating a hierarchical ordering among the academies in the high school, or students in the less prestigious academies would be systematically harmed as teachers would expect less of them (Oakes 1985/2005; Mosteller, Light, and Sachs 1996). Career academies could also target students who do not plan to go to college, and track them into classes and work experiences that direct them toward immediate entry into the labor market. Or, college-bound students could substitute career and technical classes and work experience for academic classes and experiences that would qualify them for college.

Career academies could also improve employment and wages of the disadvantaged by raising high school graduation rates. Employment rates of those without a high school diploma are unacceptably low. The employment rates of those who left school without a high school diploma are about 50 percent, nearly 20 percentage points lower than their counterparts with a high school diploma. These rates are significantly worse for blacks and Latinos, especially men. Over the initial fifteen years after leaving school, this gap declines only slightly, to ten percentage points (Stoll 2010). Moreover, it is well known that high school completion rates are low, especially for the disadvantaged in poor urban school districts.

Any significant increase in high school graduation rates would therefore significantly and positively influence employment rates of those who graduate. The evidence shows that career academy students have better attendance, earn more credits, obtain higher grades, and, more important, were more likely to graduate than a comparison group (Raby 1995).

The combined evidence points to some beneficial effects of school-to-work programs and career academies and provides rather compelling evidence that participation in some school-to-work programs increases education and employment and decreases idleness, especially for men. Going forward, there will be enormous opportunity to design career academies that train students in skills demanded in growing sectors, particularly in the heath-care sector and in green-tech jobs, industries that are primed for growth over the near term. California, for example, recently passed legislation providing significant resources to expand these academies. Moreover, career academies focusing on green-tech jobs would be ripe for creation since there are currently big federal pushes to expand this industry and that there are relatively few green-tech academies in existence at this time. This is also important since many green jobs will likely require at least a high school diploma.

The Obama administration has understood to some extent that poor job skills and market frictions (discussed below) will limit how fully disadvantaged workers will be able to access growing numbers of green-sector jobs and jobs of the future more broadly. As part of this recognition, the American Recovery and Reinvestment Act provided up to $750 million for a Pathways Out of Poverty grant to train hard-to-serve populations for green jobs using state-of-the-art training approaches and practices.

OUTSIDE-SCHOOL APPROACHES TO WORKFORCE DEVELOPMENT: PROMISING PRACTICES

The assumption of limited success of past employment and training programs as well as a greater understanding of the new realities of job skill requirements in low-skill labor markets has led to greater experimentation in program design for workforce development. What are these promising workforce development practices, and why might they be effective in further improving labor market outcomes given new realities?[6]

Employer Links

Not surprisingly, workforce development programs with links to employers have shown more success in raising employment, retention, and earnings levels than programs without such connections (Bliss 2000; Melendez and Harrison 1998). The greater success of these training programs is likely attributable to a number of factors. First, training programs with employer involvement are more likely to have current information on work standards, skill requirements, and state-of-the-art technologies of jobs, and are therefore more likely to meet employers' skill needs. Second, such programs provide employers with incentives to hire program participants. Employers involved in training programs are likely to reduce their search and training costs because of greater access to an appropriately trained labor supply.[7] These factors are likely to lead to greater placement and employment rates, wages, and retention for participants trained in programs with employer involvement. At the same time, firms that participate in external training programs also benefit through increased productivity, increased profits through lower search and training costs, and greater retention of employees (U.S. Department of Labor 1995).

Relevant and Timely Skills Training

Given the rising skill requirements of jobs and the rate of computerization of work, relevant and timely skills training seems mandatory to successfully link low-skill workers to jobs. But actual training in relevant skills has historically been absent in previous employment and training models, especially those that follow "work-first" strategies. In large part, employer involvement in training will help agencies overcome this absence and accomplish relevant and timely training. Another way to accomplish it is to contract with other training agencies that have proven track records of successfully training workers in relevant and timely skills. For example, in the Casey Foundation's St. Louis Jobs Initiative, the Better Family Life (BFL) community-based organization, which was responsible for coordinating training efforts as part of this initiative, approached the local St. Louis Community College to conduct its training because of the college's success in doing so in the past and its larger facilities and better equipment. This led to the creation of the WorkLink program, whereby BFL concentrates on "soft" skills and other pre-employment training, and the community college provides training in "hard" skills (Annie E. Casey Foundation 2000).

The establishment of standardized curricula for various skill sets is another way to effectively train workers in relevant skills. Mature occupations are usually defined by skills standards, which establish consistent information about the skills required for particular jobs. The National Skills Standards Board defines these standards as "performance specifications that identify the knowledge, skills, and abilities an individual needs to succeed in the workplace" (Northwest Center for Emerging Technologies 1999, 4). Hence, standards allow employers, trainers, and educational institutes to determine the exact skill requirements of jobs. Once established, standards allow job trainers to develop curricula to train workers in specific skills; by definition, such training should produce somewhat consistent skill outcomes across different training sites. This consistency allows programs to certify their program graduates, which plays two roles. It gives employers certainty about the bundle of skills that the potential worker possesses, and provides the potential worker with a marketable credential.

The timing of skills training is also an important factor to consider. The literature indicates that training in "hard," in addition to "soft," skills *before* job placement produces the greatest positive effect on job retention. For example, San Francisco Works found that instruction in "hard" skills such as computer training for jobs in the financial and banking sector before employment or internship placements produced longer job retention rates for participants than when it occurred simultaneously (Bliss 2000). Presumably, training before placement in employment or internships led to greater familiarity with the computer skills and components, which in turn led to greater confidence and ability to do the actual job.

In this regard, community colleges will play a big role in workforce development. Expanding the role of community colleges (and other workforce development networks in the region that connect with these institutions) will be key to successfully training workers for growing industries, such as health-care and green-sector jobs. This is partly because many community colleges already have associate's degree programs in these areas, and they have the classroom space, buildings, instructor access, and knowledge of state standards to ramp up fairly quickly to meet the growing demand for workers in these sectors. This is also partly because community colleges share many of the characteristics that have been identified as best practices in the workforce development field, including those just mentioned: links to employers and the ability to train for timely skills.

Community colleges will also become more important in the training of workers in growing industries partly because the Obama administration has allocated about $12 billion over the next decade specifically to community colleges for this effort. This investment is based on the belief that community colleges will be increasingly adept at preparing two-year graduates for practical professions, be able to swiftly respond to changing state standards, add certification programs for jobs in demand in this sector, and have the needed connections to local and regional labor markets.

Mixed Approaches to Training

Work-first employment programs clearly indicate that assistance in job search and training in workplace norms and customs are important components of training, particularly for those participants who have been out of the labor force for significant periods of time. A 1995 study by the General Accounting Office indicates that successful training programs include "soft" skills training in addition to job-specific "hard" skills (U.S. Department of Labor 1995). The Annie E. Casey Foundation's New Orleans Jobs Initiative follows this strategy and has shown positive preliminary evaluation results (Annie E. Casey Foundation 2000). Welfare-to-work programs such as Riverside's GAIN program, Florida's Family Transition Program, and the Baltimore OPTIONS program also followed this balanced approach, with signs of program success (Strawn 1998).

Post-Employment Assistance

Finally, post-employment assistance can help participants learn new skills quickly and continuously, which is important given the increase and changes in task requirements of jobs and the growing concern over job retention. The objectives of these programs are to strengthen or update skills for the current job or to facilitate career advancement.

Post-employment assistance is most effective when it addresses the range of issues that confront disadvantaged workers. Indeed, these forms of assistance are particularly important for reducing absenteeism and increasing job retention. Well over half of the absenteeism problems of welfare recipients at work are due to child-care and transportation problems

(Holzer and Stoll 2001). Post-employment programs are particularly effective when developed in conjunction with employers and are sensitive to specific workplace dynamics (Bliss 2000).

Some examples of post-employment assistance include skill enhancement, such as continued on-the-job training or formal apprenticeship programs, in which employers provide continued instruction in job skills. The Cooperative Health Care Network of New York, Philadelphia, and Boston provides continued in-service training and career upgrading programs for its graduates (Strawn 1998). The Chicago Commons Employment and Training Center provides comprehensive on-site support services, transportation assistance, and child care for their program graduates (Strawn 1998).[8]

MARKET FRICTIONS THAT AFFECT HOW WELL WORKFORCE DEVELOPMENT PROGRAMS PERFORM

Even with improvements in workforce development training programs, there will likely be many potential applicants for training programs who will fall outside the system, or situations where market frictions from new realities in labor markets will limit the effectiveness of these programs. Such limits are likely to be especially serious for certain demographic groups, in particular less-educated racial and ethnic minorities. This is significant since they represent a disproportionate share of those who receive workforce development assistance. In 2003, for example, 32 and 22 percent of program participants in federal workforce development programs were black and Latino, respectively, although they each made up about 10 percent of the labor force (Conrad 2005). Spatial and information frictions in labor markets create "extra" barriers for these workers. If not dealt with, these frictions will limit current and future employability of those groups about which we are most concerned.

Spatial Frictions

Many training programs have overlooked spatial frictions in labor markets, which arguably are responsible for the inferior labor-market outcomes and persistent poverty of many disadvantaged groups, especially African Americans. Geographic isolation from areas with skill-appropriate jobs can increase workers' costs in several ways, thereby reducing employment opportunities. First are the additional time and out-of-pocket costs of an extra mile of travel during the job search. For example, each additional mile of private auto travel during the search requires more out-of-pocket costs for such items as (especially!) gas, and traffic congestion and using public transportation increase the time costs of travel during search. Workers residing far from areas with skill-appropriate jobs must travel farther and thus must incur more costs to access jobs than those residing closer (Stoll 1999). Second, workers residing far from areas with skill-appropriate jobs must exert greater effort to acquire information about such opportunities.[9]

Place-Based and People-Based Approaches to Workforce Development   A spatial and regional strategy for workforce development is one good way to improve workforce development outcomes. Traditionally, there have been two main approaches to address the employment challenges of less-educated workers in mostly jobs-poor, inner-city minority communities: place-based and people-based policies. Place-based policies concentrate resources in economically distressed areas as a revitalization strategy, while people-based policies target resources to disadvantaged individuals, irrespective of place. Hybrids of the two are the people-place polices that focus attention on disadvantaged individuals in disadvantaged communities.

In the United States, one major place-based policy is enterprise zones (under the Reagan and Bush I administrations) and, subsequently, empowerment zones (under Clinton). Enterprise zone strategies use financial incentives such as job creation and wage credits, employer income tax credits, selective hiring credits, and investment and property tax credits to encourage firms to locate or expand in specified zones, usually in distressed urban or rural communities (Erickson and Friedman 1991; Green 1991).

The results of this strategy have largely been disappointing. Such policies generate few jobs and instead induce firms to move to zones from nearby locations (Ladd 1994). If a goal of enterprise zone policies is to increase minority employment more generally in distressed areas, then a spatial redistribution of employment may be viewed as a policy benefit. Nevertheless, this interpretation is tempered by results that indicate zone residents' employment is largely unaffected. Another concern is that such policies are expensive, ranging from $40,000 to $60,000 per new job added in a zone (Ladd 1994).

Two general people-place approaches are available to increase minority residents' physical access to jobs. The first is a residential mobility approach that aims to increase minority access to suburban housing. Residential mobility policies provide incentives and supports for low-income, mostly minority residents living in high-poverty areas to move to low-poverty suburban neighborhoods. The Gautreux program, implemented in the 1970s in Chicago to move mostly black families from mostly poor to moderate-income communities, appears to have had some success in improving the economic and social outcomes of adults and children (Rosenbaum and Popkin 1991). The results have been mixed for the "Moving to Opportunity" (MTO) program, a U.S. Department of Housing and Urban Development (HUD) five-city demonstration residential mobility program that helped move residents from high-poverty to low-poverty neighborhoods. (Katz, Kling, and Liebman 2001; Johnson, Ladd, and Ludwig 2002).

Only about 50 percent of the treatment group who received incentives to move to low-poverty suburban areas actually moved, and those who did tended to move to areas not far from their original homes (Katz, Kling, and Liebman 2001; Johnson, Ladd, and Ludwig 2002). Thus, most did not fundamentally change the nature of place in their moves, electing to live in or near areas close to the home they left, which means that the new location likely did not have appreciably different economic or social characteristics (Raphael and Quigley 2008). These problems limit our ability to apply the MTO findings, leaving one unable to completely rule out the idea that place influences social and economic opportunities.

A major concern with residential mobility approaches is the problem of going to scale. Suburban housing discrimination and limited availability of low-income housing in suburban low-poverty areas may limit the extent to which the minority poor could move there. Thus, such a policy would affect few people relative to the number who are spatially disadvantaged in the labor market. Such programs are also likely to be politically controversial and costly, in both economic and social terms (Briggs 1997; Haar 1996). The latter suggests that leaving family, friends, and other social institutions that help define and build family social capital is difficult and potentially costly.

Another concern about expanding the MTO program is that the characteristics of the sample who participated in it are likely to be different from those of the poverty population as a whole. Most participants were long-term public housing residents who had very little, if any, labor-market attachment and very limited job skills, and thus may have been more disadvantaged in the labor market than poor people generally. It is therefore not surprising that the children of these participants had more favorable economic or social outcomes from moving to low-poverty areas than the adults. Skill deficits and other social and program support problems would likely act to limit the extent to which such adult residents could take advantage of potentially increased economic opportunities in these areas, so extrapolating from the results of the MTO may be misleading.

Even without relocation policies, increased residential mobility for low-skill workers could occur through elimination or mitigation of suburban housing market discrimination and mortgage lending discrimination.

Policies to achieve these goals include tougher enforcement of the 1988 Fair Housing Act (Yinger 1995) and increased development of suburban low-income housing. However, each strategy faces its own unique economic and political challenges.

The second people-place approach takes residential location as a given and attempts to improve physical access to suburbs by subsidizing commutes, providing van pools to suburbs, or improving public transportation and its connections between central-city and suburban routes. An example of this kind of program is HUD's "Bridges to Work" initiative, which is designed to improve central city workers' access to suburban jobs by emphasizing job placement and transportation assistance ("reverse commute") programs. These policies are generally less costly per participant and are less politically controversial than residential mobility programs.

These options have several limitations. They do not deal with other potentially negative effects of residing in concentrated minority or poor neighborhoods. Second, they may have limited success if the wage benefits gained as a result of having suburban jobs are not sufficient to compensate for the additional travel costs. An interim report on "Bridges to Work" indicates that the demonstration program experienced high attrition early on in part because of the excessive commuting costs associated with travel to distant suburbs (Elliot, Palubinsky, and Tierney 1999). This problem may occur more for programs that focus on public transit and van or carpooling than on private car-access policies, such as subsidies to increase car ownership or car-sharing arrangements because of the additional travel costs of the former. Indeed, Steven Raphael and Michael A. Stoll (2001) estimate that car-access policies for less-educated minorities have large positive impacts on their employment.

A third concern is that these policies may increase potential negative externalities associated with increased private-auto work commutes and nonwork trips, such as traffic congestion and air pollution. The fact that many of the new trips are reverse commutes and are likely to occur during non-peak hours, when less-skilled minority workers are increasingly employed, are likely to mitigate these concerns (O'Regan and Quigley 1999).

Emerging Regional-Metropolitan Workforce Development Coordination   A second regional approach to reducing spatial frictions is the emerging strategy of coordination of workforce development across political jurisdictions. Typically, agencies providing job training and placement services in metropolitan areas are fragmented by separate municipalities of jurisdiction. Agencies that assist workers in central cities thus often lack information about suburban jobs. Moreover, agencies in suburban areas have little information about city workers who could fill jobs and few incentives to serve such workers. Thus, program participants are often trained in job skills that are not demanded by employers (Berkeley Policy Associates 2002).

Metropolitan-wide workforce development coordination efforts could help overcome these obstacles to effective training. Currently, the main federal workforce development program, the Workforce Investment Act (WIA), does not have an explicit metropolitan-wide planning component. WIA did, however, establish Workforce Investment Boards (WIBs) to oversee employment programs in local communities. While WIA allows states the option of developing unified plans and encourages states to look across programs for opportunities to coordinate local employment initiatives, few have done this at the regional or metropolitan area level. Most states have, however, conformed with WIA by establishing local WIBs with heavy private sector involvement to ensure that local employers have significant input into how training programs are designed and operated (Rhodes and Malpani 2000). But because WIBs are local, it is likely that only local private employers are invited to the table, thus limiting the possibility of broader participation of employers in the metropolitan area. Regional information about employment needs and opportunities is likely not transmitted across jurisdictions.

There are a few exceptions to this trend. The U.S. Department of Labor, through its Employment and Training Administration, launched the Workforce Innovation in Regional Economic Development (WIRED) initiative in 2005. The WIRED program brings together state, local, and federal agencies, academic institutions, private investment groups, foundations, and private business at the regional level to address challenges associated with regional growth and global competition. WIRED encourages the creation of data tools at the regional level that incorporate economic research and development, and real-time job information (U.S. Department of Labor 2007).

Since WIRED is relatively new, as yet there are no program evaluations to examine its effectiveness. Given problems of spatial mismatch in regional economies, we should expect somewhat measurable benefits from such coordination efforts in the form of improved program participant outcomes. Yet, there will surely be difficulties in realizing these potential benefits. Whether the programs provide proper incentives for continued department, agency, or stakeholder participation, whether there are clear lines of communication and authority, whether responsibilities for tasks and jobs are clearly defined, and whether there is institutional and resource commitment from the highest levels are all factors that will influence the extent to which the potential workforce development gains are realized by regional coordination.

Information Frictions: Labor Market Discrimination and Offender Status

Discrimination in the labor market remains a persistent barrier to employment for many disadvantaged groups, but is generally not taken into account when employment and training programs are designed, which reduces their effectiveness. Discrimination can result from a variety of factors and sources and can affect or target different worker characteristics. Two worker characteristics that consistently show up as being strong signals in low-skill labor markets are race and ex-offender status.

Recent innovative research has identified persistent prima facie discrimination in labor markets on the basis of race, though the underlying source of that discrimination (customer-, employer-, or statistically driven discrimination) remains in question. For example, Mariane Bertrand and Sendhil Mullainathan (2004), using matched pairs of testers, found that qualified applicants with typically "white"-sounding names, such as Brad and Emily, triggered a callback rate from employers that was 50 percent higher than for equally qualified applicants with typically black names, such as Jamal and Lakisha.[10] Their study also indicated that improving applicants' qualifications benefited white applicants but not blacks, thus leading to a wider racial gap in response rates to those with higher skills.

Similarly, Devah Pager and Bruce Western used matched testers to study the effects of race and criminal background status on employment and obtained similar results (Pager 2003; Pager and Western 2005). Employers were roughly twice as likely to hire a white applicant as an equally qualified black applicant. Further, they were as likely to hire a white applicant just released from prison as they were an equally qualified black or Hispanic applicant with no history of criminal involvement.

The new realities of the recent prison boom mean that this problem is of particular concern because of growing numbers of men, especially African American men, with criminal records. The Bureau of Justice Statistics (BJS) estimated that current and former prison inmates combined accounted for 4.9 percent of the adult male population in 2001. By race, 2.6 percent of non-Hispanic white males, 16.6 percent of non-Hispanic black males, and 7.7 percent of Hispanic males had served prison time (U.S. Department of Justice 2007). Thus, a large and growing fraction of all men—and black men in particular—who are seeking work do so with criminal records.

Employment opportunities for ex-offenders are likely to be scarce relative to the supply of ex-offenders, even though legitimate, paid employment is critically important for their successful reintegration.[11] To start, having served time is likely to diminish one's value to potential employers, as a worker's job skills may depreciate while incarcerated as he fails to accumulate additional work experience. Incarceration may also negatively affect the "soft skills" that employers value.

Ex-offenders are also likely to encounter reluctance among potential employers to hiring workers with criminal records for reasons beyond poor skills. Businesses that entail frequent customer contact may avoid hiring ex-offenders in the belief that former inmates are likely to victimize customers, exposing the employer to potential legal liability. Moreover, employers in certain industries and hiring into certain occupations are legally prohibited from hiring ex-offenders.

In this context, blacks who are non-offenders are quite likely to be harmed. It is well known that arrest and incarceration rates among young black men are very high, and employers are likely to be aware of this. General perceptions and recent research indicate that ex-offenders have a very difficult time finding employment, in part because of their personal characteristics (such as poor skills and work experience, and substance abuse problems), and in part because employers are less willing to hire these workers for a variety of reasons. Employers who cannot accurately distinguish between those who do and do not have criminal backgrounds might tend to avoid hiring those whom they *suspect* of having criminal records—namely, black men.

Employers have very imperfect information on exactly which applicants engage in crime. Because only about half of employers regularly check criminal backgrounds of job applicants, they may become more reluctant to hire any young black men because of perceived criminality among this group. This would be a form of statistical discrimination, where employers make hiring decisions on the basis of the perceived or real characteristics of the groups to which individuals belong, because it is too costly to gain more information about the individuals themselves. This intuition is consistent with recent research: employers that use criminal background checks do in fact hire more black men than those that do not (Holzer, Raphael, and Stoll 2006).

Antidiscrimination, Testing, and Certification

Discrimination on the basis of race and criminal record status surely depresses labor-market attachment, lowers employment by increasing the length of joblessness, and could be a key factor in the declining labor-force participation rates of key groups such as black men. The lack of employment for these groups surely slows the accumulation of human capital and thereby depresses skills acquisition on the job and undercuts these men's ability to develop networks that may be crucial in obtaining information about jobs. Thus, reducing discrimination against certain less-educated workers could have clear human capital–enhancing effects.

How could this be accomplished? Of course, greater enforcement of antidiscrimination laws should be pursued to protect black workers. Monitoring discrimination may be difficult—research suggests that much of the statistical discrimination against black men on the basis of perceived criminality occurs in smaller firms that are exempt from the Equal Employment Opportunity Commission's regulations. An alternative, indirect approach of working with labor-market intermediaries, especially with those who have strong links to employers, could remove or reduce statistical discrimination. To the extent that employers begin to see certain workforce development programs as credible and important to their business needs, they may be more willing to hire program participants irrespective of the color of their skin. Best-practice research demonstrates quite clearly that intermediaries that work with and vouch for these men are fairly successful in placing them into jobs, so this approach may also help to reduce the stigma of a criminal record for African American ex-offenders.

This view is consistent with the idea that gaining skills certification limits discrimination against stigmatized groups (Levy and Murnane 1996). To the extent that employers' attitudes about certain minority groups are negative and fixed, they will be less likely to approach and less willing to deal with programs that have such workers as their clients. This is why antidiscrimination enforcement is necessary and should be strengthened. Skill tests could also be helpful in this regard. Minority workers are more likely to be hired when objective and job-relevant skill tests are administered, all else equal (Autor and Scarborough 2008). In the absence of these tests, employers appear to assume skill proficiencies of workers differ across racial (and other) groups, and (wrongly) conclude that blacks and others don't have the requisite skills. Thus, employers whose discrimination is statistical in nature may be influenced to hire members of minority groups from these programs because of the added information infusion produced in these relationships. Targeting minority employers is likely to be particularly effective in this regard, since they are much more likely than other employers to hire minority workers (Boston 2006; Stoll, Raphael, and Holzer 2004).

Another appropriate policy intervention to lessen employment discrimination against blacks and others who have never been incarcerated might be to promote accurate criminal background checks as a workforce development policy. Recent research in Los Angeles suggests that employers have grown more willing to engage in criminal background checks, as the Internet makes it easier and cheaper to do so (Holzer, Raphael, and Stoll 2007). If so, greater use of checks could improve the employment prospects of less-skilled young black men more broadly, even while it makes it more difficult for those who have actually been offenders in the recent past.

Especially where employers exert themselves to obtain more information about criminal backgrounds, it is critically important that the information be accurate. Unfortunately, Internet providers of such information to employers do not always distinguish arrest from conviction information, though only the latter should inform employer decisions. Even the conviction information can contain errors.

For ex-offenders, training programs could also be effective, particularly those that increase skills and work experience before and immediately after release from prison. Subsidizing short-term "transitional jobs" for those released could be an important way of providing them with some solid work experience while indicating to employers that they are job-ready. Federal bonds to insure employers against the financial liabilities they might incur when hiring ex-offenders could be effective and are currently available at low cost, but the value, currently set at $5,000, might need to increase.

Since a large number of black ex-offenders are also noncustodial fathers, efforts to link ex-offenders with "fatherhood" support programs and services might be crucial. The tendency of states to garnish up to two-thirds of wages for men who are in arrears on their child support greatly reduces their incentive to accept low-wage jobs, where they could gain on-the-job experience and a work history. Thus, reforms in the procedures by which child support orders are set for low-income young men, and forgiveness of large arrears for those trying to keep up with their current payments, especially for men recently released from prison, might be also a necessary measure for improving the employment profile of these job seekers.

CONCLUSIONS

This chapter discusses important policies and approaches that could improve the employment and wages of less-educated workers, especially in an economic period of high unemployment and anemic economic growth. These workers are far more likely to have attended poor-quality secondary schools, which are also not currently well positioned to prepare students with job skills necessary for success in the new realities of the modern economy. These job seekers may also have failed to earn a high school diploma. They are also most likely to be hit hardest by high unemployment, and to be the last to benefit from economic growth. To enhance their employment and wages we must continue efforts to improve these schools and increase the rate of college-going. This could be accomplished, as many have argued, through a variety of efforts including enhancing school resources, improving teacher quality, reducing school size, and raising expectations in high school. Still, even with these changes, it is unlikely that all who attend high school will graduate from college.

Consequently, we should address the new realities of education and training needs of those not college-bound while meeting employers' needs for a highly trained and relevantly skilled workforce. For those still in school, responding to this dual concern will require changes in education that go beyond providing basic opportunities to learn. Changes must include integration of work experience with many of the traditional hallmarks of a college preparatory curriculum, such as analytical and problem-solving skills. In this respect, career academies are a good approach because they can engage students and keep them in school by providing concrete links between schooling and career options. Academies can prepare students for multiple trajectories and changes in skill requirements in the new labor market, partly through an experiential learning curriculum that allows for reflection and problem-solving in the classroom.

For those out of school, we must consider a different set of workforce development approaches that offer solutions in these new circumstances. These include approaches that better link less-educated minorities to jobs for which they qualify, that increase their competitiveness in local labor markets, and that reduce market frictions that affect labor-market success. To accomplish this, policies that reduce the distance between residence and work, that lessen discriminatory employer practices, and that promote regional coordination of workforce development efforts are likely to be particularly effective. So, too, would policies that raise the skills of less-educated workers, such as employment and training programs that incorporate "best practices" in the field. The returns to these efforts are best when labor markets are tight and economic growth is strong. This is why federal efforts to strengthen the economy and promote strong job growth are important components of improving the economic welfare of workers with limited education, particularly those who live in disadvantaged communities.

NOTES

1. In the recent past, these kinds of school-to-work programs were being squeezed out because of the growing emphasis on testing as a result of No Child Left Behind.

2. Still, a comprehensive review demonstrates the cost effectiveness of many workforce development programs, especially those that combine significant employer-based training in relevant job skills with basic education, "soft" skills training, and post-employment assistance (Strawn 1998). Experimental evaluation of JTPA demonstrated labor-market impacts on employment and earnings of about 10 percent on average for men and women with modest program costs of about a thousand dollars per participant. Even with the fading out of positive impacts, in terms of returns per net dollar, the JTPA program quite easily pays for itself over five years (Holzer 2008).

3. The goal of making WIA services more universal has clearly been achieved, as low-income individuals now make up only about 20 percent of WIA's nondislocated adult registrants and just over half of those receiving training (Holzer 2008). In contrast, nondislocated adults served under both CETA and JTPA were primarily disadvantaged. Broader targeting was done partly to remove any stigmas in the eyes of employers that might have been associated with publicly provided employment and training services.

4. Likewise, frictions in labor markets, such as discrimination in employment against certain groups, could dampen these program successes if the frictions are not taken into account. I discuss labor-market frictions and policies to address them later in this chapter.

5. Over the entire forty-eight-month follow-up period, monthly earnings impacts were 18 percent and 4 percent for young men and young women, respectively. Impacts for young men considered at medium or high risk of dropping out of school were almost as large as the overall ones, and those for minorities were large as well. Impacts on hourly wages accounted for nearly half of the monthly earnings impact.

6. This literature review examined a broad set of training organizations, including, among others, community-based organizations, community technology centers, community colleges, and publicly and privately sponsored initiatives and training intermediaries. This discussion highlights a select number of promising practices, and should not be viewed as exhaustive.

7. Employers spend a nontrivial amount of money to keep any one low-skill job filled, particularly when the high turnover rates that are characteristic of these jobs are factored in. Employers' search costs for low- to semi-skilled workers are between $300 and $1,500, depending on how difficult it is to find appropriate labor, and training costs for these workers range from $700 to $3,000, depending on the type of training required (Frazis et al. 1998; Bishop 1994).

8. Finally, positive labor-market outcomes have been associated with mentoring and "youth development" programs such as Big Brothers and Big Sisters (Herrera 1999). Such programs adopt a different approach than those discussed in this chapter.

9. See Margaret C. Simms and Winston J. Allen (1995) for a discussion of whether job-poor areas that are strategically located, such as near downtowns, represent competitive advantages and opportunities for economic development.

10. Those believed to be whites received callbacks in 10.06 percent of cases, compared with 6.70 percent for blacks. Callback rates were slightly higher for women than men, but overall levels of discrimination differed little by gender.

11. Arrests (Grogger 1995) and imprisonment (Freeman 1992) both tend to be associated with lower employment and earnings, evidence consistent with an effect of incarceration on the general employability of former inmates.

REFERENCES

Annie E. Casey Foundation. 2000. *Stronger Links: New Ways to Connect Low-Skill Workers to Better Jobs.* Baltimore, Md.: Annie E. Casey Foundation.

Autor, David H., Lawrence F. Katz, and Melissa S. Kearney. 2008. "Trends in U.S. Wage Inequality: Revising the Revisionists." *Review of Economics and Statistics* 90(2): 300–323.

Autor, David H., Frank Levy, and Richard Murnane. 2003. "The Skill Content of Recent Technological Change: An Empirical Exploration." *Quarterly Journal of Economics* 118(4): 1279–1334.

Autor, David H., and David Scarborough. 2008. "Does Job Testing Harm Minority Workers? Evidence from Retail Establishments." *Quarterly Journal of Economics* 123(1): 219–77.

Berkeley Policy Associates. 2002. *Evaluation of the Regional Workforce Preparation and Economic Development Act.* Oakland, Calif.: Berkeley Policy Associates.

Bertrand, Mariane, and Sendhil Mullainathan. 2004. "Are Emily and Greg More Employable than Lakisha and Jamal? A Field Experiment on Labor Market Discrimination." *American Economic Review* 94(4): 991–1013.

Bishop, John. 1994. "The Incidence of and Payoff to Employer Training." Working paper 94-17. Ithaca, N.Y.: Cornell University, Center for Advanced Human Resource Studies.

Blackburn, McKinley, David E. Bloom, and Richard B. Freeman. 1990. "The Declining Economic Position of Less Skilled American Men." In *A Future of Lousy Jobs? The Changing Structure of U.S. Wages*, edited by Gary Burtless. Washington, D.C.: Brookings Institution.

Blank, Rebecca M. 1997. *It Takes a Nation: A New Agenda for Fighting Poverty.* New York and Princeton, N.J.: Russell Sage Foundation and Princeton University Press.

————. 2008. "Economic Change and the Structure of Opportunity for Less-Skilled Workers." Discussion paper 1345-08. Madison: University of Wisconsin, Institute for Research on Poverty.

Bliss, Steven. 2000. *San Francisco Works: Toward an Employer-Led Approach to Welfare Reform and Workforce Development.* New York: Manpower Demonstration Research Corporation.

Boston, Thomas D. 2006. "The Role of Black-owned Businesses in Black Community Development." In *Jobs and Economic Development in Minority Communities: Realities, Challenges, and Innovation,* edited by Paul Ong. Philadelphia: Temple University Press.

Bound, John, and Richard B. Freeman. 1992. "What Went Wrong? The Erosion of the Relative Earnings and Employment Among Young Black Men in the 1980s." *Quarterly Journal of Economics* 107(1): 201–32.

Briggs, Xavier. 1997. Moving Up Versus Moving Out: Neighborhood Effects in Housing Mobility Programs. *Housing Policy Debate* 8(1): 195–234.

Buck, Maria. 2002. *Charting New Territory: Early Implementation of the Workforce Investment Act.* New York: Public/Private Ventures.

Cappelli, Peter. 1996. "Technology and Skill Requirements: Implications for Establishment Wage Structure." *New England Economic Review* (May–June): 139–56.

Card, David. 1996. "The Effects of Unions on the Structure of Wages: A Longitudinal Analysis." *Econometrica* 64(4): 957–80.

Cellini, Stephanie R. 2006. "Smoothing the Transition to College? The Effect of Tech-Prep Programs on Educational Attainment." *Economics of Education Review* 25(4): 394–411.

Conrad, Cecilia A. 2005. *A Mixed Record: How the Public Workforce System Affects Racial and Ethnic Disparities in the Labor Market.* Washington, D.C.: Joint Center for Political and Economic Studies.

Danziger, Sheldon, Reynolds Farley, and Harry J. Holzer. 2000. *Detroit Divided.* New York: Russell Sage Foundation.

Dayton, Charles, Alan Weisberg, and David Stern. 1989. *California Partnership Academies: 1987–88, Evaluation Report.* Berkeley: University of California, Policy Analysis for California Education.

DiNardo, John, Nicole Fortin, and Thomas Lemieux. 1996. "Labor Market Institutions and the Distribution of Wages, 1973–1992: A Semi-Parametric Approach." *Econometrica* 64(5): 1001–44.

Elliot, Mark, B. Palubinsky, and Joseph Tierney. 1999. *Overcoming Roadblocks on the Way to Work.* Philadelphia: Public/Private Ventures.

Erickson, Rodney A., and Susan W. Friedman. 1991. "Comparative Dimensions of State Enterprise Zone Policies." In *Enterprise Zones: New Directions on Economic Development,* edited by Roy Green. Newbury Park, Calif.: Sage.

Frazis, Harley, Maury Gittleman, Michael Horrigan, and Mary Joyce. 1998. "Results from the 1995 Survey of Employer-Provided Training." *Monthly Labor Review* 121(6): 3–13.

Freeman, Richard. 1992. "Crime and Employment of Disadvantaged Youth." In *Drugs, Crime and Social Isolation: Barriers to Urban Opportunity*, edited by Adele Harrell and George Peterson. Washington, D.C.: Urban Institute Press.

Friedlander, Daniel, and Gary Burtless. 1995. *Five Years After: The Long-Term Effects of Welfare-to-Work Programs*. New York: Russell Sage Foundation.

Green, Roy, ed. 1991. *Enterprise Zones: New Directions on Economic Development*. Newbury Park, Calif.: Sage.

Grogger, Jeffrey. 1995. "The Effect of Arrests on the Employment and Earnings of Young Men." *Quarterly Journal of Economics* 110(1): 51–71.

Haar, Charles M. 1996. *Suburbs Under Siege: Race, Space and Audacious Judges*. Princeton, N.J.: Princeton University Press.

Harrison, Bennett, and Marcus Weiss. 1998. *Workforce Development Networks: Community-Based Organizations and Regional Alliances*. Thousands Oaks, Calif.: Sage.

Herrera, Carla. 1999. *School-Based Mentoring: A First Look into Its Potential*. Philadelphia: Private/Public Ventures.

Holzer, Harry J. 1996. *What Employers Want*. New York: Russell Sage Foundation.

———. 2008. "Workforce Development as an Antipoverty Strategy: Up, Down, and Back Up?" Discussion paper 1353-08. Madison: University of Wisconsin, Institute for Research on Poverty.

Holzer, Harry J., Steve Raphael, and Michael A. Stoll. 2002. "Can Employers Play a More Positive Role in Prisoner Re-Entry?" Urban Institute Reentry Roundtable discussion paper. Washington, D.C.: Urban Institute.

———. 2006. "Perceived Criminality, Background Checks, and the Racial Hiring Practices of Employers?" *Journal of Law and Economics*, 49(2): 451–80.

———. 2007. "The Effect of an Applicant's Criminal History on Employer Hiring Decisions and Screening Practices: Evidence from Los Angeles." In *Barriers to Reentry: The Labor Market for Released Prisoners in Post-Industrial America*, edited by David F. Weiman, Michael A. Stoll, and Shawn Bushway. New York: Russell Sage Foundation.

Holzer, Harry J., and Michael A. Stoll. 2001. *Employers and Welfare Recipients: The Effect of Welfare Reform in the Workplace*. San Francisco: Public Policy Institute of California.

Jaynes, Gerald D., and Robin M. Williams, eds. 1989. *A Common Destiny: Blacks and American Society*. Washington, D.C.: National Academy Press.

Johnson, M. P., Helen F. Ladd, and Jens Ludwig. 2002. "The Benefits and Costs of Residential Mobility Programmes for the Poor." *Housing Studies* 17(1): 125–38.

Kasarda, John D. 1995. "Industrial Restructuring and the Changing Location of Jobs." In *State of the Union: America in the 1990s*, edited by Reynolds Farley. Vol. 1, *Economic Trends*. New York: Russell Sage Foundation.

Katz, Lawrence, Jeff Kling, and Jeffrey Liebman. 2001. "Moving to Opportunity in Boston: Early Results of a Randomized Mobility Experiment." *Quarterly Journal of Economics* 116(2): 607–51.

Kemple, James J. 2001. "Career Academies: Impacts on Students' Initial Transitions to Post-Secondary Education and Employment." New York: Manpower Demonstration Research Corporation.

———. 2005. "Making an Impact on the Transition from School to Work: Evidence from Career Academies." Unpublished manuscript. New York: Manpower Demonstration Research Corporation.

———. 2008. "Career Academies: Long-Term Impacts on Labor Market Outcomes, Educational Attainment and Transitions to Adulthood." New York: Manpower Demonstration Research Corporation.

Kemple, James J., and Joshua Haimson. 1994. "Florida's Project Independence: Program Implementation, Participation Patterns, and First-Year Impacts." New York: Manpower Demonstration Research Corporation.

Kemple, James J., and Jason C. Snipes. 2000. "Career Academies: Impacts on Students' Engagement and Performance in High School." New York: Manpower Demonstration Research Corporation.

Ladd, Helen, F. 1994. "Spatially Targeted Economic Development Strategies: Do They Work?" *Cityscape: A Journal of Policy Development and Research* 1(1): 193–218.

Lee, David S. 1999. "Wage Inequality in the U.S. During the 1980s: Rising Dispersion or Falling Minimum Wage?" *Quarterly Journal of Economics* 114(3): 977–1023.

Lerman, Robert. 2007. "Career-Focused Education and Training for Youth." In *Reshaping the American Workforce in a Changing Economy*, edited by Harry J. Holzer and Demetra S. Nightingale. Washington, D.C.: Urban Institute Press.

Levy, Frank, and Richard Murnane. 1996. *Teaching the New Basic Skills.* New York: Free Press.

Manski, Charles F., and Irwin Garfinkel, eds. 1992. *Evaluating Welfare and Training Programs.* Cambridge, Mass.: Harvard University Press.

Melendez, Edwin, and Bennett Harrison. 1998. "Matching the Disadvantaged to Job Opportunities: Structural Explanations for the Past Successes of the Center for Employment Training." *Economic Development Quarterly* 12(1): 3–11.

Mishel, Lawrence, Jared Bernstein, and John Schmitt. 2003. *The State of Working America 2002–03.* New York: M. E. Sharpe.

Moss, Philip, and Chris Tilly. 2001. *Stories Employers Tell.* New York: Russell Sage Foundation.

Mosteller, Fredrick, Richard J. Light, and Jason A. Sachs. 1996. "Sustained Inquiry in Education: Lessons in Skill Grouping and Class Size." *Harvard Education Review* 66(4): 707–842.

Neumark, David, and Donna Rothstein. 2006. "School-to-Career Programs and Transitions to Employment and Higher Education." *Economics of Education Review* 25(4): 374–93.

Northwest Center for Emerging Technologies. 1999. *Building a Foundation for Tomorrow: Skill Standards for Information Technology.* Bellevue, Wash.: NWCET.

Oakes, Jeannie. 1985/2005. *Keeping Track: How Schools Structure Inequality.* New Haven: Yale University Press.

Ong, Paul, and Veronica Terriquez. 2008. "Can Multiple Pathways Offset Inequalities in the Urban Spatial Structure?" In *Beyond Tracking: Multiple Pathways to College, Career, and Civic Participation,* edited by Jeannie Oakes and Marisa Saunders. Cambridge, Mass.: Harvard Education Press.

O'Regan, Katherine M., and John M. Quigley. 1999. "Spatial Isolation of Welfare Recipients: What Do We Know?" Program on Housing and Urban Policy working paper W99-003. Berkeley: University of California.

Orr, Margaret Terry, Thomas Bailey, Katherine L. Hughes, Gregory S. Kienzl, and Melinda Mechur Karp. 2007. "The National Academy Foundation's Career Academies: Shaping Postsecondary Transitions." In *Improving School-to-Work Transitions,* edited by David Neumark. New York: Russell Sage Foundation.

Pager, Devah. 2003. "The Mark of a Criminal Record." *American Journal of Sociology* 108(5): 937–75.

Pager, Devah, and Bruce Western. 2005. *Race at Work: Realities of Race and Criminal Record in the NYC Job Market.* New York: Schomburg Center for Black Culture.

Raby, Marilyn. 1995. "The Career Academies." In *Education through Occupations in American High Schools,* edited by W. Norton Grubb. Volume 1. New York: Teachers College Press.

Raphael, Steven, and John Quigley. 2008. "Neighborhoods, Economic Self Sufficiency, and the MTO." *Brookings-Wharton Papers on Urban Affairs* 9(2008): 1–46.

Raphael, Steven, and Michael A. Stoll. 2001. "Can Boosting Minority Car Ownership Rates Narrow Inter-Racial Employment Gaps?" *Brookings-Wharton Papers on Urban Affairs* 2: 99–137.

Reller, Dorothy. 1984. *The Peninsula Academies: Final Technical Evaluation Report.* Palo Alto, Calif.: American Institutes for Research.

Rhodes, Eric, and Sonal Malpani. 2000. *A Metropolitan Approach to Workforce Development.* New York: Century Foundation. Available at: www.tcf.org/list.asp?type=PB&pubid=305; accessed July 9, 2010.

Rosenbaum, James E., and Susan J. Popkin. 1991. "Employment and Earnings of Low-Income Blacks Who Move to Middle-Class Suburbs." In *The Urban Underclass,* edited by Christopher Jencks and Paul E. Peterson. Washington, D.C.: Brookings Institution.

Simms, Margaret C., and Winston J. Allen. 1995. "Is the Inner City Competitive?" *Review of Black Political Economy* 24(2–3): 213–20.

Stern, David, Marilyn Raby, and Charles Dayton. 1992. *Career Academies: Partnerships for Reconstructing American High Schools.* San Francisco: Jossey-Bass.

Stern, David, and Roman Stearns. 2009. "Combining Academic and Career-Technical Courses to Make College an Option for More Students: Evidence and Challenges." In *Multiple Perspectives on Multiple Pathways,* edited by Marisa Saunders and Jeannie Oakes. Cambridge, Mass.: Harvard Education Press.

Stern, David, Christopher Wu, Charles Dayton, and Andrew Maul. 2007. "Learning by Doing Career Academies." In *Improving School-to-Work Transitions,* edited by David Neumark. New York: Russell Sage Foundation.

Stoll, Michael A. 1999. "Spatial Job Search, Spatial Mismatch, and the Employment and Wages of Racial and Ethnic Groups in Los Angeles." *Journal of Urban Economics* 46(1): 129–55.

———. 2005. "Geographic Skills Mismatch, Job Search, and Race." *Urban Studies* 42(4): 695–717.

———. 2010. "Labor Market Advancement of Young Men: How It Differs by Educational Attainment and Race/Ethnicity During the Initial Transition to Work." *Journal of Students Placed at Risk* 15(1): 66–92

Stoll, Michael A., Harry J. Holzer, and Keith R. Ihlanfeldt. 2000. "Within Cities and Suburbs: Racial Residential Concentration and the Distribution of Employment Opportunities Across Sub-Metropolitan Areas." *Journal of Policy Analysis and Management* 19(2): 207–31.

Stoll, Michael A., Steven Raphael, and Harry J. Holzer. 2004. "Black Job Applicants and the Hiring Officer's Race." *Industrial and Labor Relations Review* 57(2): 267–87.

Strawn, Julie. 1998. *Beyond Job Search or Basic Education: Rethinking the Role of Skills in Welfare Reform.* Washington, D.C.: Center for Law and Social Policy.

U.S. Department of Justice, Bureau of Justice Statistics. 2007. "Education and Corrections Populations." Report. Washington: U.S. Department of Justice. Available at: http://www.ojp.gov/bjs/abstract/ecp.htm; accessed February 9, 2009.

U.S. Department of Labor, 1995. *What's Working (and What's Not): A Summary of Research in the Economic Impacts of Employment Training Programs.* Washington: U.S. Department of Labor.

———. 2007a. "Workforce Initiative in Regional Economic Development [WIRED]—Selected Regions." Fact sheet. Washington: U.S. Department of Labor, Employment and Training Administration. Available at: www.doleta.gov/pdf/wired fact sheet.pdf; accessed July 9, 2010.

Wilson, William J. 1996. *When Work Disappears: The World of the New Urban Poor.* New York: Knopf.

Yinger, John. 1995. *Closed Doors, Opportunities Lost: The Continuing Costs of Housing Discrimination.* New York: Russell Sage Foundation.

CHAPTER 4

CREATING OPPORTUNITY AT THE BOTTOM: THE ROLE OF SKILL DEVELOPMENT AND FIRM-LEVEL POLICIES IN IMPROVING OUTCOMES FOR LOW-WAGE EMPLOYEES

PAUL OSTERMAN

In the past several decades the American labor market has gone through a remarkable number of changes. The nature of the employment relationship has evolved as firms have reduced the types of commitments they are willing to make to their employees and, as part of this reconsideration, introduced new employment arrangements such as contingent employment systems and contract employment. New threats have arisen as employers outsource jobs throughout the globe. The channels for employee voice have narrowed as unions have lost strength. The characteristics of the workforce have changed as immigration surged. At the same time, much work has been transformed in positive directions as jobs have become broader and more complex and as the demand for skill has grown.

At the same time that these long-run shifts have taken place, the job market also experienced the shock of the Great Recession. The painfully high unemployment and underemployment focused American's attention on the labor market. Data from recent downturns show that the consequences of job loss are severe. Among workers with a high school diploma, only 54 percent reported themselves reemployed, and for workers with a college degree the rate was still only 71 percent. Reemployment itself does not make employees whole. Thirteen percent of those losing full-time jobs were reemployed in part-time work, and among those who did manage to find new full-time work the average wage loss was 11 percent for high school workers and 13 percent for those with college (Farber 2005). The evidence is that these earning losses persist (Kletzer 1998).

At the same time, the shock and pain associated with the Great Recession may have diverted attention away from the ongoing and important issue of job quality, the topic of this chapter. While the labor market has shifted in important ways, the fraction of employees who find themselves trapped in low-wage work or in insecure employment has remained high. This chapter emphasizes policies aimed at the low-wage labor market but will make the case that executing them will require efforts to connect the traditional second-chance system both to employers and to efforts to aid workers in higher reaches of the job market.

The broad argument made here is that there is a mismatch between the labor-market institutions that were created after World War II and that persist today and the new realities of the job market. I begin by describing the contours of these precarious labor markets, and I will then show that our policy regime has not caught up to the shifts in the job market. In the second half of the chapter I will offer some suggestions for moving forward.

THE CHALLENGES WE FACE

We face two broad challenges in the job market. The first is that despite decades of effort the low-wage labor market is large, and many adults are trapped in it. Second, in recent years the job market has become riskier and more volatile even for those higher up the ladder (see Hacker, this volume, chapter 2).

In 2007, 24 percent of adults earned less than two thirds of the median wage, or about $11 an hour. The figure was 30 percent less for women and 19 percent less for men. These percentages of workers that are making what is essentially a poverty wage are strikingly high.[1] Furthermore, adults in low-wage employment are often trapped. Among low earners in six years starting in the early 1990s, only 27 percent raised their incomes enough to rise consistently above the poverty line for a family of four (Holzer 2004). A more recent study using the Panel Survey on Income Dynamics comes to a similar conclusion (Theodos and Bednarzik 2006).

TABLE 4.1   Percentage Below Two Thirds of Median Wage in 2007, for Various Groups

All	24.0%
Men	18.9
Women	29.6
High school dropout	59.5
High school diploma	34.0
Some college	22.0
College degree	8.2
White	22.8
African American	33.4
Hispanic	44.1
Government employment	13.3
Private for-profit employment	27.1
Employment covered by union contract	8.5
Full-time employment	20.0
Part-time employment	49.2

Source: Author's compilation based on data from U.S. Census Bureau (2007).

Who are the people whose earnings fall below our $11-per-hour standard, and where do they work? Answering these questions will help us think about policy and how to meet the challenges. Table 4.1 provides some initial clues.

It is not surprising to learn that women and nonwhites face a greater likelihood than white men of holding a below-standard job, since these are the groups that have long faced discrimination in the job market and difficulty in penetrating into the best jobs. It is also not surprising to learn that better-educated people have better jobs. Indeed, the effect is dramatic: the chances of holding a substandard job are nearly 60 percent for high school dropouts and under 10 percent for college graduates.

The importance of the organizational characteristics of the job itself is obvious in the last several lines of the table. Government employment is much less likely to be below standard than is private-sector work. If the work is covered by a union contract the chances the job will be below standard fall dramatically. Finally, those with part-time jobs (less than thirty-five hours a week) are clearly disadvantaged. There are reasonable arguments that on average, part-time work should pay less than full-time (for example,

TABLE 4.2   Company Size and Below-Standard Wages[a]

Company Size (By Number of Employees)	Percentage of Employees Paid Below Standard	Distribution of Workers Paid Below Standard	Distribution of All Employees
Fewer than 25	40.1%	33.1%	20.5%
25 to 99	27.9	15.4	13.6
100 to 499	22.3	13.6	15.1
More than 500	18.4	37.7	50.6
Total		100	100

Source: Author's compilation based on data from U.S. Census Bureau (2007).
Note: Data are for civilian wage and salary employees between the ages of 25 and 64.
[a] An hourly wage of $11 (in 2007 dollars) or less is below standard.

there are less opportunities for on-the-job training in part-time work), but there are no good reasons for part-time work to fall below our basic standard for decent employment.

There also are wide variations across industries. At the extremes, only 8 percent of jobs in professional services fall below the standard, whereas 70 percent of jobs in the food and drink service industries (restaurants and bars) do. Predictably, the industries that are most likely to offer below-standard jobs are retail, restaurants and bars, personal services, and hotels. It is striking that nearly a third of all below-standard jobs are concentrated in just two industries, retail trade and food and drink service, and that if we add health services and manufacturing to the list we are up to half of the bad jobs. Clearly understanding the characteristics of particular industries must be part of any strategy to improve the low-wage labor market.

A final key question is the relationship between firm size and below-standard work. The risk of working for wages below the standard is much higher in small than in large firms. Forty percent of employees in the smallest firms are below the standard, while the figure is less than half that in the largest firms. As the third column of table 4.2 shows, over half of all employees are in very large firms whereas only about 20 percent are in the smallest. Again, however, the rate of risk has to be combined with the size of the risk pool in order to see where the most people in difficulty are located. The middle column shows that although a third of below-standard workers are in the smallest firms, a bit more than that are in the very largest. Put differently, it is clear that any overall strategy must be prepared to address the special difficulties facing small employers, but this does not mean that large enterprises are off the hook.

EXPLAINING BELOW-STANDARD JOBS

The most common explanation for the persistence of low wages and for growing earnings inequality is that demand for skill is growing and that people with low earnings are unable to qualify for better-paying work. This diagnosis leads naturally to an emphasis on education and job training as the policy solutions (Stoll, this volume, chapter 3).

This chapter takes a somewhat different position: that in addition to focusing on skill deficiencies, it is important to look at the decisions that firms make about how to organize work and to improve the regulatory and "employee voice" environment. Having said this (and the arguments will be elaborated on), it is nonetheless true that skills play a significant role. The perception of the central role of skill rests on the standard story relating supply and demand to wages. Beginning in the 1960s, the fraction of the workforce with at least some college education grew substantially, yet despite this increase in supply, college graduates' wages increased relative to those of other employees without that level of education. In standard economic models, the explanation of a rising price (the relative wage) in the face of increasing supply is that the demand curve is "shifting out," meaning that employers want more college-educated people at the same wage than they did in the past. This shifting out of demand is typically attributed to the nature of technological change, which is biased in favor of more-educated workers.

The wage data are persuasive but not bulletproof, particularly since in recent years the relative wages of the college-educated have stagnated (while the wages of those with more than a B.A. degree have grown). A more direct approach is to see what projections of occupational demand and trends in the organization of work imply for the future demand for skill. Every several years the Bureau of Labor Statistics projects future occupational distribution. The projections are that between 2006 and 2016 the economy will add 15.6 million jobs. This is the net new job figure that is often used to calculate how the occupational distribution will change, such as when it is stated that "between 2006 and 2016, X percent of job growth will occur in Y occupation" (Dohm and Shniper 2007).

Net new jobs are the key information over a very long time horizon, yet over any short- or intermediate-term period, replacement hiring is also important because it helps determine what jobs will be open for new entrants and for job changers. This is particularly significant because of the imminent retirement of large numbers of baby boomers. In fact, replacement hiring means that even in occupations that are declining as a share of the workforce there will still be substantial new hiring.[2] Put differently, the "hollowing out of the middle class" discussion is considerably exaggerated.

Occupational projections themselves are difficult to interpret in terms of the need, or lack of need, to upgrade the educational level of the workforce. However, the BLS makes an effort to translate the data into demand for education. These data show a trend toward more jobs requiring at least some college education, but the trend is modest: in 2004, 22.9 percent of jobs were in the two highest educational categories, and the projection is that by 2014, ten years later, the fraction will have climbed to just 24.6 percent. At the low end, 13.2 percent of jobs required just a high school education in 2004, and that is projected to fall to 12.5 percent by 2014. In short, according to the BLS the demand for post-secondary skills is increasing, but at a modest rate.

The skill challenges in the low-wage labor market have been complicated by the surge of immigrants. Whereas in 1980 immigrants accounted for 6.5 percent of the nation's workforce, in 2005 their share was 14.9 percent (Mishel, Bernstein, Allegretto 2007, 179). A large number of immigrants are very highly skilled, as illustrated by the efforts of high technology firms to expand the H1-B visa program. But a far larger number of immigrants work at the bottom of the job market. The largest group of immigrants is Mexicans. In 2000, 63 percent of Mexican men and 57 percent of Mexican women were high school dropouts and only 11 percent of the men and 16 percent of the women had more than a high school education (Mishel, Bernstein, Allegretto 2007, 180). Although the country benefits in numerous ways from immigration, to some extent the surge of immigrants places pressures on wages and employment opportunities at the bottom of the job market.

THE DEMAND SIDE

Although most discussion of low-wage work focuses on skill issues and the implied shortcomings of low-wage workers, in fact employers have some discretion about how they organize work. Many commentators point to the contrasting employment policies of Costco and Walmart, with respect to how they reward their employees. One might as readily highlight the employment situation of room cleaners in unionized and nonunionized hotels. Much of this thinking has been captured in the labels "high-road" and "low-road" employment practices—terms that imply that employers can make choices in their hiring practices.

More formal econometric research also finds that, even after controlling for companies' measurable characteristics, such as their capital stock and the industry they are in, companies that seem equivalent can vary considerably in their wage policies (Groshen 1991). Additional research that points to an important role for company decisionmaking is the recent work of Nicholas Bloom and John Van Reenen (2007). They surveyed companies' management practices, particularly their human resource policies, and found very substantial variation, with many firms using what the authors characterize as "suboptimal practices."

The case for improving the human resource practices of low-wage firms is strengthened by the fact that in many of the industries that employ low-wage adults—sectors such as hotels, restaurants, and nursing homes—working conditions have stagnated or deteriorated, but lack of technology and skills is not the culprit (Appelbaum, Bernhardt, and Murnane 2003). An example is outsourcing of food preparation or laundry in hotels. This implies that there is a kind of "HR syndrome"—a negative feedback loop in which firms' human resources practices reinforce the difficulties of low-wage workers.

One element of this negative feedback loop is the low level of training available to employees at the bottom. American companies devote considerable resources to training their workforce, but that training in private companies is biased away from low-skilled frontline workers. A substantial labor economics literature has documented that people with higher levels of education receive disproportionately more training (for a review of the literature, see Lerman, McKernan, and Riegg 2004). One representative finding is from the National Household Education Survey of 1995, which found that only 22 percent of workers in the bottom quintile of earnings reported receiving employer-supported education compared with 40 percent in the top quintile (Ahlstrand, Bassi, and McMurrer 2003, 329)

The failure to train lower-wage workers makes it harder for them to advance. Companies' HR practices contribute to these difficulties, which also include the growing tendency to outsource lower-skill work and hence to remove the jobs from the companies' internal labor market, or job ladders, as well as a more general deterioration of internal mobility paths.

POLICY MISMATCHES

After World War II, a labor-market policy regime was put into place that reflected the nature of the job market at that time. The realities have changed, but the policy regime persists even today. Elsewhere I have described in detail the key features of the postwar job market and the policies that flowed from it, as well as the changes that disrupted that market

(Osterman 1999; Osterman et al. 2001). Here I will focus on the mismatches that challenge the low-wage labor market and create employment volatility.

Mismatch Between Skill Supply and Demand

Demand for skill is growing but the employment and training system is underfunded. Our second-chance training system consists of the Workforce Investment Act (WIA) programs that are aimed at poor adults and Adult Basic Education (ABE) funded by the Department of Education and states. In addition, as I will describe later in this section, community colleges also play a central role.

The appropriations for WIA have steadily declined in both absolute and real dollars. For example, adult formula funding in WIA went from $945 million in fiscal year 2002 to $864 million in fiscal year 2006 (Rubinstein and Mayo 2007, 12). In addition, the fraction of the expenditure devoted to training has declined over time and the average spending per trainee is quite low. By any reasonable measure these efforts fall far short of meeting the need. Much the same could be said of the adult basic education system. Only 21 percent of participants received more than 150 hours of instruction (Comings, Sum, and Uvin 2000, xi), and 50 percent of those in adult education classes drop out before completing 35 hours, or ten weeks (Jobs For The Future 2004, 9).

The Employment and Training (E&T) system is often perceived as ineffective, but this is unfair. A number of careful evaluations have demonstrated that E&T programs can pay off for adults.[3] Even though the gains are statistically significant, the typical program makes a small investment with a correspondingly small return. A sense of the potential gains from a longer-term investment in people can be gained from an evaluation of Project QUEST in San Antonio, Texas. This program, which has won a number of national awards, trains working adults for eighteen months and cooperates closely with the employer community to identify job needs and to design the training curriculum. Although the "gold standard" of random assignment has not been used, two independent pre-post evaluations found very substantial wage gains. One study (Osterman and Lautsch 1996) reported an increase in participants' income of about $5,000 to $7,500 a year, and this was confirmed by another independent evaluation (Grote and Roder 2005). Supportive evidence also comes from an evaluation of Capital Idea, a program modeled on Project QUEST, that found very large positive impacts (over $4,000 increment in annual earnings) relative to a comparison group (Smith, King, and Schroeder 2007).

Mismatch Between Firms' Decisionmaking and Training System

Companies are making decisions about how to organize work that have important consequences for employee welfare, yet traditionally the employment and training system has been isolated from the private sector. Despite the importance of companies' decisionmaking, an historical weakness of the employment and training system has been that it has been perceived as isolated from the concerns of the mainstream economy. Most employers view the system as an extension of the welfare system and do not turn to it for assistance in meeting their human resource needs. For example, a recent survey of manufactures found that only 4.6 percent of responding firms reported using Workforce Investment Boards (WIBs) or one-stops to meet their human resource needs, whereas 30.8 percent used community colleges, 46 percent used industry associations, and 40 percent used temp firms (Partnership for Employer-Employee Responsive Systems 2003, 14).

Poor Communication Between Workers and Regulatory Bodies

Labor standards and employee voice are both under pressure in the low-wage labor market, yet both enforcement mechanisms and labor laws are broken. The postwar period has seen a steady decline in the power of unions, and this has had a significant impact on the well-being of low-wage employees. The potential of unions to raise the wages of those at the bottom of the earning distribution is clear in the data. For example, among people with a high school diploma or less, 9.7 percent of union members are low-wage workers, compared to 32.3 percent of nonunion employees (Osterman 2008). The real concern about the role unions might play in reducing low-wage employment is not whether they improve employment conditions when they are successful, but rather the fact that their success rate in organizing nonunion workers is poor. The rate of private-sector unionization has fallen from 25 percent in 1973 to just over 7 percent today.

Declining Labor Standards

An issue of growing importance in the low-wage labor market is employers' evasion of wage and hours laws. This evasion is significantly enabled by what can only be described as the abdication of enforcement. Between 1975 and 2004, the number of U.S. Department of Labor workplace inspectors declined by 14 percent and the number of compliance actions declined by 36 percent, while during the same period, the number of covered employees in the labor force grew by 55 percent and the number of covered establishments grew by 112 percent (Ruckelshaus 2008, 376) In 2004, there were only 788 Department of Labor inspectors nationwide. To make matters worse, the enforcement strategy is based almost entirely on worker complaints, which is a big problem in low-wage industries, and particularly in those with many immigrant workers. The decline of unions has exacerbated this problem, since the presence of unions is associated with stronger enforcement (Weil 1991).

There is considerable evidence that lack of enforcement has led to substantial difficulties in the low-wage labor market as some companies use a variety of tactics to evade labor standards. Some of these tactics are perfectly legal but lead to abuses. The leading example here is the use of subcontractors in a wide range of settings. For example, in hotels, laundry service and food preparation is increasingly subcontracted out (Bernhardt 2003). Although legal, the nature of the process is that the client firm pits contractors against each other in a cost competition, and the consequence is that the subcontractor faces substantial pressure to cut costs via illegal means.

The two most common illegal forms of cutting costs, practiced by both subcontractors and large mainstream employers, are misclassification of employees and violation of wage and hour laws. When employees are misclassified as independent contractors instead of as employees, they are paid, and their pay is reported to the IRS, as independent contractors via a 1099 form rather than as regular employees via a W-2 form. The consequence is that the employer need not pay unemployment insurance, benefits, and his or her share of Social Security and Medicare taxes. In addition, the 1099 employees are typically not protected by wage and hour and labor organizing laws. The second form of violation, not paying overtime or not paying the minimum wage, is more straightforward.

There is a substantial accumulation of evidence that these practices are increasingly common. For example, a recent three-and-a-half year study of employment practices in thirteen New York industries (groceries, retail, restaurant, home health care, residential construction, laundry, food and apparel manufacturing) found widespread use of these practices and widespread violation of labor law and labor standards (Bernhardt, McGrath, and DeFilipis 2007). Nor were these behaviors the work of only a few bad apples. A network of employment brokers and storefront employment agencies systematically recruited and placed people in these jobs in which violations were common.

Other geographically specific case studies have found similar patterns, such as widespread overtime violations found in contractors working for the nation's largest homebuilder in the Phoenix area (Interfaith Workers Justice 2008). A recent view of the national literature concluded that

> labeling employees "independent contractors" is a broad problem and affects a wide range of jobs. A DOL [Department of Labor] study found that up to 30 percent of firms misclassify their employees as independent contractors. At least eleven states have studied the problem and found high rates of misclassification. As many as four in ten construction workers were found to be misclassified. An Illinois study completed in December 2006 found that nearly 20 percent of audited employers misclassified their employees as independent contractors. This was a 21 percent increase from 2001 to 2005. (Ruckelshaus 2008, 381)

This research went on to note that evidence suggests that 50 percent of day laborers suffer wage theft, that 60 percent of nursing homes are out of compliance, and that nearly 100 percent of poultry plants are out of compliance with wage and hour laws.

The Problem of Labor-Market Volatility

Institutions whose purpose is to reduce the risk of labor-market volatility have not been updated to reflect new realities. When it comes to policies aimed at ameliorating the consequences of volatility, our institutions are substantially out of date. Today only about 19 percent of the unemployed turn to the Employment Service (ES), a federal-state program, compared to about 30 percent three decades ago (Eberts and Holzer 2004, 27). No doubt this is partly due to the emergence of alternative intermediaries, but the performance of the ES itself is an issue. Very few employers use the ES to fill openings. In one study, only 2.6 percent of employers reported that they had used the ES to fill their last job opening (Eberts and Holzer 2004, 26).

The unemployment insurance system also faces substantial challenges. Only about one third of unemployed people receive unemployment insurance (Kletzer and Rosen 2006) and for those who do receive assistance the replacement rate is about 55 percent compared to a European average of 80 percent (Freeman 2007, 15). About one third of unemployment insurance recipients exhaust their benefits before finding a new job (Kletzer and Rosen 2006). Underlying these indicators is that the nature of unemployment has changed. Increasingly, job loss is permanent rather than temporary, as with the layoffs that characterized the system when it was established. Furthermore, as more and more people work in part-time or temporary jobs, they find that they do not meet the unemployment insurance eligibility tests required by most states.

Summary

Today's labor-market policies suffer from the problem of too few resources, but the problem is deeper. These policies were created for an economic regime that is no longer operative. The pressures on employers are different, the nature of work has shifted, and the norms of the labor market regarding employee voice and labor standards have also deteriorated. It would be a mistake to argue that all of these changes are negative. The fact is that in many respects work is more skilled and more interesting than in the past. But to enable people to take advantage of these opportunities, and to assist employees who find themselves in difficulty, a new set of policies is in order. The next section of the chapter describes some ways to move forward.

MOVING FORWARD: A NEW FRAMEWORK

The challenge today is to rebuild labor-market institutions in a manner that is more congruent with the realities of the modern job market. For example, as we have seen, unemployment insurance has become an increasingly ineffective system, yet the heightened volatility in the labor market makes it all the more important. A variety of steps would make the program more relevant to more people, improvements such as shifting from an earnings test to an hours test for eligibility, easing eligibility requirements for re-entrants, and permitting a search for part-time work to meet the job-search test. (Hacker suggests "wage insurance" as an alternative to unemployment insurance for long-term joblessness; see Hacker, this volume, chapter 2.)

Clearly, skill acquisition remains central, and there is important work to be done in improving community colleges, as well as the Workforce Investment Act and adult basic education. Community colleges are especially important. Community colleges enroll around 40 percent of all postsecondary students, and these students tend to be the ones of most concern with regard to inequality in the labor market. Fifty-five percent of students in occupational programs are twenty-four or older, 39 percent are minority, and two thirds attend part-time (Bailey et al. 2004). Eighty percent of community college students work full- or part-time while in school (Brock, LeBlanc, and McGregor 2005, 2) Another indication is that among first-time community college students between the ages of twenty-five and sixty-four in the 1995-to-1996 academic year, 71 percent were in the lower two income quintiles, as compared with 50 percent of younger students (Prince and Jenkins 2005, 2).

Given the centrality of community colleges to employment preparation, it is also important to understand that the returns are positive. The payoff is clear for students who enroll for a substantial amount of credits (such as a full year's worth) or who receive an associate's degree. Research for both the 1980s and the late 1990s finds (after controls for test scores, family background, and a range of demographic characteristics) that a full-time equivalent (FTE) year of study returns about a 6 percent annual income gain. An associate's degree (about two years of study) returns about a 14 percent gain (Kane and Rouse 1999; Marcotte et al. 2005).

There are, however, some nontrivial flies in this ointment. A strikingly low fraction of students who enter community colleges attain even an FTE year of credits, much less an associate's degree. In a careful study that examined outcomes in six states for both full- and part-time students six years after entry (a time period more generous and reasonable than the federal standard, and a more inclusive group of students), Jobs For the Future found that if one added up three outcomes—an associate's degree or a certificate of achievement or transfer to a four-year school—the success rate ranged from 31 percent to 45 percent (Jobs For the Future 2008). Another study found that among students who entered community colleges and who did not receive an associate's degree, the average schooling in the community college was .16 of an FTE year (Marcotte et al. 2005, 162). Among people who completed only a semester of community college courses, there is no economic benefit for men but some gain for women (Marcotte et al. 2005, 170), and it is reasonable to believe that the .16 FTE year leads to no gain for anyone.

Several significant efforts, led by national foundations as well as organizations such as Jobs For the Future and the Manpower Development Research Corporation, are aimed at improving the performance of community colleges (see Scrivener, Weiss, and Teres 2009). A variety of other ideas have been proposed to remedy the deficiencies of the second-chance training system (Rubinstein and Mayo 2007; Osterman 2006). (See Stoll, this volume, chapter 3, for a more detailed discussion of workforce development programs.)

On balance, less thought has gone into improving the quality of jobs—influencing the demand side of the job market. Since working on the demand side is a relatively new strategy, I will focus the remainder of this chapter on how best to think about it and what new policy ideas seem promising.

TABLE 4.3   Policy Choices

Goal	Standard Setting	Programmatic
Make bad jobs good	• Minimum wage • Living wages • Unionization	• Career ladders • Intermediaries • Sectoral programs
Create more good jobs	• Community benefit agreements • Managed tax incentive	• Extension services • Sectoral programs • Consortia or partnerships under business or union auspices

Source: Author's compilation.

An important distinction between policy options is what might be termed "standard setting" on the one hand and "technical assistance" or "programmatic interventions" on the other. Examples of the former include unionization, minimum- and living-wage legislation, and community-benefit agreements. Examples of the latter are sectoral training programs, labor-market intermediaries, and variants of manufacturing extension services.

A second useful distinction is between interventions aimed at improving the quality of existing jobs ("making bad jobs good") and interventions aimed at creating, or retaining, more good jobs. Examples of the first set of policies are efforts to raise the wages or to create job ladders in the existing job base—for example, in the retail, health, or hospitality industries. Examples of the second category are economic development programs that use labor-market tools to attract good jobs or to assist existing firms in competing more effectively and hence maintain the base of good jobs that already exist.

Table 4.3 shows possible policy levers in terms of these distinctions. The distinctions in this chart are to some extent arbitrary, but they do represent a useful way of thinking about the universe of policy interventions on the demand side. There are also opportunities for fruitful interactions across the different boxes. For example, when tax incentives are restricted to jobs above a certain quality threshold, it makes sense to provide programmatic assistance to firms to enable them to meet the standards.

Programmatic Options That Work with Firms

Some programs that work with firms aim to redesign jobs to create career ladders or to enlarge the content of existing jobs. These strategies imply both working with management to redesign work and providing training and support to employees so that they can meet the additional responsibilities and move up in the workplace. An alternative approach is to encourage firms to increase the quantity of training that they make available to lower-paid employees in the hope that this will lead to career advancement.

The new program models vary along a number of dimensions: target groups, the auspices under which the programs are managed, and the nature of the services that are provided. What is striking, however, is that they have also coalesced around a common set of what might be termed "best-practices" elements. These elements are what move these innovations beyond the traditional approach of E&T programs and make these new programs distinctive and important.

The most important of these best-practice elements is driven by an understanding that employment and training efforts work best if they connect effectively to both sides of the labor market—to employers as well as employees. To accomplish this, they work hard to become knowledgeable about the human resource needs of their target group of firms, and in some cases they also seek to understand how they can contribute to the competitive success of the firms. In short, they seek to shape their appeal to firms as a business proposition, not as a charity, public relations, or welfare effort.

The second feature is that best-practice programs make substantial investments in their clients. They reject the quick and dirty training, short-term investments, and simple-minded job-search assistance models that characterize much of the traditional E&T system. The investments that the new programs make take a variety of forms: long training periods, more sustained involvement with companies, and higher levels of support to clients in terms of financial assistance and counseling.

There are, however, important differences across the programs. Their auspices vary and include community groups, unions, community colleges, employer organizations, and state governments. The programs also vary in the extent to which they work with workers who currently hold jobs versus job seekers.

Much, but not all, of the discussion around these new models tends to focus on two broad program types: labor-market intermediaries and sectoral programs. Labor-market intermediaries are organizations that consciously look both ways in the job market, attempting to work with both employers and with individuals. (See Sandfort, this volume, chapter 8, for a discussion of intermediaries in other social policy arenas.) The most creative intermediaries provide a range of services to employers, including what might be termed "human resources consulting," aimed at improving job quality. These intermediaries also work with individuals by providing training and placement for their client firms. Sectoral programs perform the same functions as intermediaries, but they specialize in a particular industry. Both sets of organizations try not only to improve access to jobs but also to help make bad jobs better and to create more good jobs. The relative weight put on these goals varies across different programs. These programs have various strategies for improving job quality, but the most common are attempts to create career ladders and to enlarge jobs.

The formal evaluation evidence on these initiatives is promising, but incomplete and thin. A pre-post evaluation of Project QUEST found very large gains for participants; as part of that evaluation a study of participant files suggested that the gains could not be attributed to creaming and self-selection effects (Osterman and Lautsch 1996). A qualitative evaluation reached positive conclusions about the ability of sectoral programs to achieve their goals (Pindus et al. 2004), and a pre-post evaluation of six intermediary and sectoral programs by Public/Private Ventures found that twenty-four months after program completion, there were gains in hourly wages for five of the organizations, and these gains ranged from $1 to $5 per hour (Grote and Roder 2005).

Overall the greatest success seen in programs that work with companies has been in industries such as health care. This is because the overall shape of employment in the health sector is conducive to career ladders because there are multiple levels of jobs and a progression path. This effect is boosted by that fact that health-care employers are local; they cannot pull up stakes and move to a location with lower wages. Furthermore, in their operations they tend to be dependent on various public policies: licenses, approvals, and the like.

There are significant challenges in working with both large and small firms. Small firms are difficult targets because of the tremendous effort required to reach a substantial number of workers via small firms. Yet even in large firms there is often no advocate for transforming the work of low-wage employees. Furthermore, many managers in both large and small firms are skeptical of the gains that could be achieved by upgrading their low-wage workers. Only when top management "gets religion" does an opportunity open up to work with a company. The task of spreading that religion within an organization is slow and difficult.

In addition to the career-ladder model, some other programs aim to increase employers' investment in training. A number of states provide tax credits to companies for employees who complete certified retraining programs, but there have been no efforts to assess these programs, either

in terms of direct impact or in their ability to expand the scope of training rather than simply subsidize firms for what they would have done in
any case.[4] In addition, a number of states have established programs that
give direct grants to firms to subsidize or provide incentives for improved
practices.

Standard Setting and Enforcement

The goal of standard setting is to set a floor to the quality of jobs. The
great attraction of this approach is that it is relatively straightforward and
has the potential of reaching a scale well beyond what is possible with
more programmatic interventions. Standard-setting policy falling has two
subgroups: policies put in place by government, such as minimum wages,
and policies set by private actors such as unions.

The best-known standard aimed at the low-wage labor market is the
minimum wage. The minimum wage has stagnated for many years when
measured as a percentage of the pay of the average nonsupervisory private-
sector worker. States have responded to this stagnation; well over half of
them now have set minimum wages above the federal level.

The discussion of the minimum wage is typically framed in terms of its
impact upon the wages and employment of directly affected employees. The
balance of opinion has shifted to the view that the negative impact, if any, is
small. However, a broader view suggests that more is at stake. By establishing a wage floor, a minimum wage may prevent low-wage employers from
competing on the basis of wage costs with firms that are willing to pay
above the minimum. Such competition, if permitted, would drive down the
overall wage structure.

Related to the line of argument that the minimum wage is about more
than just wage levels is the view that a higher minimum wage would lead
firms to adopt a different bundle of human resource practices. This idea has
been around for a long time; in the union literature it has been characterized
as the "shock effect." The argument is that an enforced higher wage forces a
company to redesign its employment and production system to increase efficiency and obtain the productivity that is necessary to pay the higher wage.

The second set of standards issues is about enforcement of wage and
hours laws. Obviously, it is important to reverse the decline in the number of inspection and enforcement personnel. Beyond this, several other
steps seem important. One is to move from a complaint-driven inspection
regime to one in which inspections are strategically targeted in order to
have the greatest impact (Weil, forthcoming). Second, core aspects of

employment law need to be strengthened. For example, confusion about the definition of an employee enables some firms to evade their responsibility for a range of employment protections.

A good deal of internal effort is being made by unions to raise their rate of organization success. These efforts include putting more resources into organizing, being more strategic in designing organizing campaigns, and considering new models of representation such as membership organizations without collective bargaining rights. On the national agenda are attempts to reform labor law to speed up union elections and to reduce the incentives of employers to delay and to engage in unfair labor practices. There is little agreement among union advocates as to the best approach for improving (or bypassing) the National Labor Relations Act, but it is clear that finding ways to level the playing field for unions in the low-wage labor market is an important component of any strategy to improve the situation of low-wage workers.

Community Benefit Agreements

Community benefit agreements (CBAs) combine living-wage campaigns and efforts to control location subsidies. The central idea is to identify a large development project that requires city approval, and then a coalition of community groups negotiates with the developer regarding first source hiring, wage standards, and other topics such as parking, affordable housing, and recreation. If an agreement can be reached, the coalition becomes an ally of the developer in obtaining the relevant approvals. Among the most active geographies for CBAs has been Los Angeles, where coalitions organized and supported by the Los Angeles Alliance For A New Economy (LAANE) have negotiated agreements in the Los Angeles airport, the Staples Center, and Century Boulevard developments. Similar efforts have been initiated in Denver, Milwaukee, Boston, Seattle, and Chicago. As promising as CBAs are, they have obvious limitations (for a description of CBAs see Gross, LeRoy, and Janis-Aparicio 2005). They typically only benefit residents in the area of the large-scale development, and the labor standards tend to be modest.[5] Nonetheless, they are a creative addition to the repertoire of ways to use a combination of political and standard-setting power to upgrade job quality.

Conclusion

Strategies to improve conditions in the low-wage labor market should include programs to improve our second-chance training system, to work with firms to upgrade the quality of work that is offered, and to strengthen labor-market regulation. Beyond these specifics, we need to think about a national framework or set of institutions for supporting efforts to upgrade low-quality jobs. In the long run a model based on foundation support, which is a fair description of the current situation, is not sustainable, nor can it operate on the appropriate scale.

A second broadly strategic issue is that initiatives aimed at low-wage jobs should also be linked to efforts to help employees in better circumstances who are nonetheless hurt by the increased volatility of the labor market. Effective training programs and an improved labor exchange could meet this objective. The advantage is both substantive, in terms of what the programs can accomplish, and political. A broader constituency for such an initiative can be created if labor-market policies are of value to a wider range of workers. The historical isolation of the employment and training systems each from the other has been a long-standing source of weakness.

Today's labor market is volatile, and there is widespread understanding that people need skills to do well up and down the income scale. There is also a broad understanding that labor-market institutions that enable people to make successful transitions are important. Companies face a newly competitive environment, and many recognize that a key to their success is the quality of their human resources. In short, recognition of what it takes to achieve success in a volatile world bolsters the case for a strong set of programs and standards, a system in which the federal role is to stimulate innovation and to leverage other labor-market actors to build ladders that lead to success.

NOTES

1. This is calculated from the Census Outgoing Rotation Group for 2007 and refers to people between the ages of twenty-five and sixty-four.
2. The impact of this can be illustrated dramatically in the case of the broad category of jobs the BLS labels "production" occupations. In 2016 there will be, according to the BLS, 528,000 fewer of these blue-collar jobs than in 2006, and one might conclude that the occupation has no future. But despite the negative net job creation, replacement needs in the same period will lead to 2.3 million job openings.
3. The national Job Training Partnership Act (JTPA) evaluation was a random assignment study of 15,981 people who were served by JTPA. The people were tracked for thirty months after leaving in 1989. The sample was drawn from sixteen service delivery areas around the country; they were not chosen randomly but were chosen to be demographically representative of the nation. Within each SDA, random assignment was used to assign clients to the program or to a control group. People in the control

group did not receive JTPA training but could receive training and services from other sources (Bloom et al. 1997).

4. Brian Bosworth reports that these tax credits are available in Rhode Island, Georgia, Arizona, Colorado, Connecticut, Kentucky, Louisiana, and Mississippi (Bosworth 2006, 43)

5. In the Staples agreement the wage standards for 70 percent of the jobs in the project were set at between $7.72 and $8.97 an hour, and $100,000 was set aside to support training.

REFERENCES

Ahlstrand, Amanda, Lauri Bassi, and Daniel McMurrer. *Workplace Education for Low Wage Workers.* 2003. Kalamazoo, Mich.: W. E. Upjohn Institute for Employment Research.

Appelbaum, Eileen, Annette Bernhardt, and Richard J. Murnane, eds. 2003. *Low-Wage America: How Employers Are Reshaping Opportunity in the Workplace.* New York: Russell Sage Foundation.

Bailey, Thomas, Timothy Leinbach, Marc Scott, Mariana Alfonso, Gregory Kienzl, and Benjamin Kennedy. 2004. "The Characteristics of Occupational Students in Post-Secondary Education." CCRC brief no. 21. New York: Teachers College, Community College Research Center.

Bernhardt, Annette. 2003. "The Coffee Pot Wars." In *Low-Wage America: How Employers Are Reshaping Opportunity in the Workplace,* edited by Eileen Appelbaum, Annette Bernhardt, and Richard J. Murnane. New York: Russell Sage Foundation.

Bernhardt, Annette, Siobhan McGrath, and James DeFilipis. 2007. "Unregulated Work in the Global City." Report. New York: New York University Law School, Brennan Center For Justice.

Bloom, Howard, Larry Orr, Stephen Bell, George Cave, Fred Doolittle, Winston Lin, and Johannes Bos. 1997. "The Benefits and Costs of JTPA Title II-A Programs: Key Findings from the National Job Training Partnership Act Study." *Journal of Human Resources* 32(3): 549–76.

Bloom, Nicholas, and John Van Reenen. 2007. "Measuring and Explaining Management Practices Across Firms and Countries." *Quarterly Journal of Economics* 122(4): 1351–1408.

Bosworth, Brian. 2006. "Strengthening Employer Support for the Postsecondary Education of Working Adults." Somerville, Mass.: Futureworks.

Brock, Thomas, Allen LeBlanc, and Casey McGregor. 2005. "Promoting Student Success in Community College and Beyond: The Opening Doors Demonstration." New York: Manpower Development Research Corporation.

Comings, John, Andrew Sum, and Johan Uvin. 2000. "New Skills for a New Economy; Adult Education's Role in Sustaining Economic Growth and Expanding Opportunity." Boston: MassINC.

Dohm, Arlene, and Lynn Shniper. 2007. "Occupational Projections to 2016." *Monthly Labor Review* 130(11): 86–125.

Eberts, Randall, and Harry Holzer. 2004. "Overview of Labor Exchange Policies and Services." In *Labor Exchange Policy In the United States*, edited by David Balducchi, Randall Eberts, and Christopher O'Leary. Kalamazoo, Mich.: W. E. Upjohn Institute.

Farber, Henry. 2005. "What Do We Know About Job Loss in the United States? Evidence from the Displaced Workers Survey, 1984–2004." Working paper no. 498. Princeton, N.J.: Princeton University, Industrial Relations Section.

Freeman, Richard. 2007. *America Works: Critical Thoughts on the Exceptional U.S. Labor Market*. New York: Russell Sage Foundation.

Groshen, Erica. 1991. "Sources of Intra-industry Wage Dispersion: How Much Do Employers Matter?" *Quarterly Journal of Economics* 106(3): 869–84.

Gross, Julian, Greg LeRoy, Madeline Janis-Aparicio. 2005. *Community Benefits Agreements*. Washington, D.C.: Good Jobs First.

Grote, Mae Watson, and Anne Roder. 2005. "Setting the Bar High: Findings from the National Sectoral Employment Initiative." New York: Public/Private Ventures.

Holzer, Harry. 2004. "Encouraging Job Advancement Among Low-Wage Workers: A New Approach." Brookings Institute policy brief no. 30 (May).

Interfaith Workers Justice. 2008. Available at: www.wagetheft.org; accessed July 30, 2010.

Jobs For the Future. 2004. *Breaking Through: Helping Low-Skilled Adults Succeed in College and Careers*. Boston: Jobs for the Future.

———. 2008. *Test Drive: Six States Pilot Better Ways to Measure and Compare Community College Performance*. Boston: Jobs for the Future.

Kane, Thomas, and Cecilia Rouse. 1999. "The Community College: Educating Students at the Margin Between Education and Work." *Journal of Economic Perspectives* 13(1): 63–84.

Kletzer, Lori. 1998. "Job Displacement." *Journal of Economic Perspectives* 12(winter): 115–36.

Kletzer, Lori, and Howard Rosen. 2006. "Reforming Unemployment Insurance for the Twenty-First-Century Workforce." Washington, D.C.: Brookings Institution, Hamilton Project.

Lerman, Robert, Signe-Mary McKernan, and Stephanie Riegg. 2004. "The Scope of Employer-Provided Training in the United States: Who, What, Where, and How Much?" In *Job Training Policy in The United States*, edited by Christopher O'Leary, Robert Straits, and Stephen Wander. Kalamazoo, Mich.: W. E. Upjohn Institute for Employment Research.

Marcotte, David, Thomas Bailey, Carey Borkoski, and Greg Kienzl. 2005. "The Returns of a Community College Education: Evidence From the National Education Longitudinal Survey. *Educational Evaluation and Policy Analysis* 27(2): 157–175.

Mishel, Larry, Jared Bernstein, and Sylvia Allegretto. 2007. *The State of Working America*. Ithaca, N.Y.: Cornell University Press.

Osterman, Paul. 1999. *Securing Prosperity: The American Labor Market: How It Has Changed and What To Do About It*. Princeton, N.J.: Princeton University Press.

————. 2006. "Employment and Training Policies: New Directions for Less Skilled Adults." In *Workforce Policies for a Changing Economy*, edited by Harry Holzer and Demetra Nightingale. Washington, D.C.: Urban Institute Press.

————. 2008. "Improving Job Quality: Policies Aimed at the Demand-Side of the Low Wage Labor Market." In *A Future of Good Jobs?*, edited by Timothy Bartik and Susan Houseman. Kalamazoo, Mich.: W. E. Upjohn Institute for Employment Research.

Osterman, Paul, Thomas Kochan, Richard Locke, and Michael Piore. 2001. *Working in America: A Blueprint for a New Labor Market*. Cambridge, Mass.: MIT Press.

Osterman, Paul, and Brenda Lautsch. 1996. "Project QUEST: A Report to the Ford Foundation." Cambridge, Mass.: MIT, Sloan School of Management.

Partnership for Employer-Employee Responsive Systems. 2003. "Workforce Intermediaries: Generating Benefits for Employers and Workers." Boston: Jobs for the Future.

Prince, David, and David Jenkins. 2005. "Building Pathways to Success for Low-Income Adult Students: Lessons for Community College Policy and Practice from a Statewide Longitudinal Tracking Study." Olympia: Washington State Board for Community and Technical Colleges.

Pindus, Nancy, Carolyn O'Brien, Maureen Conway, Conaway Haskins, and Ida Rademacher. 2004. "Evaluation of the Sectoral Employment Demonstration Program." Washington, D.C.: Urban Institute Press.

Rubinstein, Gwen, and Andrea Mayo. 2007. "Training Policy in Brief: An Overview of Federal Workforce Development Policies." 2d ed. Washington, D.C.: Workforce Alliance.

Ruckelshaus, Catherine. 2008. "Labor's Wage War." *Fordham Urban Law Journal* 35(March): 373–407.

Scrivener, Susan, Michael J. Weiss, and Jedediah J. Teres. 2009. "More Guidance, Better Results? Three-Year Effects of an Enhanced Student Services Program at Two Community Colleges." New York: Manpower Development Research Corporation.

Smith, Tara Carter, Christopher T. King, and Daniel G. Schroeder. 2007. *Local Investments in Workforce Development: Initial Evaluation Findings—Final Report*. Austin: University of Texas, Lyndon B. Johnson School of Public Affairs, Ray Marshall Center for the Study of Human Resources.

Theodos, Brett, and Robert Bednarzik. 2006. "Earnings Mobility and Low-Wage Workers in the United States." *Monthly Labor Review* 129(6): 34–47.

U.S. Census Bureau. 2007. *Current Population Survey*. "Outgoing Rotation Groups; Civilian Wage and Salary Employees Between Ages of 25 and 64." Available at: www.nber.org; accessed July 30, 2010.

Weil, David. 1991. "Enforcing OSHA: The Role of Labor Unions." *Industrial Relations* 30(1): 20–36.

————. Forthcoming. "A New Strategy for Labor Market Regulation." *International Labor Review*.

CHAPTER 5

ASSET-BASED POLICIES AND FINANCIAL SERVICES: TOWARD FAIRNESS AND INCLUSION

MICHAEL SHERRADEN

As the editors of this volume suggest in the opening chapter, we may be in an era of social policy transformation. Policies that were put into place during the twentieth century, in the United States and abroad, today are experiencing strain, questioning, and revision. Although typically discussed in the political terms of left and right, the sources of policy strain are primarily technological and economic.[1] Social policies of the twentieth century were designed for an industrial society with low-skilled and relatively stable labor markets. When a household was without labor income due to death, disability, job loss, age, or some other factor, social policy was designed to provide income to support basic consumption. These policies were successful in many respects, notwithstanding the fact that America's social policy was never as comprehensive or generous as most policies in Western Europe.

In the twenty-first century, we live in a world where technological changes have produced very different labor markets. Greater skills are needed, jobs are less stable, more than one job is often required to support a middle class lifestyle, and income inequality is growing (Osterman, this volume, chapter 4; Stoll, this volume, chapter 3). Jacob S. Hacker (2004, 2006;

this volume, chapter 2) finds increased income volatility and downward mobility, with income instability in the mid-1990s to be several times higher than in the early 1970s. He also points out that employment-based social benefits and government programs have eroded, and risks have shifted from collective intermediaries (governments, employers, and insurance pools) to individuals and families. Although specifics might be debated, this key observation is accurate. What we are now witnessing may be a major revision in the social contract that was worked out for the industrial era.

In this environment, the growth of income inequality and increased risks shouldered by individuals should certainly be understood as an issue of social injustice and human hardship—but also as an issue of a rapidly changing political economy in the information age. In this environment, the direct and indirect income supports suggested by Hacker, Sandfort, Heymann, and other authors in this volume are fundamental. But at the same time, it is no longer clear that collective forms of income support will be the singular policy response to household economic and social challenges going forward.

In the first years of the twenty-first century, there is declining public and political support for means-tested programs in the United States and many other countries, and perhaps even declining support for some types of social insurance, a primary pillar of the twentieth-century welfare state. Although usually discussed in terms of values and politics, the underlying dynamics of change are operating on the larger stage of technology and history. Industrial-era policies are being questioned, and new policy directions are being considered and explored in many countries. No one can predict the outcome of this era of social policy transformation, nor can we even be optimistic that new policies will be constructive for families, communities, and nations. So far, we have reason to be disheartened and pessimistic about what is happening. We live in a time of increased inequality, hardship, and uncertainty.

At the same time, there are opportunities for positive change. As with the creation of welfare state policies in the twentieth century, there is a sense that major new reforms may be required, although we do not know what they will be. Searching policy discussions, creative innovations, and applied research projects are under way. In this volume and elsewhere, many committed people and bright minds are engaged in this task.

ASSET-BASED POLICY AND LOW-INCOME HOUSEHOLDS

As one part of the larger tapestry of policy transformation, an active discussion of asset inequality and asset-based policy arose in the United States in the 1990s (Oliver and Shapiro 1995; Sherraden 1991). This has led to a growing body of theory, policy innovation, and research. In simple terms, asset-based policy suggests that individual, household, and community well-being (or "welfare") is derived not solely from a certain level of income and consumption, but also from building assets to invest in life goals and to enhance long-term economic stability and social protections. Asset building is viewed, in part, as a constructive response to information age economies and labor markets. In addition to greater financial stability, assets may yield positive psychological, social, and political effects. This growing discussion has led to policy innovations and testing of asset-building policies, as well as financial services that can be more inclusive and fair for the whole population. The key observations and reasoning for asset-based policy can be briefly summarized.

Inclusion, productivity, and security across a lifetime are based on a wide range of social and economic resources. Economically, the two major resources are income (flows) and assets (stocks). Although income and assets are closely connected, they have distinctive properties, and very likely distinctive effects. Building assets may enable individuals, families, and communities to expand their capabilities and security in ways that income alone does not. Asset-based policy typically focuses on building financial and tangible wealth aimed at both social protections and social and economic development. Because asset holding is inevitably intertwined with financial services, consideration of asset-based policy must include financial services as well.

Dimensions of poverty and its distribution are different when approached from an assets perspective. Asset poverty (low stocks of economic resources) may leave people vulnerable to unexpected economic events and unable to take advantage of opportunities offered by a prosperous society. Many studies have found that the rate of asset poverty is extremely high, reaching 37 percent for the whole population and 61 percent for blacks and Hispanics, when the asset poverty measure is the equivalent of three months of income at the poverty line (Haveman and Wolff 2005).[2] These figures indicate that many U.S. families have little financial cushion to sustain them in the event of a job loss, illness, or other income disruption (Hacker, this volume, chapter 2). Also, social and economic development of these families may be truncated because of a lack of resources to invest in education, experience, home, business, and other key assets (Sherraden 1991). Moreover, as noted below, patterns of asset holding define and perpetuate racial and class divisions (Oliver and Shapiro 1995; Shapiro 2004).

Thus, income- and asset-based policies address different types of social and economic issues, and are complementary. A proposal for asset building is not in any sense a proposal to reduce income supports.

Asset-based policy is not new. The United States and many other countries already have large asset-based policies. In most cases, these operate through the tax- and employer-based systems so that public transfers occur via tax benefits—for example, the home mortgage interest deduction; tax deferments for 401(k) accounts, Individual Retirement Accounts (IRAs), and a variety of other retirement accounts; tax benefits for College Savings Plans; and other emerging policies, such as Health Savings Accounts.

Asset-based policies are largely a phenomenon of the second half of the twentieth century, along with the rapid expansion of home mortgage financing and tax benefits after World War II; IRAs, created in 1974; 401(k) plans, created in 1978; College Savings Plans, also called 529 plans (for Section 529 of the Internal Revenue Code, which created these types of savings plans in 1997); and Health Savings Accounts, created in 2004. These asset-based policies have grown rapidly in recent years and today are approaching $400 billion per year in tax expenditures, representing the bulk of federal tax subsidies to individuals, and at least 25 percent of all "welfare state" expenditures. A fundamental point about these policies is that they are highly regressive. Nearly all of the public subsidies go to the non-poor (Howard 1997; Seidman 2001; Sherraden 1991; Woo and Buchholz 2007).

Interestingly, over the same period, the U.S. household savings rate declined. The savings rate was 9.0 percent in 1985, 4.6 percent in 1995, and 0.4 percent in 2005, becoming the lowest among economically advanced nations. (With the sharp recession in 2008 and 2009, the U.S. household savings rate has gone up as of this writing, reversing at least temporarily the decades-long decline.) It is possible that the proliferation of asset-building policies has provided psychological assurances that have led to an overall decline in household saving.

Although some well-intentioned people may believe that the poor cannot or do not need to accumulate assets, this view is inaccurate. Building assets is a concept that applies to the rich and poor alike—every household must have some savings to smooth consumption and respond to emergencies, and must in some form build assets for security and development. But low-income individuals and families typically do not participate in existing asset-based mechanisms. The poor are less likely to own homes, investments, and retirement accounts, where most asset-based policies are targeted. The poor have little or no tax incentives, or other incentives, for asset accumulation. And asset limits in means-tested transfer policies may discourage saving by the low-income population. Altogether, the poor face a very different—and inferior—asset-based policy structure.

DISTRIBUTION OF ASSETS AND LIABILITIES

Asset-based policies should be considered in light of the overall distribution of wealth in the society. Data from the Survey of Consumer Finances indicate that the top 10 percent of U.S. households (ranked by income) earn 42 percent of the nation's income, but hold 67 percent of household net worth, while the bottom 60 percent earn 18 percent of the income and hold less than 10 percent of the net worth (Bucks, Kennickell, and Moore 2006).

The Center for Social Development at Washington University in St. Louis has worked with the Urban Institute and the New America Foundation on a comprehensive review of theory and evidence on household assets and policy implications, published by Urban Institute Press as *Asset Building in Low-Income Families* (McKernan and Sherraden 2008). As part of this larger project, Adam Carraso and Signe-Mary McKernan (2008) summarize disparities in household assets and liabilities.[3] Their conclusions illuminate what is happening in households with limited incomes.

Looking first at assets, the typical bottom-quintile family has assets of $17,000, less than one ninth as much as families in the third (middle) quintile. Most bottom-quintile families do not own a home (60 percent), have no retirement account (90 percent), and have no business equity (96 percent). Social Security and Medicare entitlements, if considered wealth, make up roughly 90 percent of expected wealth for low-income families. Turning to liabilities, the typical bottom-quintile family may hold debt of $7,000, one sixth the debt of third-quintile families. The combination of assets and liabilities for bottom-quintile families results in median net worth of $7,500, one tenth that of third-quintile families.

The typical single-headed family may own a home (55 percent), have a car (77 percent), and have a checking or savings account (88 percent). In total, a typical single-headed family may own assets worth $83,400, less than one third of the assets owned by the typical married or cohabiting family. Most single-headed families do not own retirement accounts, financial assets beyond their checking and savings accounts, or any business equity. Turning to liabilities, the typical single-headed family holds debt valued at $24,000, about one quarter that owed by married or cohabiting families. The reason for the disparity is that, very similar to less-educated families, only 32 percent of single-headed families owe mortgage debt compared with 59 percent of married or cohabiting families. The typical debts owed by a single-headed family are credit card debt (41 percent) or installment loan debt (37 percent). The combination of assets and liabilities for single-parent families results in median net worth valued at $40,000, about one fourth the net worth of married or cohabiting families. The net worth gap by marital status widens sharply with age.

Turning to race and ethnicity, the typical family headed by someone who is nonwhite or Hispanic owns a vehicle (76 percent), a checking or savings account (81 percent), and a home (51 percent). Some have a retirement account (33 percent), but it is worth only $16,000. In total, a typical nonwhite- or Hispanic-headed family holds assets worth $60,000, about one quarter of the assets held by a white non-Hispanic-headed family. Looking at liabilities, the typical nonwhite- or Hispanic-headed family holds debt valued at $30,500, less than half of the debt of white non-Hispanic families. The combination of assets and liabilities for nonwhite- or Hispanic-headed families results in median net worth of $25,000, less than one sixth the net worth of white non-Hispanic-headed families.

Assets over the Life Course

In another chapter in *Asset Building in Low-Income Families,* Mark R. Rank (2008) has analyzed assets over the life course. As Rank documents, five factors stand out as important:

> *Intergenerational transmission of assets.* Many studies find that most wealth is transferred from parents. William G. Gale and John Karl Scholz (1994) estimate that intended family transfers and bequests account for 51 percent of U.S. household wealth, with an additional 12 percent of wealth acquired through funding of college by parents. Laurence J. Kotlikoff and Lawrence H. Summers (1981) argue that more than 80 percent of the net worth was the result of intergenerational transfers.

> *Race and ethnicity.* A substantial body of work (Conley 1999; Feagin 2000; Kochhar 2004; Oliver and Shapiro 1995) documents that race, particularly being African American, may constrain the ability of individuals to accumulate significant assets during their lifetimes. Thomas M. Shapiro (2004) reports that the typical black household earns about 60 cents for every dollar earned by its white counterpart, and holds only 10 cents of wealth for every dollar of wealth held by a white household. These effects are due in part to intergenerational transmission of wealth, housing-market discrimination, residential segregation, and educational opportunity.

> *Income.* Fundamentally, the accumulation of assets over the life course depends on having an income surplus. Although there is evidence that

even those in poverty have the ability to save, a critical factor in building assets is the level and stability of income over time.[*]

Family structure. Family structure and changes in family structure affect accumulation of wealth. In particular, single-mother families are at a disadvantage compared to married-couple families. Joseph Lupton and James P. Smith (1999) find a large and significant effect of marriage on the accumulation of financial assets and net worth across the life course. Jay L. Zagorsky (2005) reports that married respondents experienced a net worth increase of 77 percent over single respondents during the time of the study, while those who experienced a divorce suffered a significant drop in their overall net worth.

Timing of life events. Particular events at certain stages of the life cycle can have large effects. For example, a teenage girl who has a child out of wedlock will likely experience a cascading negative effect on her ability to build assets later in life. Likewise, the timing of other unanticipated events (unemployment, health problems, divorce) at particular points in the life course can have profound effects on later patterns of asset accumulation (Voyer 2004).

POLICY INNOVATION AND TESTING: THE SYMBOLIC AND PRACTICAL ROLE OF INDIVIDUAL DEVELOPMENT ACCOUNTS

With these social and economic patterns in mind, we turn now to policy responses. How can social policy create more inclusive (universal and progressive) asset building that is responsive to low-income households and life-course patterns?

The past twenty years have witnessed an increase in awareness of the role of assets in well-being and development of families and communities. One policy innovation has been Individual Development Accounts (IDAs), matched savings accounts which have in some respects come to symbolize inclusive asset building. As originally proposed, IDAs would be set up for everyone, provide greater support for the poor, begin as early as birth, and be used for key development and social protection goals across the lifespan such as education, homeownership, business capitalization, and retirement security in later life (Sherraden 1988, 1991). Matched funds for IDAs could come from a broad range of public, non-profit, and private sector resources.

As with more progressive policy proposals, IDAs have not been adopted as a large-scale, inclusive asset-based policy, but instead have been implemented as short-term "demonstration" programs targeted toward the poor. We can contrast this with the process of adoption of 401(k)s, which today cost approximately $100 billion in tax expenditures for the non-poor, but did not go through any demonstration and research phase. Congress did not ask for evidence that 401(k)s are a good use of public funds. This common pattern of policy formation—demonstrations and research for the programs that benefit the poor—is another aspect of class structure. Demonstrations give the appearance of doing something, but rarely result in long-term policy.

As a result of the extended demonstration period, IDA innovations and research have been widespread. In brief, we have evidence that IDA participants can save; features of IDA accounts (beyond the matching incentive) are positively associated with savings outcomes; assets can accumulate for IDA participants, particularly in the form of homeownership, and it may be that improved financial knowledge and consumer credit reduction are part of this asset-building process (Grinstein-Weiss et al. 2008; Han, Grinstein-Weiss, and Sherraden 2009; Mills et al. 2008; Schreiner and Sherraden 2007; Sherraden et al. 2005; Sherraden and McBride 2010). A fourth survey wave of a randomized IDA experiments (part of the "American Dream Demonstration") is now under way with the important mission of asking what happened to IDA participants and controls during the subprime lending meltdown and rising foreclosures. Anecdotal information from the field suggests that IDA participants have done well in holding on to their homes. We do not know if this is in fact the case. The fourth wave of experimental data will give us better information.

Since asset building and IDAs were proposed, there has been modest progress in policy. One noteworthy change has been an increase in welfare asset limits—that is, in the amount of wealth someone on welfare is allowed to own—in nearly all states in the 1990s and 2000s, influenced in part by the discussion of assets and public policy. Regarding direct public-resource allocation, IDAs were included as a state option in the 1996 "welfare reform" act. The federal Assets for Independence Act, the first public IDA demonstration, became law in 1998. Other bills to extend IDAs are regularly before the U.S. Congress (Boshara 2003; Cramer, Parrish, and Boshara 2005). Over forty U.S. states have adopted some type of IDA policy (Edwards and Mason 2003). This may appear to be a lot of policy activity, but none of these efforts is comprehensive. Together, IDA policy development represents a major change in thinking and widespread innovation, but not yet a large-scale change in policy.

IDA research has influenced other policy initiatives. It contributed to President Clinton's 1999 proposal for Universal Savings Accounts and his

2000 proposal for Retirement Savings Accounts (Clinton 1999, 2000). Research on IDAs has influenced asset-based policy developments in the United Kingdom, including the Saving Gateway and Child Trust Fund (H.M. Treasury 2001; Kempson, McKay, and Collard 2003; Kelly and Lissauer 2000; Paxton 2003); Family Development Accounts in Taipei (Cheng 2003); IDAs and the Learn$ave demonstration in Canada (Kingwell et al. 2004; Leckie, Dowie, and Gyorfi-Dyke 2008); Child Development Accounts in Korea (Sherraden and Han 2007); and asset-building programs for the poor in Australia, Uganda, Peru, China, Hungary, and elsewhere. At this writing, the Social Affairs Minister of Israel is proposing Child Development Accounts for the lowest-income Israeli households.

IDA and other matched-savings policies, services, and products continue to develop in the United States. To take some recent examples, FDIC Chairman Sheila C. Bair suggests that "IDAs are a relatively low-risk way for banks to introduce underbanked individuals to the financial mainstream. IDAs can help people of modest means build assets and can help banks tap into new markets" (Federal Deposit Insurance Corporation 2007). Hillary Clinton and John Edwards, in their 2008 primary campaigns, proposed matching the savings of middle- and low-income workers in their 401(k) plans. As president, Barack Obama has proposed an "auto IRA" that would be available to workers not covered by an employer pension plan; the auto IRA would provide a match (in the form of a refundable tax credit) of up to $1,000 annually to households earning up to $65,000. In the nonprofit sector, the United Way of America has announced a $1.5 billion initiative on Family Financial Stability that includes IDAs and savings.

Looking forward, it seems likely that after the current financial and economic crisis has ended, there will be less emphasis on credit and more emphasis on saving. In this policy environment, IDAs and other strategies for inclusive savings may play a larger role.

A PATHWAY TO INCLUSION: UNIVERSAL CHILD DEVELOPMENT ACCOUNTS

Stimulated by IDA research in the United States, a serious discussion of asset-based policy began in the United Kingdom in 2000 (Blair 2001; Blunkett 2000; Kelly and Lissauer 2000; Nissan and LeGrand 2000). In April 2001, Tony Blair, the Prime Minister, proposed a Child Trust Fund for all children in the United Kingdom, with progressive funding. Beginning in April 2005, each newborn child in the United Kingdom has been given an account, retroactive to children born from September 2002. The children have received an initial deposit of at least £250, and children in the bottom third of family income have received £500. At this writing, unfortunately, a new U.K. government has proposed stopping payments to the Child Trust Fund as a budget reduction measure.

Other countries in addition to the United Kingdom are expanding or adopting Child Development Accounts, or CDAs (Loke and Sherraden 2009). Currently Yunju Nam and others at the Center for Social Development (CSD) are working on CDAs with the government of Korea, where the plan is to provide accounts for the bottom half of the population (Sherraden and Han 2007). Expansion of this policy is also currently on hold.

In the United States, universal and progressive accounts for all children at birth have been proposed for some time (Boshara and Sherraden 2003, Cramer 2004; Goldberg 2005; Lindsey 1994; Sherraden 1991). Policy discussion on children's accounts is bipartisan and continues to be active, with at least five different bills introduced in the Congress in recent years (Boshara, Cramer, and Parrish 2005; Cramer, O'Brien, and Boshara 2007; New America Foundation 2006). CDAs are not on the front burner for the Obama administration, but Senator Charles Schumer and other congressional leaders strongly support this proposal.

Looking at the larger picture, CDAs may be a promising long-term strategy for inclusive asset building in the United States. As one perspective on this, the United States is one of the few economically advanced nations without a children's allowance, a monthly cash payment to all families with children. Western European countries spend an average of 1.8 percent of GDP on their children's allowances. For ideological and political reasons, the United States is unlikely to adopt a children's allowance, but a CDA is ideologically and politically much more feasible. Even 0.1 percent of U.S. GDP would provide enough funds for an initial deposit of $3,000 in a CDA for every newborn (see Curley and Sherraden 2000).

What do we know about the effects of CDAs on child development and educational achievement? Studies using the Panel Study of Income Dynamics (PSID), looking at the impact of wealth on child developmental outcomes, find that, controlling for many other factors, parental wealth is positively associated with cognitive development, physical health, and socio-emotional behavior of children (Shanks 2007; Williams 2003). Using the PSID Child Development Supplement, looking at three-to-twelve-year-olds, household wealth is associated with improved math outcomes and reduced problem behaviors. These results support the proposition that assets may lead to enhanced well-being of offspring, above and beyond economic well-being. The study finds that the effects occur even among very income-poor families, and that wealth seems to be a better predictor of well-being as children grow older.

Other studies suggest that CDAs may raise educational expectations and achievement. An in-depth study of first and second graders in a CDA program finds that young children can articulate that the purpose of their saving is for college (Elliott and Sherraden 2007). A study using the National Survey of Families and Households finds that asset accumulation in low-income, single-parent families is associated with higher educational expectations on the part of the mother, and later on with higher educational achievement of the children (Zhan and Sherraden 2003). In this research, when assets are included in regression models, the effects of income becomes nonsignificant, indicating that studies predicting the social outcomes of economic conditions that do not include assets (which is the vast majority) may be underspecified.

Using the National Longitudinal Survey of Youth, Amy Orr (2003) examines the influence of household wealth on math achievement scores and finds significant positive results. Orr's interpretation is that wealth may influence "cultural capital," which may enhance academic achievement over time. She suggests that household wealth may explain a good portion of the black-white achievement gap. From a somewhat different perspective, Shapiro (2004), relying on in-depth interview research, documents that many parents use wealth, sometimes even modest amounts, to create "transformative" opportunities for their children, such as moving to a better school district. Consistent with this, Dalton Conley (1999) uses the PSID to look at the influence of childhood household wealth on adult outcomes. He finds that level of parental wealth in childhood helped to predict both high school graduation and college graduation rates. Effects of wealth are stronger than the effects of income. In sum, household wealth appears to influence both outlook and behaviors regarding children's education, from early education through college graduation.

In applied research, the Ford Foundation, the Charles Stewart Mott Foundation, Lumina Foundation for Education, and several other foundations are supporting a large CDA demonstration project—the SEED (Saving for Education, Entrepreneurship, and Downpayment) initiative—whose purpose is to model, test, and inform a universal and progressive CDA policy for the United States.[5] The SEED research team is using multiple research methods. SEED has several demonstration components, including accounts at twelve community-based sites, one of which uses a quasi-experimental design, and a true experiment with random assignment in a state population. SEED also has initiatives in federal and state policy design to create children's accounts by means of 529 college saving plans and other strategies.

A universal and progressive CDA policy has been a longstanding interest of the Center for Social Development, going back to the original proposal for IDAs. SEED for Oklahoma Kids (SEED OK) began in 2008 as a large experiment to test the universal CDA concept. Social experiments in a total population (without selection) are uncommon, and therefore this project will be of interest to policy scholars. The research results will directly inform the potential of a universal policy of CDAs in the United States. We hypothesize positive impacts of SEED OK savings on parental attitudes and behaviors related to education, cognitive and educational development of children, and, within the seven-year widow of the study, children's educational achievement. The current plan is to follow the plan participants and controls for seven years. Ideally, researchers will continue to follow respondents and survey them again when they are older, perhaps at ages twelve, eighteen, and twenty-four. With effective data collection at wave 1 and successful randomization into treatment and control groups, SEED OK is now set up as a long-term "public good" that can continue to generate useful knowledge over an extended period of time.

ASSETS AND RISK: REFLECTING ON THE SUBPRIME MORTGAGE MELTDOWN

The primary emphasis in asset-based policy is on saving for long-term investments. But financial life is complex, and credit is also a necessary tool for building assets. In this regard, it would be remiss not to discuss the credit crisis in subprime lending for housing, which began in 2007 and continues at this writing. In the midst of this crisis, the country and researchers are still in a period of confusion. It is difficult at this stage to assess accurately what has happened, but we can identify some of the major outlines and issues.

The larger picture is that in the 2000s, annual household savings dropped to under 1 percent of disposable income, a level not seen since the 1930s, and total household debt mushroomed to record levels, with an increasing proportion of homeowners (reaching about 72 percent) in mortgage debt. In this context, the financial services industry tends to look at mortgage defaulters as people who should not have taken out home loans in the first place. The opposing view is that borrowers should not have been set up with loans that were sure to fail sooner or later. The first is a consumer decisionmaking view, and the latter a regulatory view. A great deal hinges on how this is finally documented and understood.

Eventually, firm data will make clear just what happened. It seems likely that most of the problem of subprime lending was due to lax regulation in an atmosphere of easy monetary policy and unethical lending practices. A few key figures may be helpful. A key point is that between 1998 and 2006, only 9 percent of subprime loans were used by first-time home buyers (Center for Responsible Lending 2007). Subprime lending consisted mostly of predatory loans to people who were already homeowners, either for refinancing (63 percent of subprime loans) or for purchasing other homes (27 percent). We do not know much about how subprime victims were doing financially before they took out subprime loans (see Reid 2005, for a thorough review of evidence on low-income homeowners), but we do know that most were already living in their own homes. Given these data, it would be a long stretch to conclude that most subprime victims are people who should not have owned homes in the first place—especially given that homeownership has been the most prominent pathway to building assets for most households (U.S. Census Bureau 2001).

As another piece of the broad outline, the press has discussed a homeownership "boom" of the 2000s, as if this has been a historical aberration, often suggesting that too many low-income people were pushed into homeownership who should not have been—with the well-meaning help of government policy and community organizations (see Rohe and Watson 2007 for a thorough review). What is the actual picture? There was a much greater percentage growth in homeownership in the 1940s and 1950s than in the 1990s and 2000s. The rate went from 44 percent to 55 percent in the 1940s, and from 55 percent to 62 percent in the 1950s (U.S. Census Bureau 2008). During the recent homeownership "boom," the percentage of owners went from 64 percent to 66 percent in the 1990s, and from 66 percent to 69 percent in the 2000s. In other words, the 1940s and 1950s witnessed an increase of about eighteen percentage points in homeownership, whereas the 1990s and 2000s have witnessed an increase of five percentage points. Prior decades' increases have been several times larger, yet they did not result in a crisis of foreclosures—indeed, just the opposite. The U.S. economy grows over time; people in the 2000s on average have greater resources than people did in the 1960s; and homeownership has been a primary source of wealth accumulation in households. Under these circumstances, it is not unreasonable to expect that percentages of homeowners would increase with an expanding economy.

There is no fixed ceiling on the desirable or appropriate percentage of homeownership, and it is not at all clear that 69 percent is too high. As an outlying example, Singapore has a homeownership rate of over 90 percent, which has created probably the most egalitarian advanced economy on earth in terms of wealth holding. The government subsidizes homeownership at the bottom through a broad range of price and fee reductions. This wealth base in households makes it possible for most low-income Singaporeans to maintain a reasonably stable life, even though there, and in most of the world, income inequality, as in much of the world, is increasing (Sherraden et al. 1995; Vasoo and Lee 2006).

Returning to the U.S. subprime crisis, the broad data indicate that this was not a home-ownership disaster, but a credit regulatory failure. People were often tricked into loans with bad terms. As a simple comparison, we regulate carefully to make sure that poisons do not end up in our drinking water or breakfast cereal, yet for some reason it has been acceptable to market toxic home loans that are sure to destroy household finances and family well-being. Given the existing broad data, it would be premature, and probably faulty, to conclude that the people affected by the subprime meltdown should not have been attempting to accumulate assets in the form of homeownership.

In light of assertions that "too many" people own their own homes who for some reason shouldn't, the long-term benefits of homeownership should be kept in mind. Returns to homeownership can be substantial. Even in low-appreciation environments, owners in low- and middle-income neighborhoods achieve modest gains in wealth after seven to ten years when compared to renters (Carraso and McKernan 2008). But the potential returns to homeownership go beyond finances. Research finds that homeownership improves outcomes for children of homeowners, such as higher educational attainment and lower teen-pregnancy rates, most likely because of homeownership's role in increased residential stability. These findings may be particularly important for low-income families (Lerman and McKernan 2008).

We return to the key policy point that nearly all current homeownership subsidies go to the top half of the income distribution. Federal spending on homeownership programs was roughly $176 billion in 2007, and 99 percent was in the form of tax subsidies (Cramer, O'Brien, and Boshara 2007). As discussed above, subsidies provided as tax breaks mostly benefit higher-income families. Of the two largest homeownership expenditures—the mortgage interest deduction and deductions for property taxes—60 percent goes to households in the top 10 percent by income, and the bottom 50 percent of households get less than 3 percent (Woo and Buchholz 2007). More low-income people would be able to own homes, and better homes, and lead more stable lives, if housing subsidies were distributed fairly to all households. For the low-income households who choose ownership, Carolina Katz Reid (2005) suggests additional research so that we can know better what is happening to them and provide the most appropriate policy supports.

DIRECTIONS FOR ASSET-BASED POLICY

The distinction between income and assets and its implications for social policy have resonated with policymakers. Demonstration projects offered evidence that low-income people can save under the right conditions. While income maintenance strategies remain prominent in antipoverty discussions, policymakers across the political spectrum now seriously consider the "assets perspective" when focusing on the long-term social and economic development of individuals, families, and communities. This policy perspective is viewed as relevant, achievable, and measurable (Sherraden 2005).

Most of the current policies for asset building are embedded in the tax code. The value of these asset-building tax expenditure programs exceeds $400 billion, including over $176 billion a year to support homeownership and over $111 billion to subsidize retirement savings (Cramer, O'Brien, and Boshara 2007). As mentioned, most low-income families are denied access to these asset-based policies delivered through the tax code because their incomes are too low to receive a tax benefit. For example, in fiscal year 2005, less than 3 percent of the benefits from federal asset-building programs went to the bottom 60 percent of households as measured by income. The top 20 percent, in contrast, received nearly 90 percent of the benefits (Woo and Buchholz 2007).

If inclusive (universal and progressive) asset accumulation is the goal, structured saving plans that represent large bundles of key constructs are likely to be an effective policy package (Clancy, Orszag, and Sherraden 2004). Current savings plans, all of them created by public policy, include 401(k) plans in the private sector, 403(b) plans in the nonprofit sector, the Thrift Savings Plan for federal employees, and state-run 529 plans for postsecondary education. Although none of these plans reach the entire population, the plans have the potential to deliver bundles of services and institutional support structures that can lead to greater inclusion. The bundles could include greater access through availability to all, outreach, and ease of registration; greater incentives at the bottom through progressive matching and elimination of fees on small savings; greater information through financial education; greater expectations though higher match limits and target savings amounts; and greater facilitation through automatic enrollment and direct deposits (Beverly and Sherraden 1999; Schreiner and Sherraden 2007; Sherraden, Schreiner, and Beverly 2003).[6]

Inclusive asset-based policy would ideally have several characteristics. First, it would provide the means to reach a large number of people, perhaps even all people. Second, it would occur throughout life and be flexible enough to adjust to changes in an individual's life course. Third, it would consider assets needed over the life course in a comprehensive and integrated fashion—from a bank account to a home or business, through retirement. Fourth, it would offer greater subsidies to people with fewer resources and greater need. It would provide incentives for building assets to low-income families (not just high-income families) and minimize disincentives—such as asset limits in means-tested public-assistance programs. And fifth, it would be substantial enough to support adequate levels of accumulation in a meaningful way (Sherraden 2005). If inclusive asset-based policy is useful as a social policy framework, policymakers may want to explore policy options that support asset building in a manner that is more universal, lifelong, flexible, progressive, and adequate.

There is no single strategy for inclusive asset building. Because assets can be held in many different forms over the life course, many policy levers can be used to help families build assets. These range from simplifying and liberating means-tested asset limits, to broadening and making tax credits refundable so that they reach low-income families, to a reformed pension system that complements Social Security (Cramer, O'Brien, and Lopez-Fernandini 2008; Perun and Steuerle 2008). Financial and tangible assets have been the primary focus of this chapter, but education and its potential outcomes are also important.

The policy goal should be lifelong asset building for everyone, using public resources at least fairly (equal subsidies for all) and, ideally, progressively (greater public subsidies for those who have less). Unfortunately, today we are a long, long way from fairness in asset-based policy, and further still from progressivity.

As is the case with the current array of tax-preferred savings accounts, a well-regulated financial services sector should play a primary role in carrying out asset-building policy because it offers a high degree of security, transparency, and efficiency. These markets can facilitate investment within the framework created by the public sector and will establish the institutional structures that maximize access, provide protections, and minimize costs. Whether the accounts are tax-preferred and for what income levels will have important implications for progressivity (Butrica et al. 2008). A focus of policy deliberations in this area should be the search for the safest and most efficient ways to achieve these positive consequences of asset accumulation for the greatest number of families.

OLD ASSUMPTIONS, NEW REALITIES, AND ASSET-BASED POLICIES

We can summarize by returning to the main theme of this volume: old assumptions and new realities. Among a potentially long list, we can focus on three old assumptions and new realities that may affect asset-based policies.

One old assumption is that certain assets (homes and shares of stock) are only for the rich, who can afford to take market risks. The new reality is that homeownership and stock market equity have reached more than half the population, and are subsidized for the non-poor but not the poor. At the same time, weak regulations have permitted predatory lending and wealth stripping of the poor. The policy implications are for at least fair (if not progressive) subsidies across the whole population, and greater market regulation of financial services for consumer protections.

A second old assumption is that few assets are required for human capital investment, and workers do not need a college degree to succeed. The new reality is that supporting a family at a middle-class level typically requires a college degree or advanced skill. Nevertheless, access to postsecondary education depends to an important degree on family wealth, and is out of reach (or believed to be out of reach) for many of the poor. The clear policy implication is to create wealth-building mechanisms for all children early in life through Child Development Accounts, ideally based on the existing platform of State College Savings (529) Plans (Clancy, Cramer, and Parrish 2005).

A third old assumption is that working-age people can live off of current income, and retirees can rely on Social Security. The new reality is that employment income is more volatile and more unequal, with many lower-income families unable to support a household. And Social Security retirement benefits very often must be supplemented by private savings and pensions, but the poor typically do not have savings or pensions. The policy implication is that lifelong savings and pension wealth should be built for the poor through IDAs, universal and progressive 401(k)s, and similar savings strategies aimed at inclusion of the whole population in building assets. (See Hacker, this volume, chapter 2, for related discussion of reforms to 401(k)s and Social Security aimed at ensuring a financially secure retirement.)

Regarding policy directions, the concept of an inclusive asset-based social policy, seldom discussed fifteen years ago, is ascendant today. The language of assets is now part of a bipartisan discussion on establishing asset-building policies for the whole population, including lower-income households. This is almost a sea change in thinking, but it is not yet widespread in policy. We have yet to see whether these discussions will yield policies that are responsive to new social and economic realities.

CONCLUSIONS

It seems possible—indeed likely—that the years ahead will bring continued questioning and reformulations of social policy. We should anticipate that a renewed social contract, which would take decades to evolve, would retain the most effective features of current social policy, including Social Security retirement as social insurance, but also incorporate new directions. In a future social contract there might be less emphasis on borrowing and making promises for tomorrow and more emphasis on saving and building assets as a foundation for future development, in public policy as well as in households and communities.

If indeed we are in this historical position (which is impossible to know when we are so close to it), it may be helpful to reflect on the emergence of the Social Security Act of 1935. This act has been the greatest single social policy success in the history of the United States, profoundly successful in reducing poverty among the elderly and protecting against risks of disability, loss of a breadwinner, and much more. This time around, can we hope to be as successful in policy reformulation? The Social Security Act sets a high bar.

How will a new social contract come about? Most likely it will be born in crisis (one thinks of soldiers' pensions coming out of the Civil War, and the Social Security Act coming out of the Great Depression). We do not know when such a crisis will present itself. Perhaps it is already beginning in the current credit and financial crisis. We do not yet know.

As in the past, a group of bright and dedicated people will have to be ready with new ideas when a major economic and social policy opportunity occurs. Wilbur Cohen, one of the architects of the Social Security Act, was my professor when I was in graduate school at the University of Michigan several decades ago. He spoke very convincingly about incrementalism in social policy—the step-by-step movement toward a desired end. He never talked about big changes happening all at once. But as a graduate student I could not help but notice that Cohen's incrementalism was successful only because it occurred in the context of the biggest vision for social policy in the history of the United States. A constructive tension between large vision and small steps may again present itself.

We are a long way from being able to replicate an achievement on the scale and with the positive impacts of the Social Security Act, and we have no choice but to be humble in the face of huge challenges. But a similar scale of social policy change may be necessary in the decades ahead. We cannot know what the characteristics of this new policy formulation will be, but given current trends we have reason to believe that asset building in the form of universal and progressive individual accounts will play a growing role in twenty-first-century American social policy.

If this is correct, the greater risk ahead will not be that people own assets, but that they do not. Using the language of risk, we might call this *access* risk, which is more fundamental than *investment* risk. To illustrate, in the current economic downturn, owing to investment risk, some unfortunate people have lost 30 percent or more of the value of their subsidized retirement accounts. But owing to access risk, many people do not have subsidized retirement accounts at all. While most of the attention is on the people with accounts, the people without accounts are far more disadvantaged. As emphasized throughout this chapter, the primary challenge for an asset-based policy will be inclusion and protection of the whole population.

NOTES

1. The dominant relationships appear to be: Technology shapes economic organization, and economic organization shapes social issues and policy responses of the state. These are not new observations. These simple relationships were the underlying theme—and perhaps most important contribution—of Karl Marx (1867/1967), and they have been reiterated by a wide range of scholars in economics and sociology.
2. The rate of income poverty in recent years, by contrast, has been between 11 and 14 percent.
3. Most of the wealth data in this section come from tables produced by Brian Bucks, Arthur B. Kennickell, and Kevin B. Moore (2006), using the 1995 to 2004 Survey of Consumer Finances (SCF); Robert I. Lerman (2005), using the 2001 Survey of Income and Program Participation (SIPP); and Lupton and Smith (1999) using the 1992 Health and Retirement Study (HRS). To allow comparisons over time and across data sets from different time periods, all values are converted to 2004 dollars using the Consumer Price Index for All Urban Consumers.
4. Hacker (this volume, chapter 2) discusses income support policy options to cushion earnings losses resulting from unstable employment. The chapters by Paul Osterman and Michael A. Stoll in this volume discuss policy options for improving wage levels and working conditions.

5. SEED is a demonstration and research partnership among the Corporation for Enterprise Development, CSD, the School of Social Welfare at the University of Kansas, the New America Foundation, the RTI International, the Aspen Institute Initiative on Financial Security, and others.
6. See Cramer, Sherraden, and McKernan (2008) for further discussion of policy options.

REFERENCES

Beverly, Sondra, and Michael Sherraden. 1999. "Institutional Determinants of Saving: Implications for Low-income Households and Public Policy." *Journal of Socio-economics* 28(4): 457–473.

Blair, Tony. 2001. "Savings and Assets for All." Speech. London: 10 Downing Street (April 26, 2001).

Blunkett, David. 2000. "On Your Side: The New Welfare State as an Engine of Prosperity." Speech. Department of Education and Employment, London (June 7, 2000).

Boshara, Ray. 2003. "Federal Policy and Asset Building." *Social Development Issues* 25(1–2): 130–41.

Boshara, Ray, Reid Cramer, and Leslie Parrish. 2005. *Policy Options for Achieving an Ownership Society for All Americans.* Issue brief no. 8. Washington, D.C.: New America Foundation.

Boshara, Ray, and Michael Sherraden. 2003. "For Every Child, a Stake in America." *New York Times,* July 23, 2003.

Bucks, Brian, Arthur B. Kennickell, and Kevin B. Moore. 2006. "Recent Changes in U.S. Family Finances: Results from the 2001 and 2004 Survey of Consumer Finances." *Federal Reserve Bulletin* 92(1): 1–38.

Butrica, Barbara, Adam Carasso, C. Eugene Steuerle, and Desmond J. Toohey. 2008. "Children's Savings Accounts: Why Design Matters." Opportunity and Ownership Project report 4. Washington, D.C.: Urban Institute.

Carraso, Adam, and Signe-Mary McKernan. 2008. "Asset Holding and Liabilities." In *Asset Building and Low-Income Families,* edited by Signe-Mary McKernan and Michael Sherraden. Washington, D.C.: Urban Institute Press.

Center for Responsible Lending. 2007. *Subprime Lending: A Net Drain on Homeownership.* Issue paper no. 14. Durham, N.C.: Center for Responsible Lending.

Cheng, Li-Chen. 2003. "Developing Family Development Accounts in Taipei: Policy Innovation from Income to Assets." *Social Development Issues* 25(1–2): 106–17.

Clancy, Margaret, Reid Cramer, and Leslie Parrish. 2005. *Section 529 Savings Plans, Access to Post-Secondary Education, and Universal Asset Building.* Washington, D.C.: New America Foundation.

Clancy, Margaret, Peter Orszag, and Michael Sherraden. 2004. *College Savings Plans: A Platform for Inclusive Saving Policy?* St. Louis, Mo.: Washington University, Center for Social Development.

Clinton, William Jefferson. 1999. "State of the Union Address." Washington: U.S. Executive Office of the President.

———. 2000. "State of the Union Address." Washington: U.S. Executive Office of the President.

Conley, Dalton. 1999. *Being Black, Living in the Red: Race, Wealth and Social Policy in America.* Berkeley: University of California Press.

Cramer, Reid. 2004. *Accounts at Birth: Creating a National System of Savings and Asset Building with Children's Development Accounts.* Washington, D.C.: New America Foundation.

Cramer, Reid, Rourke O'Brien, and Ray Boshara. 2007. *The Assets Report 2007: A Review, Assessment and Forecast of Federal Assets Policy.* Washington, D.C.: New America Foundation.

Cramer, Reid, Rourke O'Brien, and Alejandra Lopez-Fernandini. 2008. *The Assets Agenda 2008: Policy Options to Promote Savings and Asset Ownership by Low-and Moderate-Income Americans.* Washington, D.C.: New America Foundation.

Cramer, Reid, Leslie Parrish, and Ray Boshara. 2005. *Federal Assets Policy Report and Outlook.* Washington, D.C.: New America Foundation.

Cramer, Reid, Michael Sherraden, and Signe-Mary McKernan. 2008. "Policy Implications." In *Asset Building and Low-Income Families,* edited by Signe-Mary McKernan and Michael Sherraden. Washington, D.C.: Urban Institute Press.

Curley, Jami, and Michael Sherraden. 2000. "Policy Lessons from Children's Allowances for Children's Development Accounts." *Child Welfare* 79(6): 661–87.

Edwards, Karen, and Lisa Marie Mason. 2003. "State Policy Trends for Individual Development Accounts in the United States, 1993–2003." *Social Development Issues* 25(1–2): 118–29.

Elliott, William, and Margaret S. Sherraden. 2007. "College Expectations Among Young Children: The Potential Role of Savings." CSD working paper 07-06. St. Louis: Washington University, Center for Social Development.

Feagin, Joe R. 2000. *Racist America: Roots, Current Realities, and Future Reparations.* New York: Routledge.

Federal Deposit Insurance Corporation. 2007. "IDAs and Banks: A Solid Match." *FDIC Quarterly* (June).

Gale, William G., and John Karl Scholz. 1994. "Intergenerational Transfers and the Accumulation of Wealth." *Journal of Economic Perspectives* 8(4): 145–60.

Goldberg, Fred. 2005. "The Universal Piggy Bank: Designing and Implementing a System of Universal Accounts for Children." In *Inclusion in the American Dream: Assets, Poverty, and Public Policy,* edited by Michael Sherraden. New York: Oxford University Press.

Grinstein-Weiss, Michal, Jung-Sook Lee, Johanna K. P. Greeson, Chang-keun Han, Yeong H. Yeo, and Kate Irish. 2008. "Fostering Low-Income Homeownership Through Individual Development Accounts: Results of a Longitudinal, Randomized Experiment." *Housing Policy Debate* 19(4): 711–40.

Hacker, Jacob S. 2004. "Privatizing Risk Without Privatizing the Welfare State: The Hidden Politics of Social Policy Retrenchment in the United States." *American Political Science Review* 98(2): 243–60.

———. 2006. *The Great Risk Shift: The New Economic Insecurity and the Decline of the American Dream.* New York: Oxford University Press.

Han, Chang-Keun, Michal Grinstein-Weiss, and Michael Sherraden. 2009. "Assets Beyond Savings in Individual Development Accounts." *Social Service Review* 83(2): 221–44.

Haveman, Robert, and Edward N. Wolff. 2005. "Who Are the Asset Poor? Trends, Levels, and Composition, 1983–1998." In *Inclusion in the American Dream: Assets, Poverty, and Public Policy,* edited by Michael Sherraden. New York: Oxford University Press.

H.M. Treasury. 2001. *Saving and Assets for All: The Modernisation of Britain's Tax and Benefit System, number eight.* London: H.M. Treasury.

Howard, Christopher. 1997. *The Hidden Welfare State: Tax Expenditures and Social Policy in the United States.* Princeton, N.J.: Princeton University Press.

Kelly, Gavin, and Rachel Lissauer. 2000. *Ownership for All.* London: Institute for Public Policy Research.

Kempson, Elaine, Stephen McKay, and Sharon Collard. 2003. *Evaluation of the CFLI and Saving Gateway Pilot Projects.* Bristol, U.K.: University of Bristol, Personal Finance Research Centre.

Kingwell, Paul, Michael Dowie, Barbara Holler, and Liza Jimenez. 2004. *Helping People Help Themselves: An Early Look at Learn$ave.* Ottawa: Social Research and Demonstration Corporation.

Kochhar, Rakesh. 2004. *The Wealth of Hispanic Households.* Washington, D.C.: Pew Hispanic Center.

Kotlikoff, Laurence J., and Lawrence H. Summers. 1981. "The Role of Intergenerational Transfers in Aggregate Capital Accumulation." *Journal of Political Economy* 89(4): 706–32.

Leckie, N., Michael Dowie, and Chad Gyorfi-Dyke. 2008. *Learning to Save, Saving to Learn: Early Impacts of the Learn$ave Individual Development Account Demonstration.* Ottawa: Social Research and Demonstration Corporation.

Lerman, Robert I. 2005. "Are Low-Income Households Accumulating Assets and Avoiding Unhealthy Debt? A Review of the Evidence." Opportunity and Ownership Project Brief No. 1. Washington, D.C.: Urban Institute.

Lerman, Robert I., and Signe-Mary McKernan 2008. "Benefits and Consequences of Holding Assets." In *Asset Building and Low-Income Families,* edited by Signe-Mary McKernan and Michael Sherraden. Washington, D.C.: Urban Institute Press.

Lindsey, Duncan. 1994. *The Welfare of Children*. New York: Oxford University Press.

Loke, Vernon, and Michael Sherraden. 2009. "Building Assets from Birth: A Global Comparison of Child Development Account Policies." *International Journal of Social Welfare* 18(2): 119–29.

Lupton, Joseph, and James P. Smith. 1999. "Marriage, Assets, and Savings." RAND working paper series 99-12. Santa Monica, Calif.: RAND Corporation.

Marx, Karl. 1867/1967. *Capital: A Critique of Political Economy*. New York: International Publishers.

McKernan, Signe-Mary, and Michael Sherraden, eds. 2008. *Asset Building and Low-Income Families*. Washington, D.C.: Urban Institute Press.

Mills, Gregory, William G. Gale, Rhiannon Patterson, Gary V. Englehardt, Michael D. Eriksen, and Emil Apostolov. 2008. "Effects of Individual Development Accounts on Asset Purchases and Saving Behavior: Evidence from a Controlled Experiment." *Journal of Public Economics* 92(5–6): 1509–30.

New America Foundation. 2006. *Savings Accounts for Kids: Current Federal Proposals*. Washington, D.C.: New America Foundation.

Nissan, David, and Julian LeGrand. 2000. *A Capital Idea: Start-up Grants for Young People*. Policy report no. 49. London: Fabian Society.

Oliver, Melvin, and Thomas Shapiro. 1995. *Black Wealth/White Wealth*. New York: Routledge.

Orr, Amy. 2003. "Black-White Differences in Achievement: The Importance of Wealth." *Sociology of Education* 76(4): 281–304.

Paxton, Will, ed. 2003. *Equal Shares? Building a Progressive and Coherent Asset-Based Welfare Policy*. London: Institute for Public Policy Research.

Perun, Pamela, and C. Eugene Steuerle. 2008. "Why Not a 'Super Simple' Saving Plan for the United States?" Opportunity and Ownership Project report 3. Washington, D.C.: Urban Institute.

Rank, Mark R. 2008. "Asset Building Across the Life Course." In *Asset Building and Low-Income Families*, edited by Signe-Mary McKernan and Michael Sherraden. Washington, D.C.: Urban Institute Press.

Reid, Carolina Katz. 2005. "Achieving the American Dream? A Longitudinal Analysis of the Homeownership Experiences of Low-Income Households." CSD working paper no. 05-20. St. Louis: Washington University, Center for Social Development.

Rohe, William M., and Harry L. Watson. 2007. *Chasing the American Dream: New Perspectives on Affordable Homeownership*. Ithaca, N.Y.: Cornell University Press.

Schreiner, Mark, and Michael Sherraden. 2007. *Can the Poor Save? Savings and Asset Building in Individual Development Accounts*. New Brunswick, N.J.: Transaction.

Seidman, Laurence. 2001. "Assets and the Tax Code." In *Assets for the Poor: Benefits and Mechanisms of Spreading Asset Ownership*, edited by Thomas Shapiro and Edward Wolff. New York: Russell Sage Foundation.

Shanks, Trina R. Williams 2007. "The Impacts of Household Wealth on Child Development." *Journal of Poverty* 11(2): 93–116.

Shapiro, Thomas M. 2004. *The Hidden Cost of Being African American: How Wealth Perpetuates Inequality*. New York: Oxford University Press.

Sherraden, Margaret S., and Amanda M. McBride. 2010. *Striving to Save: Creating Policies for Financial Security in Low-Income Families*. Ann Arbor: University of Michigan Press.

Sherraden, Margaret S., Amanda M. McBride, Stacie Hanson, and Lissa Johnson. 2005. "The Meaning of Saving in Low-income Households." *Journal of Income Distribution* 13(3–4): 76–97.

Sherraden, Michael. 1988. "Rethinking Social Welfare: Toward Assets." *Social Policy* 18(3): 37–43.

———. 1991. *Assets and the Poor: A New American Welfare Policy*. Armonk, N.Y.: M. E. Sharpe.

———, ed. 2005. *Inclusion in the American Dream: Assets, Poverty, and Public Policy*. New York: Oxford University Press.

Sherraden, Michael, and Chang-Keun Han. 2007. "Social Investment State and Asset-Based Policy: Implications for Korean Social Policy." *Proceedings of International Symposium*, 29–50. Seoul: Seoul Welfare Foundation.

Sherraden, Michael, Sudha Nair, S. Vasoo, Nam Tee Liang, and Margaret S. Sherraden. 1995. "Social Policy Based on Assets: The Impact of Singapore's Central Provident Fund." *Asian Journal of Political Science* 3(2): 112–33.

Sherraden, Michael, Mark Schreiner, and Sondra Beverly. 2003. "Income, Institutions, and Saving Performance in Individual Development Accounts." *Economic Development Quarterly* 17(1): 95–112.

U.S. Census Bureau. 2001. *Did You Know? Homes Account for 44 Percent of All Wealth*. Current Population Reports Series P70-75. Washington, D.C.: U.S. Government Printing Office.

———. 2008. *Historical Census of Housing Tables*. Washington, D.C.: U.S. Bureau of the Census.

Vasoo, S., and James Lee. 2006. "Promoting Social Development Through the Central Provident Fund and Public Housing Schemes in Singapore." *Social Development Issues* 28(2): 71–83.

Voyer, Jean-Pierre. 2004. *A Life-Course Approach to Social Policy Analysis: A Proposed Framework*. Discussion paper. Toronto: Government of Canada, Policy Research Initiative.

Williams, Trina R. 2003. "The Impact of Household Wealth and Poverty on Child Outcomes: Examining Asset Effects." Ph.D. diss., Washington University.

Woo, Lillian, and David Buchholz. 2007. "Subsidies for Assets: A New Look at the Federal Budget." Report prepared for Federal Reserve System/CFED Research Forum on Asset Building. Washington, D.C.: Corporation for Enterprise Development.

Zagorsky, Jay L. 2005. "Marriage and Divorce's Impact on Wealth." *Journal of Sociology* 41(4): 406–24.

Zhan, Min, and Michael Sherraden. 2003. "Assets, Expectations, and Educational Achievement." *Social Service Review* 77(2): 191–211.

CHAPTER 6

ENSURING THAT AMERICANS CAN SUCCEED AT HOME AND AT WORK IN A GLOBAL ECONOMY

JODY HEYMANN AND ALISON EARLE

TRANSFORMATIONS IN WHERE AMERICANS LIVE AND HOW THEY WORK

In the early 1800s, most American adults worked out of their homes and farms. They grew their own food, made their own clothes, and produced goods largely for their own families and a small quantity for sale. The United States was a country of rural communities and small towns, and Americans who did live in cities still often worked out of their homes or in shops connected to their residences. When children weren't apprenticing in work themselves, they were cared for in close proximity to their parents' workplaces. There were few elderly Americans.

In the beginning of the twenty-first century, most Americans work at distance from their homes, are supervised by managers who determine their work hours, and are contracted to employers who determine their working conditions. Whereas only 6 percent of Americans lived in cities in the beginning of the 1800s, 79 percent lived in cities in the beginning of the 2000s (U.S. Census Bureau 2000a, 2000b). Only a minority of parents are able to care for their preschool children during daytime hours or

150

for their school-age children as soon as school lets out. The number of older Americans climbed dramatically over the twentieth century. In 1900 there were 3.1 million people in the United States age sixty-five and over; that number had shot up to 38.9 million by 2008. This age group constituted only 4.1 percent of the U.S. population in 1900; in 2008, it made up 12.6 percent (U.S. Census Bureau 2010).

While the industrial labor force disproportionately drew American men in the 1800s, men were not the first workers to enter these jobs. In the early 1800s, at the dawn of the industrial revolution, single women were the first to work, particularly in clothing factories. As these jobs began to be seen as more desirable, men increasingly took over these roles. Moreover, bans and bars against married women's work meant that two thirds of women ceased paid work in the formal labor force once they married (Kessler-Harris 1982). Not until World War II, when large numbers of women were needed to fill the jobs held by men who had gone to war, did a dramatic decline in discrimination against married women occur in hiring. In 1890, just 5 percent of married women worked in the paid labor force; by 1940, this number had only risen to 16 percent; but between World War II and the end of the twentieth century, the number of married women in the paid labor force rose markedly, until over 60 percent were doing paid labor. In contrast, more than 40 percent of single women had been in the paid labor force since before 1890 (U.S. Census Bureau 1976a; U.S. Bureau of Labor Statistics 2009a).

Just one example of the discriminatory barriers: Prior to the war, three out of five school districts refused to hire married women, and half fired women who married while they were employed. After the war, only one in five school districts refused to hire married women, and only 10 percent fired those who married while teaching. Although African American women had long worked in the paid labor force in higher numbers than European American women, the discrimination against the employment of married women affected them as well. It was not until the second half of the twentieth century that the majority of married women of any racial or ethnic group held paid jobs in the nonagricultural labor force (Goldin 1990).

These demographic and employment changes resulted in profound transformations in American families. In 1830, 70 percent of American children lived in farm families; by 1930, the numbers had flipped, and only 30 percent lived on farms. In 1830, only 15 percent of children had a father who was a wage earner; by the 1920s, the majority of children's fathers earned wages. The increase in the labor-force participation of women with children occurred in the second half of the twentieth century. In 1940 only 11 percent of women with school-age children were in the labor force; by the end of the twentieth century this had increased to nearly 77 percent. Whereas only 6 percent of women with preschool-age children were in the labor force in 1940, this number had risen to 64 percent by the end of the twentieth. By 1990 more than 70 percent of American children already lived in households in which both parents were in the labor force (Hernandez 1993; U.S. Census Bureau 1943,1976b; U.S. Bureau of Labor Statistics 2009b).

PUBLIC POLICY RESPONSES: AN UNFINISHED REVOLUTION AT WORK

Public policy in the United States responded to the new needs of American families when families first became dependent on wage earners in the 1800s and early 1900s. Workers' compensation laws passed in states across the country to ensure that workers and their families would continue to have an income in the event of a work-related injury. Unemployment insurance, old-age pensions, and survivors' insurance passed first at state levels and then at the federal level to ensure that Americans had income when wage-work was lost or when earners were too old to continue to labor. Workers' compensation had been adopted by ten states as of 1911, and by forty-two states as of 1920. The combined rise of unions' political power and the economic necessity of the Great Depression spurred these developments. In 1929, old-age assistance—income security for those too old to work for wages—was mandated in California for the first time. Unemployment insurance was first adopted in Wisconsin in 1932 (Day 1997). The Social Security Act of 1935 gave a nationwide guarantee of income for the elderly and unemployed through federal insurance programs.

Yet, as Heymann argued in *The Widening Gap* a decade ago, American policy had not caught up with the movement into the workplace of second workers in two-parent families and of sole earners in single-parent families (Heymann 2000a); this still holds true today. Workers' compensation and unemployment, old-age, and disability insurance have met needs that arose in the era when a single worker per family entered the formal labor force, but U.S. policy does not effectively meet the needs of the majority of families today, in which all caregivers work for pay. American public- and private-sector policies do little to ensure that adults can simultaneously earn a living and care for sick children (or even healthy children) or aging parents. Among many other unresolved issues, policies currently in place do not yet answer such critical questions as: How can parents work for pay and also play an essential role in their preschool children's development and school-age children's learning? Who cares for the elderly when they can no

FIGURE 6.1   Average Length of School Term, 1870 to 2006, in Days

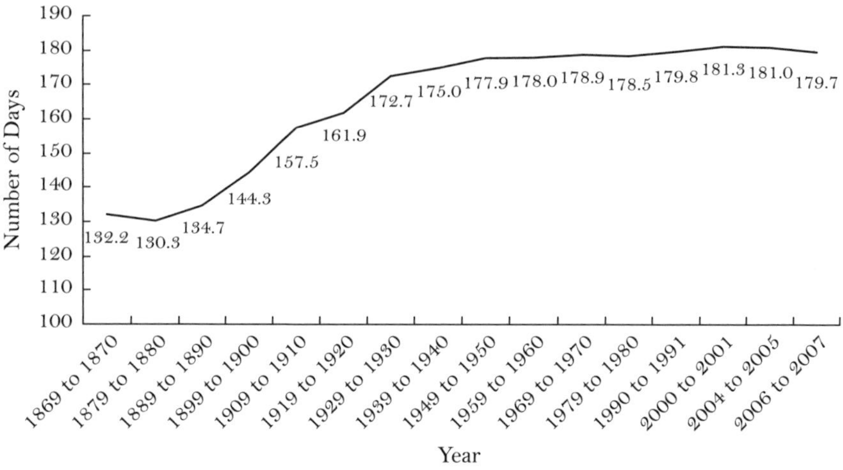

Source: Authors' compilation based on data from the U.S. Department of Education, National Center for Education Statistics (1997, 1999, 2008).

longer care for themselves? What happens to children when parents must work evenings and nights? The U.S. federal government did nothing to ensure that all Americans would have paid maternity or paternity leave, paid parental or family medical leave, the ability to breastfeed while working, or the ability to meet personal or family needs during an annual leave.

Just as the United States has failed to adopt social insurance and working conditions to enable adults to survive economically while succeeding at caring for family members, it has failed to update programs for children in light of the dramatic historical changes in families. The average length of the school year in 1870—when this country was an agrarian economy—was 132 days. The short school year was sufficient to provide children and youth with basic reading and arithmetic skills, the formal skills they needed in the 1870s. The skills needed for work were learned primarily through apprenticing. This short school year allowed plenty of time for children to assist on family farms and in household labor. By World War II, the school year had gradually climbed to 178 days. But as figure 6.1 shows, the length of the school year across the United States remained virtually unchanged between World War II and the beginning of the twenty-first century. During this period of rapid transformation in women's labor-force participation, family structure, and the number of children being raised in households in which all adults worked outside of the home, the school year continued to be short—

designed for children to assist with agricultural work that no longer occurred in over 98 percent of families. Likewise, nothing was done to provide early-childhood care and education—critical to the quality of education for children in all families and essential to care in households where all adults work for pay. As the jobs in America became increasingly competitive and children needed to acquire markedly more advanced skills in school, the educational system failed to expand.

COLLISION WITH GLOBALIZATION

Changes in public policy take time and are swayed by many forces. Just as voices were beginning to be raised in the United States in favor of paid family leave and other similar policies, the economy was increasingly globalizing. Over the course of the 1980s and the 1990s, companies' ability to do business across borders increased exponentially as faxes, email, the Internet, instant messaging, video conferencing, and other mechanisms dramatically lowered the cost and increased access to instantaneous communications. Equally important, the opening of the Chinese and Indian economies and the transformation of the economies in the former Soviet Union doubled the size of the global labor force open to capital investment during this period (Freeman 2005). These forces—together with the signing of an increasing number of multilateral and bilateral free-trade agreements, meant that the barriers to companies moving jobs across borders dropped dramatically. Manufacturing jobs left the United States for Mexico and Central America and then for China and Asia. Business services jobs, from call centers to billing, followed next, departing the United States for India and other nations. Jobs that remained for low-skilled American workers were by and large service jobs with lower wages than those that had been lost. Companies increasingly claimed that in order to keep any jobs in the United States, they would have to decrease employees' benefits (Ross 1997; Tonelson 2000). Policymakers also argued that it would be hard for the United States to compete economically while guaranteeing working families a floor of decent conditions (U.S. Senate 2007).

WORKING CONDITIONS AND SOCIAL SUPPORTS: WHERE DOES THE UNITED STATES STAND?

Public policy lagged behind the new realities of American families, and so, too, did the public discourse. Working poor families in the United States recognized the significant barriers they were facing, but the challenges they faced received little public attention. For most of the last half of the twentieth century, the academic and public debate focused on poor families who lacked jobs and whose income came from government welfare programs. Discussions of "working families" revolved almost entirely around two-parent upper-middle-class families.

In the 1990s, researchers began to document what American families already understood all too well: the great need for transformation in our public policy relating to work and families (for example, Heymann 1994; Heymann, Earle, and Egleston 1996; Waldfogel 1998; Gornick, Meyers, and Ross 1998; Kamerman and Kahn 1997; Blau and Ehrenberg 1997). Our research group carried out the first studies to look across the whole country at the extent of work disruptions to care for family members; across social classes at the availability of paid leave, flexibility, and other workplace adaptations to ensure that all adults could care for children, disabled adults, and elderly parents; and at the impact that the United States' near complete failure to develop policies for working families has had on Americans' health and education (Heymann and Earle 1996, 1998, 1999; Heymann and Bergstrom 1999; Heymann, Toomey, and Furstenberg 1999).

We have studied over ten thousand Americans from across the country. We carried out in-depth interviews with working mothers and fathers, grandparents, healthcare and childcare providers, and employers. We conducted a national survey of the intersection between Americans' efforts at work, at home caring for family members, and in the community. We examined national, state, and local policy and analyzed national data collected by the U.S. government and academics on families across every state, income group, employment sector, family type, and racial and ethnic group to better understand their successes and challenges as they sought to succeed at work and in caregiving. We sought to answer the key questions at the core of the obstacles families faced: First, how often do work and family responsibilities come into conflict? Second, for whom do these conflicts arise most frequently? Do men and women experience them similarly? Are the experiences of poor working families and middle-income working families the same or different? Do young adults experience more or fewer conflicts than older adults? Third, which family members are affected by these conflicts? In particular, is work-family policy all about taking care of children, as often seems to be the assumption? Are elderly parents and spouses also in need of assistance? Should other family members and friends also be considered? Fourth, what types of problems are working Americans helping their family members deal with? Are most work interruptions due to child-care problems or to elderly parents' illnesses, or is the spectrum of needs much broader? The answers to these questions were striking.

FIGURE 6.2   Cutbacks from Work to Care for Others,
                by Age of Respondent

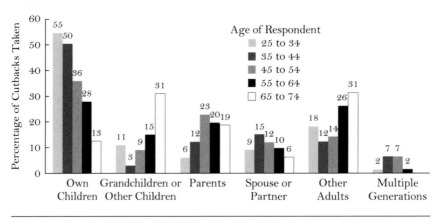

Source: Authors' adaptation of previous research (Heymann 2000a).

Limited Leave from and Flexibility at Work

Industrial and postindustrial work schedules, designed in the 1800s and
early 1900s, are based on the assumption that employees' contributions will
be uninterrupted. Yet the reality is that the demands placed on individuals
by families are neither predictable nor confined to nonworking periods. In
one study we asked a nationally representative sample of over one thousand
Americans about their daily lives. We called working Americans eight days
in a row and asked whether they had needed to cut back the time they spent
on any of their normal activities during the previous twenty-four hours as
a result of a family member's need for assistance. We examined a sample of
currently employed adults and the instances when they had to cut back on
their work time for family needs.

During the interview week, 30 percent of the respondents needed to cut
back on work hours on at least one day in order to meet the needs of family
members, and 12 percent needed to cut back on two or more days. All of
these working adults had significant caregiving responsibilities, but those
age thirty-five to forty-four were shouldering the greatest burden of dual
work and caregiving responsibilities (figure 6.2). Thirty-five percent of this
age group needed to cut back their work time on at least one day a week.
Although women were more likely to take cutbacks than men, men still
had a large number of cutbacks to meet family members' needs: 35 percent
of women and 24 percent of men had to cut back on at least one day in a given

FIGURE 6.3   Respondents' Reasons for Taking Cutbacks from Work, by Age of Respondents

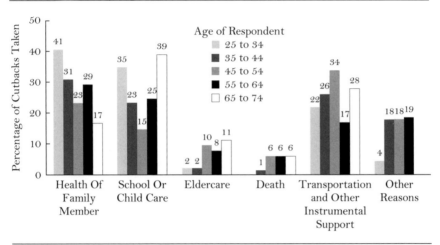

Source: Authors' adaptation of previous research (Heymann 2000a).

week. These findings are consistent with other research documenting that fathers have increased the time they spend with children, although men continue to perform less household work that women (Bianchi et al. 2000; Bianchi 2000). While there were more cutbacks for respondents with children than for any other single group, at 42 percent, they did not account for a majority. Fifteen percent of cutbacks were taken to care for parents, 12 percent for spouses or partners, 7 percent for other children, and 24 percent for other family members (Heymann 2000a).

Family members' needs were far more varied and complex than those addressed by many public policy proposals. Twenty-two percent of the cutbacks were taken to address problems with child care, 5 percent to provide for eldercare, 3 percent to provide for children's educational needs, 10 percent to provide transportation for family members, 16 percent to provide other instrumental support, 3 percent to cope with a death, 1 percent to deal with divorce, and 15 percent to provide emotional and other support. Figure 6.3 shows that the reasons for cutting back on working time varied by the age of the workers. For young workers, meeting family members' health needs was the most common reason to work fewer hours. The amount of work missed because of school or child-care needs followed a U-shaped curve, with workers between the ages of twenty-five and thirty-four and those between the ages of sixty-five and seventy-four being the

FIGURE 6.4   Parents' Lack of Paid Leave from Work, by Income[a]

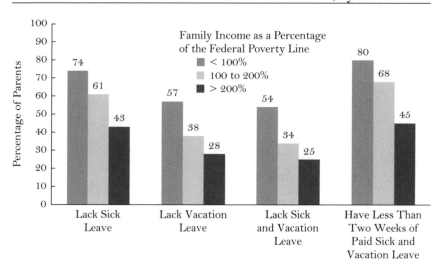

Source: Authors' adaptation of previous research (Heymann et al. 2002).
[a] Bars represent parents who lacked benefits some or all of the time they worked between 1994 and 1998.

two groups most likely to take time off from work in order to provide this care. In other words, both younger parents and grandparents were providing such care. Adults in mid-life, between ages forty-five and sixty-four, are more likely to be providing care for aging parents and other adult family members.

While the needs of working men and women to be able to address family issues were great, our research in the 1990s and early 2000s into national labor conditions also documented that the availability of leave from work to meet these needs—paid time off as well as flexible work schedules— was limited for all workers, and particularly so for low-income families (Heymann 2000a, 2000b, 2002; Heymann and Earle 1998, 2000; Heymann et al. 2002; Earle and Heymann 2004). Over a five-year period, between 1994 and 1998, 43 percent of Americans with incomes above 200 percent of the poverty line, 61 percent of families with incomes between 100 percent and 200 percent of the poverty line, and a stark 76 percent of families with incomes below 100 percent of the poverty line lacked paid sick leave some or all of the time (figure 6.4). Although more Americans had paid vacation leave[1] than paid sick leave, the availability of vacation leave still followed a clear income gradient: 28 percent of families with incomes above 200 per-

FIGURE 6.5   Types of Job Inflexibility, by Family Income

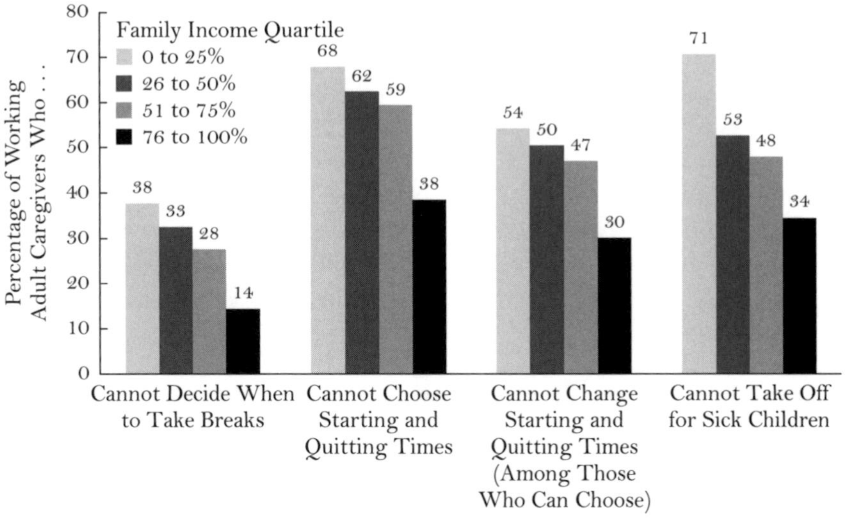

Source: Authors' adaptation of previous research (Heymann 2000a).

cent of the poverty line, 38 percent of families with incomes between 100 percent and 200 percent of the poverty line, and 57 percent of families with
incomes below 100 percent of the poverty line lacked paid vacation leave
some or all of the time.

Being able to adjust the starting and ending times of their workdays
can make an enormous difference in working parents' ability to ensure
that young school-age children are not alone in the morning or at the
end of the day. Yet 59 percent of upper-middle-income families, 62 percent
of lower-middle-income families, and 68 percent of Americans in the bottom
income quartile lacked the flexibility to adjust their work schedules in this
way (figure 6.5). Whereas 37 percent of low-income families reported they
did not have a choice in how their job was performed, only half as many families in the top income quartile (18 percent) lacked this kind of decisionmaking latitude.

A gradient in how much say adults have in planning their work environment also exists. Fifty percent of families in the bottom income quartile
lacked this kind of autonomy, while 43 percent of lower-middle income
families, 40 percent of upper-middle income families, and 31 percent of
high-income families did. Women were the most disadvantaged: they

carried more caregiving responsibilities, yet their jobs provided them with less paid sick leave, less paid annual leave, less autonomy, and less flexibility than men (Heymann 2000a).

Gradients documented in the 1990s continued in the 2000s. Researchers found that only 33 percent of workers in the bottom quartile could decide when to take breaks at work compared with 57 percent of workers in the middle and top quartiles. More than twice as many middle- and high-income workers as lowest-income workers were able to adjust their starting and ending time on a daily basis: 26 percent versus 12 percent. These are just two of the twelve measures of flexibility on which workers at the bottom of the income spectrum are at a significant disadvantage (Bond and Galinsky 2006).

Research has also shown that the social gradients around many types of paid leave have not significantly changed in the years since our studies were first conducted. In 2009, 86 percent of families in the top income quartile received paid sick leave, compared with only 37 percent of families in the lowest-income quartile.[2] The gap between families in the second quartile and lowest income quartile workers is 30 percentage points, or three times as large as the gap between the third and second quartiles. This pattern of the lowest-earning workers being markedly worse off than the workers just one quartile above in terms of access to paid sick leave holds true across industries (U.S. Bureau of Labor Statistics 2010a). A similar pattern also exists for access to paid leave that can be used for children's health needs and paid leave that can be used for one's own preventive care (Lovell 2004).

Access to paid leave around the birth or adoption of a child is even more limited than access to paid sick or vacation leave. Moreover, because there is an income gradient to this availability, the lowest-income workers have almost no access. In 2007, 11 percent of workers earning fifteen dollars or more per hour received paid or unpaid family leave, compared to only 5 percent of workers earning under fifteen dollars per hour. Workers in managerial and professional positions are more likely to have paid or unpaid family leave than service and blue-collar workers (Institute for Women's Policy Research 2007).

Many working parents, and poor working parents in particular, lack not only adequate paid leave and flexibility, but the hours and schedule they are being asked to work also bring the potential for greater conflict with family responsibilities. During the post–World War II period, as all adults in American families were increasingly becoming part of the labor force, the frequency of evening and night work also increased. Harriet Presser's research has demonstrated the detrimental impact of evening and night work on marriage quality and stability (Presser 2000). We examined the impact of these work schedules on children's educational outcomes. For every hour a parent regularly worked in the evening, the probability of their child scoring in the bottom quartile on math tests increased by 17 percent. When parents had to work night shifts, the probability of their child being suspended from school increased by 172 percent. These increases occurred even when controlling for parental education, family structure, and income (Heymann 2000a).

The lack of working protections took a great toll on children's health and families' incomes. Although families who received paid leave were five times as likely to be able to care for their sick children themselves, the majority of workers received no such leave (Heymann, Toomey, and Furstenberg 1999). In addition, while the availability of paid sick leave increased the likelihood that workers would retain their jobs after major illnesses, the paucity of sick leave in America has resulted in workers' illnesses and the illnesses of their children being among the most important causes of job loss, along with the birth of a new child (Earle, Ayanian, and Heymann 2006; Earle and Heymann 2002). As Jacob Hacker compellingly illustrates in chapter 2 of this volume, when a serious illness or injury occurs, families can end up risking everything, from income loss to bankruptcy, in a desperate effort to meet family health needs and pay their medical bills.

The amount of public attention and, in a few cases, the passage of legislation to address these issues have increased since the first studies on the extremely limited availability of adequate working conditions for families emerged. In 2002, California passed a paid family leave law that was 100 percent employee-funded through the state disability insurance program. This initiative, which came into effect in July of 2004, provides working Californians with up to 55 percent of their wages for up to six weeks to care for a newborn, a newly adopted child, or a seriously ill family member (State of California 2002). In 2007, Washington State passed the Family Leave Insurance law, securing workers' right to five weeks of paid leave to care for a newborn or newly adopted child with protected income of up to $250 per week. But the source of funding for the Washington state proposal was not specified (State of Washington 2007). In 2008, New Jersey followed California's and Washington's leads to become the third state to enact laws ensuring paid family leave for workers, guaranteeing a total of six weeks of paid leave in any twelve-month period to tend to the care needs of children and family members. It pays two thirds of workers' regular weekly earnings up to a maximum of $524 per week (State of

New Jersey 2008). This was funded entirely by an employee payroll tax, without contributions from employers.

Millions of Americans who did not live in the few states or cities that passed legislation remained uncovered. In 2007, only 57 percent of Americans working in the private sector had access to paid sick leave. This number fell to 44 percent among Americans earning less than fifteen dollars per hour. Among all employees—public and private—75 percent had paid annual leave, with only two out of five of those in the bottom income decile receiving paid annual leave. Among the minority of low-wage workers who received annual leave, most received less than six days in the first year of employment with a given employer (Institute for Women's Policy Research 2007; U.S. Bureau of Labor Statistics 2010a, 2010b).

Inadequate Availability of Early Childhood and After-School Care

Unfortunately, social programs and services that support working families are no more available than basic workplace benefits. Here we discuss two types of programs that provide care while adults are at work: early-childhood care and education and after-school care. In the United States, unlike in many other industrialized nations, there is little public provision or financing of early-childhood care. Although the vast majority of four-year-olds in the U.S. attends some type of early-childhood education or care program, just under half of those enrolled, and 39 percent of all four-year-olds, are in a publicly funded program. Only 52 percent of all three-year-olds are in some type of preschool program, and less than 25 percent of those enrolled (14 percent of all three-year-olds) attend a public program (National Institute for Early Education Research 2008). One study estimates that only 5 percent of children age two and under are served in publicly financed care (OECD 2001).

Federal dollars for child-care assistance fall far short of the needs of low-income working families. The main federal program providing assistance to low-income families is the Child Care and Development Block Grant, but recent estimates are that only one in seven children eligible for child-care assistance actually receives it (Mezey, Greenberg, and Schumacher 2002). Head Start, the program that directly serves and provides early education and care and has been around for more than forty years, now serves only about half of all eligible preschool-age children, and Early Head Start serves less than 3 percent of eligible infants and toddlers (Center for Law and Social Policy 2008).

The District of Columbia and thirty-eight states have stepped in to try to fill the gap, funding pre-kindergarten programs, but some serve only a small percentage of children at risk and operate only part of the day, and a number of them lack adequate quality standards (National Institute for Early Education Research 2008). Parents face not only a lack of available early-childhood care and education but also high costs. In thirty-three states and the District of Columbia, the annual cost of center-based child care for a preschooler is more than the annual tuition at a four-year public university (Children's Defense Fund 2008; Giannarelli and Barsimantov 2000). Many working families, especially those living below the poverty line, have to spend a large share of their monthly earnings (32 percent) on child care (Smith and Gozjolko 2010).

Working parents may need to secure fewer hours of care and supervision when children enter school, but the supply of quality after-school and summer programs is grossly inadequate. Nationwide, 26 percent of all school-age children—over 15 million—are on their own after school, including over a million children in elementary school (Afterschool Alliance 2009a). Eighty-six cities' mayors reported that only one third of children needing after-school care were receiving it, and only 4 percent of companies nationwide offer after-school care (U.S. Conference of Mayors 2003). According to national data, of the 28 million school-age children whose parents work outside the home, only 8.4 million are enrolled in after-school programs while an additional 18.5 million would participate if a quality program were available in their community (U.S. Bureau of Labor Statistics 2010c; Afterschool Alliance 2009a). In a 2009 survey by the Afterschool Alliance of nearly 1,500 after-school programs, 86 percent respondents said that more children in their community needed after school care than could be served. Nearly one third of programs say they would need at least to double capacity to serve all the children in their communities who need after-school care (Afterschool Alliance 2009b).

After-school care and supervision, like other social supports, are not equitably available. The gaps in access follow the same social gradient as access to work supports. Low-income parents are at a disadvantage when facing an underfunded public option and prohibitively expensive care. In the 2010 federal budget, the 21st Century Community Learning Centers received less than half of the $2.5 billion originally authorized in the No Child Left Behind Act (U.S. Department of Education 2010). The situation is especially critical for minorities. Far more African American parents than parents overall—61 percent versus 38 percent—report that they would have their child participate in an after-school program if one with spaces were located in their community (Afterschool Alliance 2009c). Hispanic parents are also more likely than parents in general—47 percent versus 38 percent—to say they would send their children to an after-school program if one were available. Parents cite a number of barriers to enrolling their children in after-school programs; for more than half (52 percent), cost is most insurmountable.

WHERE DO OTHER NATIONS STAND?

Americans' limited rights to care for their families while working are in sharp contrast with the rights of adults in other countries. Guarantees of basic employee protections such as paid annual leave and sick leave exist around the world and have a long history in other nations. Paid annual leave was passed for white-collar workers in 1909 in Iceland; 1910 in Austria; 1919 in Finland, Italy, and Luxemburg; and 1925 in Brazil and Chile. Manual workers started being guaranteed paid annual leave in Spain in 1919; in Czechoslovakia and Denmark in 1921; in Austria in 1922; and in Belgium in 1923. Similarly, universal paid annual leave was passed even before the Depression in Latvia, Poland, Finland, Russia, and Luxembourg (Mills 1927).

The world history of guaranteed basic rights enabling workers to care for their children is just as lengthy. Germany had unpaid maternity leave by 1878 and paid maternity leave by 1893; Austria had guaranteed unpaid leave by 1884 and paid leave by 1911; Belgium guaranteed paid leave in the 1890s; Ireland had unpaid maternity leave by 1901 and paid leave by 1913; and Denmark had unpaid leave by 1913 and paid leave by 1915 (Gauthier 1996; U.S. Social Security Administration 2008). Early paid maternity leave was not limited to Europe. Japan passed unpaid maternity leave in 1911 and paid maternity leave in 1922. Thus, most of Europe had guaranteed maternity leave prior to World War I, and much of Latin America had guaranteed maternity leave by World War II. Maternity leave policies swept the majority of Africa prior to and surrounding national independence (U.S. Social Security Administration 2008, 2009a, 2009b).

At least 177 countries guarantee women leave with income in connection with childbirth. This includes nations from all regions and of all income levels (see figure 6.6) One hundred and one of these countries offer fourteen or more weeks of paid leave. Although in a number of countries many women work in the informal sector, where these government guarantees do not always apply, the fact remains that these countries provide more than the United States, which guarantees no paid leave for mothers in any segment of the workforce. One hundred

FIGURE 6.6   Global Availability of Paid Leave for New Mothers

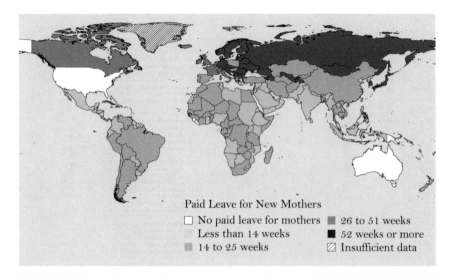

Paid Leave for New Mothers
☐ No paid leave for mothers ■ 26 to 51 weeks
   Less than 14 weeks   ■ 52 weeks or more
   14 to 25 weeks   ▨ Insufficient data

Source: Authors' adaptation of previous research (Heymann and Earle 2010).

thirty-two countries protect working women's right to breastfeed, of which 113 provide one hour or more per day.

Seventy-three countries ensure that fathers either receive paid paternity leave or have a right to paid parental leave (figure 6.7). Thirty-two of these countries offer fourteen or more weeks of paid paternal leave. The United States guarantees fathers neither paid paternity nor paid parental leave (Heymann and Earle 2010).

A global consensus has developed regarding the necessity of providing a variety of other basic guarantees that protect working adults and their families. One hundred sixty-four countries mandate paid annual leave, and 148 of these guarantee two weeks or more each year (figure 6.8). Meanwhile, the United States does not require employers to provide any paid annual leave at all. At least 157 countries require employers to provide a mandatory day of rest each week; The U.S. does not guarantee workers even this twenty-four-hour break from work. Sixty countries provide evening or night wage premiums.

Over 163 countries provide paid sick days for short- or long-term illnesses. Of these, 140 replace at least 50 percent of the lost earnings, and of these 140 countries, 58 guarantee at least 75 percent of earnings. One hundred and fifty-eight countries provide sickness benefits for a week or

FIGURE 6.7   Maximum Paid Paternity and Parental Leave Available to Fathers in Countries Providing Leave

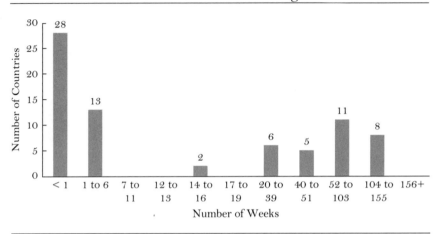

Source: Authors' adaptation of previous research (Heymann and Earle 2010).

FIGURE 6.8   Number of Weeks of Paid Annual Leave in Countries Mandating Leave

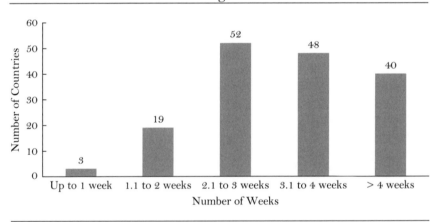

Source: Authors' adaptation of previous research (Heymann and Earle 2010).

FIGURE 6.9   Number of Days of Paid Sick Leave

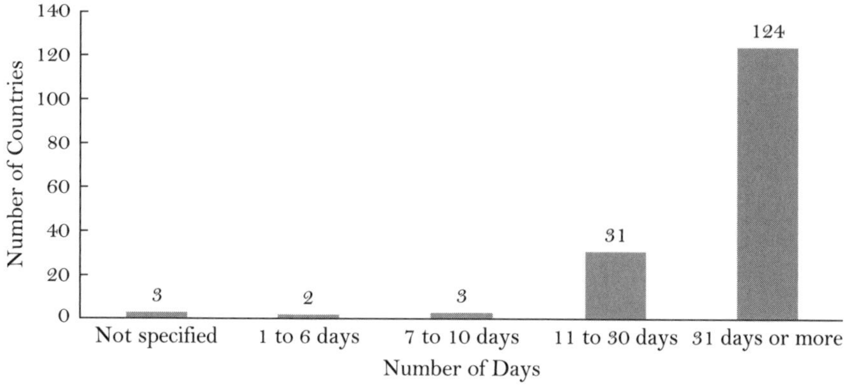

Source: Authors' adaptation of previous research (Heymann and Earle 2010).

more annually, with 98 providing sickness benefits for at least 26 weeks or until recovery (figure 6.9). The United States provides only unpaid leave for serious illnesses, through The Family Medical Leave Act (FMLA), and provides no protection for less severe illnesses. Moreover, many Americans can't afford to make use of the unpaid leave guaranteed through the FMLA, and illness is one of the leading causes of bankruptcy and mortgage foreclosure in the U.S.

The differences between the experiences of working families in the United States and those around the world are not limited to working conditions. They include access to preschool, a school day and school year that are long enough to cover more of the typical work day and year, and other services targeting the needs of both children and the elderly. To note just a few global examples: fifty-four nations have longer school years than the United States. Twenty countries have school years of over two hundred days, which is at least four weeks longer than in the United States. The United States tied with Ecuador and Surinam for thirty-ninth rank in enrollment in early-childhood care and education of three-to-five-year-olds (Heymann et al. 2004).

HOW DO WE BEGIN TO CLOSE THE GAPING HOLES?

Clearly the chasm between the old assumptions and the new realities of American working families must be bridged in American policy. It is equally evident that this is economically and politically feasible. Great adaptations are needed to ensure that Americans no longer lag behind, yet a number of steps could rapidly be implemented.

American working families need three kinds of changes. First, Americans need the guarantees of basic protections to working adults that exist the world over. These include the right to take leave from work when sick without losing your job, the right to paid annual leave, and the right to rest during the seven-day week, among others. Second, the transformation in the American labor force and in American families, which mirrors the transformation that has occurred worldwide, means that Americans now need the guarantees of basic rights at work that allow adults to provide essential care for their families while earning a living. These guarantees include paid maternity leave, paid paternity leave, the ability to breastfeed at work, and paid leave and flexibility to deal with a realistic range of critical health and developmental needs of family members. Third, the configuration of educational institutions and social supports that exist in the United States need to be brought into the twenty-first century, just as the workplace provisions do.

GUARANTEEING BASIC PROTECTIONS FOR ALL WORKERS

There are a series of basic protections that companies can readily implement that are important to the lives of American men and women. A few examples follow:

- *Paid Sick Leave:* While almost every country in the world offers paid sick leave, the United States does not. Most Fortune 100 companies in America provide paid sick leave and have demonstrated the feasibility of competing economically while doing so. Yet the majority of low-income Americans who need it the most lack paid time off for illness or injury. In 2009, 60 million Americans did not have access to paid leave to meet their health needs (U.S. Bureau of Labor Statistics 2010a).

- *Paid Annual Leave:* Paid annual leave is not only guaranteed by the overwhelming majority of countries around the world, but also by the UN's Universal Declaration of Human Rights, which all countries, including the United States, have adopted. Paid annual leave is far from a trivial consideration. Most schools in the United States break for sixteen weeks a year, and yet working parents are guaranteed no annual leave. Many families use annual leave to meet essential needs such as caring for young children when preschools are closed and transitioning elderly family members into new living situations. For families living near the poverty line, taking even two weeks of leave without pay is completely unaffordable. Clearly economically feasible and already adopted by the leading large companies in the United States, guaranteed leave would make an important difference to the millions of low- and middle-income Americans currently lacking access to paid leave.

• *Part-Time Parity:* Some adults have part-time jobs or work less than full-time schedules in order to address health needs or care for their children, parents, and disabled family members. These workers frequently lack access to health insurance, leave, disability insurance, and pensions because of their part-time status. This problem affects high-hour workers as well if they are unable to find a single full-time position and must cobble multiple part-time jobs together. Readily affordable, part-time parity legislation does not require companies to provide benefits to part-time workers that they are not providing to full-time employees. Rather, it ensures that part-time workers proportionately receive the same benefits as full-time workers.

GUARANTEEING BASIC PROTECTIONS FOR WORKING FAMILIES

Policies that support working men's and women's ability to keep their families healthy benefit not only the family members but also employers by enabling their workers to be productive and to avoid turnover. A few examples of these policies follow.

• *Paid Parental Leave:* Studies have identified numerous health benefits for both mothers and infants when new mothers have adequate time at home after giving birth. Paid parental leave increases a mother's ability to breastfeed her baby, which is known to reduce the risk of infections, child morbidity, and mortality significantly (for a summary of this evidence, see Yimyam and Morrow 2003; Kramer and Kukuma 2004). Paid leave also enables the formation of emotional bonds between parents and infants and the ability of infants to develop feelings of attachment and affection and a sense of security, which have been shown to have a significant impact on children's psychosocial development (Crouch and Manderson 1995). The lack of paid parental leave in the United States has long-term consequences for family finances. Studies have shown that women who receive paid maternity leave are more likely to return to work after the child's birth and to avoid long-term wage and income loss (Waldfogel 1998; Waldfogel, Higuchi, and Abe 1999). Without receiving paid leave from work to recover from childbirth and nurture a new infant, families often must choose between safeguarding a needed job and income and taking unpaid leave to ensure the healthy development of an infant.

Paternity leave is one of the key policies for improving gender equity at home and for contributing to the cognitive and social development of newborns.[3] Paternity leave contributes to the reduction of marital stress and helps prevent maternal depression (Coutrona and Troutman 1986). Fathers who have longer paternity leaves are more involved with their infants and families (Feldman, Sussman, and Zigler 2004). Men taking paternity leave can encourage changes in attitudes about which parent has primary responsibility for child care at home as well as expectations around who will or should take time off from work to provide care (Brandth and Kvande 2001).

• *Breastfeeding Breaks:* Around the world, including in the United States, breastfeeding newborn infants leads to a marked decrease in both morbidity and mortality. Breastfeeding decreases gastrointestinal diseases and respiratory infections by one fifth to one third (Betrán et al. 2001; Habicht, DaVanzo, and Butz 1986; Hobcraft, McDonald, and Rutstein 1985; Jason, Nieburg, and Marks 1984; Dewey, Heinig, and Nommsen-Rivers 1995). It also leads to improvements in infants' cognitive development and has important benefits to maternal health, including decreased risk of breast cancer.[4] Any company that can find a way to provide workers with breaks for lunch is also able to find a way to provide women with breaks to feed their infants. This low-cost but high-benefit guarantee should rapidly be passed in the United States, as it has been in 132 other countries (Heymann and Earle 2010).

• *Paid Leave to Care for Family Health:* Numerous studies have demonstrated that adults have better outcomes and recover faster from serious health events, including strokes and heart attacks, when they receive care from family and close friends (see, for example, Tsouna-Hadjis et al. 2000; Berkman 1995). Family care benefits children as well. The benefits of parental care have been documented for children's recovery from outpatient procedures, from illnesses and injuries requiring hospitalization, and from a wide range of chronic and acute diseases (for a summary of this literature, see Heymann, Earle, and Egleston 1996; for an example, see Kristensson-Hallstrom, Elander, and Malmfors 1997). The most straightforward way to pay for family medical leave is through a social insurance program. Although it is understandable that there would be concern about implementing such a program, in light of the state of the economy in 2010, it is important to note that the United States' Social Security system passed into law during the Great Depression. Once social insurance legislation has been passed, it will be essential to support implementation and uptake of the new programs. A recent study found that shortly after the passage of paid family and medical leave insurance in California, parents' lack of awareness about the program (only 18 percent knew about it) limited uptake, as did concerns that employers were not supportive of the policy and would fire parents who took leave (Schuster et al. 2008).

A number of policies important to all workers and their families, such as paid parental and paid family medical leave, will have impacts on federal and state budgets, either because of the need to raise new revenues in the case of the creation of a new social insurance program or the loss of tax revenues if payments during leave are financed through tax credits. Other policies—short term paid sick days, paid annual leave, part-time parity and breastfeeding breaks—will not affect public budgets. In the two states that have passed paid family and medical leave laws where employees pay the entire cost, the cost per worker is estimated to be somewhere between $33 (in New Jersey) and $65 (in California) per worker per year (State of New Jersey, Department of Labor and Workforce Development 2009; Hass 2009; Milkman 2008). Were the same limited six weeks of leave with partial wage replacement that are available in California and New Jersey made available nationally, and publicly funded, the government would need $8.5 billion to cover the approximately 130 million workers in the United States (2009 figure) (U.S. Bureau of Labor Statistics 2010c). This cost does not take into account savings from reduced job turnover and absenteeism and improved health. Even if there were no savings, the $8.5 billion is peanuts in comparison with the $700 billion bailout of the finance industry and is just as important for America's economic recovery.

The benefits to employees of having paid leave are many. Guarantees of paid leave will begin to address the root causes of families' inability to pay mortgages and other bills in the event of a major illness. Illness is one of the primary causes of job loss, bankruptcy, and housing foreclosures as a result of the simultaneous limitations of health insurance (which recent health insurance legislation began to address) and the lack of paid sick leave (Himmelstein et al. 2005). Nearly equal in frequency are the job losses that occur in connection with the birth of a child and the financial losses that occur as the gender gap in lifetime earnings reflects the lack of paid parental leave for mothers (Earle, Ayanian, and Heymann 2006; Earle and Heymann 2002; Waldfogel 1998). Paid parental and family medical leave would help address both problems.

INSTITUTIONS SERVING THE YOUNGEST AND OLDEST

When most American families lived on homesteads, in the early 1800s, they farmed their own land, grew their own food, and made their own clothes. In the 2000s, the majority purchase staple food and clothing. Since most American children in the twenty-first century are reared in households in which all adults work, it should be obvious that—unless multiyear paid parental leave comes into existence in the United States—caregivers other than parents are needed to provide quality early-childhood care and education to many of America's children. Similarly, as most older Americans find themselves with all their children in the workforce or living in distant locations, they will need services provided by someone other than their immediate family members so they can live at home as long as possible and their health needs can be met when they can no longer live at home.

Updating Policies for Preschool and School-Age Children

The 1930s brought forth major job programs to build infrastructure and public works. Our infrastructure could use an upgrade in the 2010s, but it does not lag behind the rest of the world anywhere near as much as our education system. According to the Program for International Student Assessment (PISA), among all OECD countries American students rank twenty-fifth in mathematics and twenty-first on science and literacy scales (U.S. Department of Education, National Center for Education Statistics 2007). A report issued by the Trends in International Mathematics and Science Study (TIMSS) in 2003 placed the United States behind fourteen countries in math, including Japan, Malaysia, Latvia, and Hungary, and behind eight countries in science, including Estonia, the Netherlands, Hong Kong, South Korea, and Singapore (U.S. Department of Education, National Center for Education Statistics 2003). Early-childhood care and education and quality after-school programs are essential for the competitiveness of the United States and for the quality of life of American children and adults. It is also critical to extend the length of the school year. Our twenty-first-century investments in "public works" should be in the area of education.

An Equally Important Vision for Older Americans

The U.S. grew older as a nation in the 20th century as the growth rate of the elderly far outstripped that of the total population. In 1900, the median age of the population was 22.9 years, and just 1 in 25 Americans, or 4 percent, were 65 or older (U.S. Census Bureau 2002). In 2007, the median age was just under 37, and 1 in every 8 Americans was aged 65 and over. According to the Census Bureau's projections, the number of elderly will reach 88 million by 2050 and come to represent one fifth of the population (U.S. Census Bureau 2008). If current policy continues unchanged, the Medicaid program will pay for institutional care for those older individuals who have been living independently and spent down all their savings, at a far higher expense than enabling the elderly to remain at home. Not only will the costs of caring for the elderly increase exponentially but their quality of life will spiral downward. We need to ensure that older Americans receive high-quality supports that enable them to remain at home longer, including provision of visiting care providers to help elders meet basic nutritional, medical, and daily-care needs. The evidence is irrefutable that active engagement and physical and mental activities are essential to the length of life without significant disability, so it is important to attack the roots of age discrimination, which decreases older Americans' ability to work or contribute to communities while they are still able (Treas and Torrecilha 1995; Szinovacz 1998; Pruchno and Johnson 1996).

THE FEASIBILITY OF CHANGE

Many of the necessary workplace mandates and early childhood care and education programs have long existed elsewhere in the world, so it would be reasonable to ask: Is it possible for the United States to undertake these changes in the globalized and weakened economy of 2010?

The evidence points to the feasibility of change. Global business leaders and top academics have worked together to create a global competitiveness index published each year by the World Economic Forum (WEF). Our research team examined the labor policies in the countries consistently designated to be among the most competitive over the ten-year period 1999 to 2008, as well as in the thirteen OECD countries with the lowest unemployment rates over the ten-year period from 1998 to 2007.[5] Elsewhere on the globe, none of the working conditions studied are linked with lower levels of economic competitiveness or employment. In fact, many of these guarantees are associated with increased competitiveness. Of the world's fifteen most competitive countries, fourteen provide paid sick leave, fourteen provide paid annual leave, thirteen guarantee a weekly day of rest, and thirteen provide paid leave for new mothers and twelve for new fathers. The majority of the thirteen OECD countries with consistently low unemployment rates provide many forms of paid leave. Twelve provide paid annual leave, a weekly day of rest, and paid leave for new mothers. Eleven provide paid sick leave (all but the United States and South Korea), and nine provide paid leave for new fathers.

Some may argue that economic conditions after the rapid rise in housing foreclosures in 2007 and the record-breaking fall in the stock market in 2008 and early 2009 are particularly grave and thus preclude any "social" expenditures. Yet, conditions are clearly no more dire than in the Great Depression when the United States passed some of its most important federal protections for individual workers. Unions were instrumental in the passage of major legislation in the early twentieth century to protect the movement of the first wage earners into the industrial labor force. In the twenty-first century, when American families more than ever before need the workplace to be transformed so that they can succeed economically while caring for their loved ones, unions have been declining in numbers and power for several decades. As Osterman (this volume, chapter 4) observes, their strength could once again increase if the United States were to change the laws and regulations that have limited workers' ability to organize, and if unions themselves were to find new ways of gaining membership in a dramatically transformed U.S. economy.

Whether or not there is a resurgence of work-based organizations, the means of forming coalitions are markedly increasing. Electronic forums such as MomsRising offer a new form of political opportunity for people with shared interests—in this case, parents caring for children—to organize effectively across the country. These forums have instantaneously been able to motivate thousands of people to write to legislators and senators, to attend demonstrations at state capitals, and to make appeals in person in Washington, D.C. These new means of political organization are bringing a strengthened voice to a wide range of Americans that have been deeply affected by the country's failure to enact legislation and support programs urgently needed by working adults and their families.

This chapter was made possible by the exceptional research, editorial, and staff assistance of Parama Sigurdsen, Melanie Benard, and Gonzalo Moreno. It draws on the research evidence of an extraordinary team of staff and students at Harvard and McGill who have participated in the Work, Family, and Democracy Initiative and the Project on Global Working Families. For the international comparisons, we are particularly indebted to the collaborative efforts of Jeff Hayes and Amy Raub. Special thanks are due to Megan Gerecke, Martine Chaussard, and Izabela Steflja for their new reviews of the international histories of minimum wages, annual leave, and parental leave, and to Giulia El-Dardiry for her review of current U.S. corporate policy.

NOTES

1. We use the term "vacation leave" instead of "annual leave" here because we are reporting on data gathered by the Department of Labor, which uses this terminology irrespective of whether the worker can use the paid time off for rest and leisure or must use it for family responsibilities.
2. The fraction of workers that have a benefit in a given year is larger than the fraction with access to that benefit consistently over a period of years.
3. Although the bulk of the literature has focused on the bonds between mothers and infants, there is no evidence to suggest that bonding with fathers is any less significant to children (see, for example, Nettelbladt 1983; Taubenheim 1981; Seward, Yeatts, and Zottarelli 2002).
4. Numerous studies have established the benefits of breastfeeding. For a summary, see Kramer and Kukuma (2004) and Leon-Cava et al. (2002).
5. The labor policies examined are from an Adult Labor database we developed as part of the WoRLD Initiative at the McGill Institute for Health and Social Policy. The primary source of information for this database was original legislation, both labor codes and other labor-related legislation obtained from NATLEX, the International Labour Organization's global database of legislation pertaining to labor, social security, and human rights from 189 countries as well as additional territories. Our final review of legislation was completed in August 2009. Additional sources of legislation include country websites and the law libraries of Harvard and McGill Universities and of the International Labour Organization in Geneva. For a detailed description of the sources used in compiling the Adult Labour policy database, see the appendix in Heymann and Earle (2010).

REFERENCES

Afterschool Alliance. 2009a. America After 3pm. "Key Findings." Washington, D.C.: Afterschool Alliance. Available at: www.afterschoolalliance.org/documents/AA3PM_Key_Findings_2009.pdf; accessed July 28, 2010.

———. 2009b. "Uncertain Times 2009: Recession Imperiling Afterschool Programs and the Children They Serve." Washington, D.C.: Afterschool Alliance.

———. 2009c. America After 3pm. "A Snapshot of the African-America Community After 3pm." Washington, D.C.: Afterschool Alliance. Available at: www.afterschoolalliance.org/documents/AA3PM_African-American_2009.pdf; accessed July 14, 2010.

Berkman, Lisa F. 1995. "The Role of Social Relations in Health Promotion." *Psychosomatic Medicine* 57(3): 245–54.

Betrán, Ana P., Mercedes de Onis, Jeremy A. Lauer, and José Villar. 2001. Ecological Study of Effect of Breast Feeding on Infant Mortality in Latin America." *British Medical Journal* 323(7308): 303–6.

Bianchi, Suzanne M. 2000. "Maternal Employment and Time with Children: Dramatic Change or Surprising Continuity?" *Demography* 37(4): 401–14.

Bianchi, Suzanne M., Melissa A. Milkie, Liana C. Sayer, and John P. Robinson. 2000. "Is Anyone Doing the Housework? Trends in the Gender Division of Household Labor." *Social Forces* 79(1): 191–228.

Blau, Francine, and Richard Ehrenberg, eds. 1997. *Gender and Family Issues in the Workplace.* New York: Russell Sage Foundation.

Bond, James T., and Ellen Galinsky. 2006. "What Workplace Flexibility Is Available to Entry-Level, Hourly Employees?" Supporting Entry-Level, Hourly Employees research brief no. 3. New York: Families and Work Institute, November. Available at: http://familiesandwork.org/site/research/reports/brief3.pdf; accessed July 14, 2010.

Brandth, Berit, and Elin Kvande. 2001. "Flexible Work and Flexible Fathers." *Work, Employment and Society* 15(2): 251–67.

Center for Law and Social Policy. 2008. "Early Head Start Participants, Programs, Families, and Staff in 2006." Washington, D.C.: CLASP. Available at: www.clasp.org/publications/ehs_pir_2006.pdf; accessed July 14, 2010.

Children's Defense Fund. 2008. "Children Enrolled in Head Start." In *State of America's Children 2008 Report—Early Childhood Care and Development.* Washington, D.C.: Children's Defense Fund. Available at: www.childrens defense.org/child-research-data-publications/data/state-of-americas-children-2008-report-early-childhood-care-development.pdf; accessed July 14, 2010.

Coutrona, Carolyn E., and Beth R. Troutman. 1986. "Social Support, Infant Temperament and Parenting Self-Efficacy: A Mediational Model of Post-Partum Depression." *Child Development* 57(5): 1507–18.

Crouch, Mira, and Lenore Manderson. 1995. "The Social Life of Bonding Theory." *Social Science and Medicine* 41(6): 837–44.

Day, Phyllis. 1997. *A New History of Social Welfare.* Boston: Allyn & Bacon.

Dewey, Kathryn, M. Jane Heinig, and Laurie Nommsen-Rivers. 1995. "Differences in Morbidity Between Breastfed and Formula-Fed Infants." Part 1. *Journal of Pediatrics* 126(5): 696–702.

Earle, Alison, and S. Jody Heymann. 2002. "What Causes Job Loss Among Former Welfare Recipients? The Role of Family Health Problems." *Journal of the American Medical Women's Association* 57(1): 5–10.

———. 2004. "Work, Family, and Social Class." In *How Healthy Are We? A National Study of Well-being at Midlife,* edited by Orville Gilbert Brim, Carol D. Ryff, and Ronald D. Kessler. Chicago: University of Chicago Press.

Earle, Alison, John Z. Ayanian, and Jody Heymann. 2006. "What Predicts Women's Ability to Return to Work After Newly Diagnosed Coronary Heart Disease: Findings on the Importance of Paid Leave." *Journal of Women's Health* 15(4): 430–41.

Feldman, Ruth, Amy L. Sussman, and Edward Zigler. 2004. "Parental Leave and Work Adaptation at the Transition to Parenthood: Individual, Marital and Social Correlates." *Applied Developmental Psychology* 25(4): 459–79.

Freeman, Richard. 2005. "What Really Ails Europe (and America): The Doubling of the Global Workforce." *The Globalist* (online magazine), June 3. Available at: www.theglobalist.com/StoryId.aspx?StoryId=4542; accessed July 14, 2010.

Gauthier, Anne H. 1996. *The State and the Family: A Comparative Analysis of Family Policies in Industrialized Countries.* Oxford: Clarendon Press.

Giannarelli, Linda, and James Barsimantov. 2000. "Child Care Expenses of America's Families." Assessing the New Federalism Series, occasional paper no. 40. Washington, D.C.: Urban Institute.

Goldin, Claudia. 1990. *Understanding the Gender Gap: An Economic History of American Women.* New York: Oxford University Press.

Gornick, Janet C., Marcia K. Meyers, and Katherin E. Ross. 1998. "Public Policies and the Employment of Mothers: A Cross-National Study." *Social Science Quarterly* 79(1): 35–54.

Habicht, Jean-Pierre, Julie DaVanzo, and William P. Butz. 1986. Does Breastfeeding Really Save Lives, or Are Apparent Benefits Due to Biases? *American Journal of Epidemiology* 123(2): 279–90.

Hass, Sarah. 2009. "Paid Leave in the States: A Critical Support for Low-wage Workers and Their Families." New York: Columbia University, National Center for Children in Poverty (March).

Hernandez, Donald J. 1993. *America's Children: Resources from Family, Government, and the Economy.* New York: Russell Sage Foundation.

Heymann, Jody. 1994. "Labor Policy: Its Influence on Women's Reproductive Lives." In *Power and Decision: The Social Control of Reproduction,* edited by Gita Sen and Rachel Snow. Boston: Harvard University Press.

———. 2000a. *The Widening Gap: Why America's Working Families Are in Jeopardy and What Can Be Done About It.* New York: Basic Books.

———. 2000b. "What Happens During and After School: Conditions Faced by Working Parents Living in Poverty and Their School-age Children." *Journal of Children and Poverty* 6(1): 5–20.

———. 2002. "Low-Income Parents and the Time Famine." In *Taking Parenting Public: The Case for a New Social Movement,* edited by Sylvia Ann Hewlett, Nancy Rankin, and Cornel West. Lanham, Md.: Rowman & Littlefield.

Heymann, S. Jody, and Cara A. Bergstrom. 1999. *Supervised Care for Preschool and School-Age Children: Report to the City of Cambridge.* Boston: Harvard School of Public Health.

Heymann, Jody, Renee Boynton-Jarrett, Patricia Carter, James T. Bond, and Ellen Galinsky. 2002. "Work-Family Issues and Low-Income Families." Ford Foundation report. New York: Ford Foundation.

Heymann, S. Jody, and Alison Earle. 1996. "Family Policy for School Age Children: The Case of Parental Evening Work." John F. Kennedy School of Government Center for Social Policy working paper series H-96-2. Cambridge, Mass.: John F. Kennedy School of Government.

————. 1998. "The Work Family Balance: What Hurdles Are Parents Leaving Welfare Likely to Confront?" *Journal of Policy Analysis and Management* 17(2): 312–21.

————. 1999. "The Impact of Welfare Reform on Parents' Ability to Care for Their Children's Health." *American Journal of Public Health* 89(4): 502–5.

————. 2000. "Low-income Parents: How Do Working Conditions Affect Their Opportunity to Help School-age Children at Risk?" *American Educational Research Journal* 37(2): 833–48.

————. 2010. *Raising the Global Floor: Dismantling the Myth That We Can't Afford Good Working Conditions for Everyone.* Stanford, Calif.: Stanford University Press.

Heymann, S. Jody, Alison Earle, and Brian Egleston. 1996. "Parental Availability for the Care of Sick Children." Part 2. *Pediatrics* 98(2): 226–30.

Heymann, Jody, Alison Earle, Stephanie Simmons, Stephanie M. Breslow, and April Kuehnhoff. 2004. "Work, Family, and Equity Index: Where Does the United States Stand Globally?" HSPH report, Project on Global Working Families. Boston: Harvard School of Public Health.

Heymann, S. Jody, Sara Toomey, and Frank Furstenberg. 1999. "Working Parents: What Factors Are Involved in Their Ability to Take Time Off from Work When Their Children Are Sick?" *Archives of Pediatrics and Adolescent Medicine* 153(8): 870–74.

Himmelstein, David, Elizabeth Warren, Deborah Thorne, and Steffie Woolhandler. 2005. "Market Watch: Illness and Injury as Contributors to Bankruptcy." *Health Affairs* Web Exclusive, February 2: w5-63–w5-75. Available at: http://content.healthaffairs.org/cgi/content/full/hlthaff. w5.63/DC1; accessed July 29, 2010.

Hobcraft, John N., John W. McDonald, and Shea O. Rutstein. 1985. "Demographic Determinants of Infant and Early Child Mortality: A Comparative Analysis." *Population Studies* 39(3):363–85.

Institute for Women's Policy Research. 2007. "Maternity Leave in the United States: Paid Parental Leave Is Still Not Standard, Even Among the Best U.S. Employers." Fact sheet. Available at: www.iwpr.org/pdf/parental leaveA131.pdf; accessed July 14, 2010.

Jason, Janine M., Phillip Nieburg, and James S. Marks. 1984. "Mortality and Infectious Disease Associated with Infant-Feeding Practices in Developing Countries." Part 2. *Pediatrics* 74(4): 702–27.

Kamerman, Sheila B., and Alfred J. Kahn, eds. 1997. *Family Change and Family Policies in Great Britain, Canada, New Zealand, and the United States.* Oxford: Clarendon Press.

Kessler-Harris, Alice. 1982. *Out of Work: A History of Wage-Earning Women in the United States.* New York: Oxford University Press.

Kramer, Michael S., and Ritsuko Kakuma. 2004. "The Optimal Duration of Exclusive Breastfeeding: A Systematic Review." In *Advances in Experimental*

Medicine and Biology, edited by Larry K. Pickering, Ardythe L. Morrow, Guillermo M. Ruiz-Palacios, and Richard Schanler, Vol. 554. New York: Kluwer Academic/Plenum Publishers.

Kristensson-Hallstrom, Inger, Gunnel Elander, and Gerhard Malmfors. 1997. "Increased Parental Participation on a Pediatric Surgical Daycare Unit." *Journal of Clinical Nursing* 6(7): 297–302.

Leon-Cava, Natalia, Lutter Chessa, Ross Jay, and Martin Luann. 2002. *Quantifying the Benefits of Breastfeeding: A Summary of the Evidence.* Washington, D.C.: Pan American Health Organization.

Lovell, Vicky. 2004. "No Time To Be Sick: Why Everyone Suffers When Workers Don't Have Paid Sick Leave." IWPR report B242. Washington, D.C.: Institute for Women's Policy Research. Available at: www.iwpr.org/pdf/B242.pdf; accessed July 14, 2010.

Mezey, Jennifer, Mark Greenberg, and Rachel Schumacher. 2002. "The Vast Majority of Federally-Eligible Children Did Not Receive Child Care Assistance in FY 2000." Washington, D.C.: Center for Law and Social Policy. Available at: www.clasp.org/publications/1in7full.pdf; accessed July 14, 2010.

Milkman, Ruth. 2008. *New Data on Paid Family Leave.* Report prepared for David and Lucile Packard Foundation. Los Angeles: UCLA, Institute for Research on Labor and Employment. Available at: www.familyleave.ucla.edu/pdf/NewData08.pdf; accessed July 28, 2010.

Mills, Charles M. 1927. *Vacations for Industrial Workers.* New York: Ronald Press.

National Institute for Early Education Research. 2008. *The State of Preschool 2008: State Preschool Yearbook.* Piscataway, N.J.: Rutgers University Press.

Nettelbladt, Per. 1983. "Father-Son Relationship During the Preschool Years: An Integrative Review with Special Reference to Recent Swedish Findings." *Acta Psychiatrica Scandinavica* 68(6): 399–407.

Organisation for Economic Co-operation and Development (OECD). 2001. *Starting Strong: Early Childhood Education and Care.* Paris: OECD.

Presser, Harriet B. 2000. "Nonstandard Work Schedules and Marital Instability." *Journal of Marriage and the Family* 62(1): 93–110.

Pruchno, Rachel, and Katrina Johnson. 1996. "Research on Grandparenting: Review of Current Studies and Future Needs." *Generations* 20(1): 65–70.

Ross, Andrew, ed. 1997. *No Sweat: Fashion, Free Trade, and the Rights of Garment Workers.* London: Verso.

Schuster, Mark A., Paul J. Chung, Marc N. Elliott, Craig F. Garfield, Katherine D. Vestal, and David J. Klein. 2008. "Awareness and Use of California's Paid Family Leave Insurance Among Parents of Chronically Ill Children." *Journal of the American Medical Association* 300(9): 1047–55.

Seward, Rudy R., Dale E. Yeatts, and Lisa K. Zottarelli. 2002. "Parental Leave and Father Involvement in Child Care: Sweden and the United States." *Journal of Comparative Family Studies* 33(3): 387–99.

Smith, Kristin, and Kristi Gozjolko. 2010. "Low Income and Impoverished Families Pay More Disproportionately for Child Care." Issue brief 16. Dover, N.H.: University of New Hampshire, Carsey Institute. Available at: www.peerta.acf.hhs.gov/uploadedFiles/PB_Smith_LowIncome-ChildCare. pdf; accessed July 14, 2010.

State of California. 2002. Senate Bill 1661, Disability Compensation: Family Temporary Disability Insurance. Available at: http://info.sen.ca.gov/pub/ 01-02/bill/sen/sb_1651-1700/sb_1661_bill_20020926_chaptered.pdf; accessed August 2, 2010.

State of New Jersey, Department of Labor and Workforce Development. 2009. "Family Leave Insurance Fact Sheet." Available at: http://lwd.dol. state.nj.us/labor/fli/content/fli_fact_sheet.html; accessed July 14, 2010.

State of New Jersey. 2008. "Family Leave Insurance Benefits Regulations." 41 N.J.R. 1052(c). Available at: http://lwd.dol.state.nj.us/labor/forms_ pdfs/tdi/fli_adopted_regs.pdf; accessed August 2, 2010.

State of Washington. 2007. State Laws of the State of Washington: Chapter 357, Bill No. E2SSB 5659, Family Leave Insurance. Available at: www. leg.wa.gov/CodeReviser/documents/sessionlaw/2007pam2.pdf; accessed August 2, 2010.

Szinovacz, Maximiliane. 1998. "Grandparents Today: A Demographic Profile." *The Gerontologist* 38(1): 37–52.

Taubenheim, Ann M. 1981. "Paternal-Infant Bonding in the First-Time Father." *Journal of Obstetrical, Gynecological and Neonatal Nursing* 10(4): 261–4.

Tonelson, Alan. 2000. *Race to the Bottom.* Boulder, Colo.: Westview.

Treas, Judith, and Ramon Torrecilha. 1995. "The Older Population." In *State of the Union: America in the 1990s.* Volume 2, *Social Trends,* edited by Reynolds Farley. New York: Russell Sage Foundation.

Tsouna-Hadjis, E., Kostas Nikolaos Vemmos, Nikolaos A. Zakopoulos, and Stamatis Stamatelopoulos. 2000. "First-Stroke Recovery Process: The Role of Family Support." *Archives of Physical Medicine and Rehabilitation* 81(7): 881–87.

U.S. Bureau of Labor Statistics. 2009a. *Women in the Labor Force: A Databook (2009 Edition).* "Table 4. Employment status by marital status and sex, 2008 annual averages." Available at: www.bls.gov/cps/wlftable4.htm; accessed July 29, 2010.

———. 2009b. *Women in the Labor Force: A Databook (2009 Edition).* "Table 7. Employment status of women by presence and age of youngest child, March 1975–2008." Available at: www.bls.gov/cps/wlftable7.htm; accessed July 29, 2010.

———. 2010a. *National Compensation Survey: Employee Benefits in the United States, March 2009.* "Table 30. Leave Benefits: Access, civilian workers, National Compensation Survey, March 2009." Available at: www.bls. gov/ncs/ebs/benefits/2009/ownership/civilian/table21a.pdf; accessed August 4, 2010.

————. 2010b. *National Compensation Survey: Employee Benefits in the United States, March 2009.* "Table 34. Paid vacations: Number of annual days by service requirement, Civilian Workers, National Compensation Survey, March 2009." Available at: www.bls.gov/ncs/ebs/benefits/2009/ownership/civilian/table23a.pdf; accessed July 14, 2010.

————. 2010c. Establishment Data: Historical Employment. "Table B-1. Employees on Nonfarm Payrolls by Major Industry Sector, 1960 to Date." Available at: ftp://ftp.bls.gov/pub/suppl/empsit.ceseeb1.txt; accessed July 14, 2010.

U.S. Census Bureau. 1943. *Employment and Family Characteristics of Women.* Washington: U.S. Government Printing Office.

————. 1976a. *Historical Statistics of the United States: Colonial Times to 1970.* Part I, Series D 49-62, Marital Status of Women in the Labor Force, 1870–1970. Washington: U.S. Government Printing Office. Available at: http://www2.census.gov/prod2/statcomp/documents/CT1970p1-01-05.pdf; accessed August 5, 2010.

————. 1976b. *Historical Statistics of the U.S.: Colonial Times to 1970,* Series D 63-74, Married Women (Husband Present) in the Labor Force, by Age and Presence of Children, 1948–1970. Washington: U.S. Government Printing Office. Available at: http://www2.census.gov/prod2/statcomp/documents/CT1970p1-01-05.pdf; accessed August 5, 2010.

————. 2000a. *Selected Historical Decennial Census Population and Housing Counts.* "Table 4. Population: 1790 to 1990." Available at: www.census.gov/population/www/censusdata/files/table-4.pdf; accessed August 4, 2010.

————. 2000b. American FactFinder. "United States—Urban/Rural and Inside/Outside Metropolitan Area." Available at: http://factfinder.census.gov/servlet/GCTTable?_bm=yand-geo_id=01000U.S.and-_box_head_nbr=GCT-P1and-ds_name=DEC_2000_SF1_Uand-redoLog=falseand-mt_name=DEC_2000_SF4_U_GCTH8_DI1and-format=U.S.-1; accessed July 14, 2010.

————. 2002. Demographic Trends in the 20th Century. Census 2000 Special Report, CENSR 4. "Table 5. Population by Age and Sex for the United States: 1900 to 2000." Available at: www.census.gov/prod/2002pubs/censr-4.pdf; accessed July 13, 2010.

————. 2008. *National Population Projections.* "Table 2. Projections of the Population by Selected Age Groups and Sex for the United States: 2010 to 2050." Available at: www.census.gov/population/www/projections; accessed July 30, 2010.

————. 2010. "USA Statistics in Brief—Population by Sex and Age." Available at: www.census.gov/compendia/statab/2010/files/pop.html; accessed July 14, 2010.

U.S. Conference of Mayors. 2003. "After-School Programs in Cities Across the United States." Survey. Washington, D.C.: U.S. Conference of Mayors.

U.S. Department of Education. 2010. *Fiscal Year 2011 Budget Summary.* Available at: http://www2.ed.gov/about/overview/budget/budget11/summary/edlite-section3a.html#clcs; accessed August 3, 2010.

U.S. Department of Education, National Center for Education Statistics. 1997. "Table 39: Historical Summary of Public Elementary and Secondary School Statistics: 1869–70 to 1996–97." In *Digest of Education Statistics 1997.* Washington: NCES. Available at http://nces.ed.gov/programs/digest/d97/d97t039.asp; accessed July 13, 2010.

———. 1999. "Table 127: Selected Characteristics on Eighth-Grade Students in Public Schools, by Region and State." In *Digest of Education Statistics 1999.* Washington: NCES. Available at http://nces.ed.gov/programs/digest/d99/d99t127.asp; accessed August 5, 2010.

———. 2003. "Trends in International Mathematics and Science Study (TIMSS) 2003." Table 5, "Average Mathematics Scale Scores of Eighth-Grade Students, by Country: 2003," and Table 6, "Science Scale Scores of Eighth-grade Students, By Country: 2003." Available at: http://nces.ed.gov/timss/TIMSS03Tables.asp?Quest=3andFigur==5 and http://nces.ed.gov/timss/TIMSS03Tables.asp?Quest=3andFigur==6; both accessed July 14, 2010.

———. 2007. *Highlights from PISA 2006: Performance of U.S. 15-year-old students in science and mathematics literacy in an international context. NCES 2008-016.* "Table 3: Average Scores Of 15-Year-Old Students On Mathematics Literacy Scale, By Jurisdiction: 2006." Available at: http://nces.ed.gov/pubs2008/2008016.pdf; accessed July 14, 2010.

———. 2008. "Table 130: Selected Statistics on Mathematics Education for Public School Students, by State or Jurisdiction: 2000, 2003, 2004, and 2006." In *Digest of Education Statistics 2007.* Washington: NCES. Available at: http://nces.ed.gov/pubs2008/2008022.pdf (see links for tables); accessed July 14, 2010.

U.S. Social Security Administration. 2008. "Social Security Programs Throughout the World, Europe." Available at: www.ssa.gov/policy/docs/progdesc/ssptw; accessed July 14, 2010.

———. 2009a. "Social Security Programs Throughout the World, The Americas." Available at: www.ssa.gov/policy/docs/progdesc/ssptw; accessed July 14, 2010.

———. 2009b. "Social Security Programs Throughout the World, Africa." Available at: www.ssa.gov/policy/docs/progdesc/ssptw; accessed July 14, 2010.

U.S. Senate. 2007. Committee on Health, Labor and Pensions Full Committee Hearing. "The Healthy Families Act: Safeguarding Americans' Livelihood, Families and Health with Paid Sick Days". February 13, 2007. Transcript available at: http://help.senate.gov/hearings/hearing/?id=0d8dd92b-b098-3934-f368-71667eef92e6; accessed October 4, 2010.

Waldfogel, Jane. 1998. "The Family Gap for Young Women in the United States and Britain: Can Maternity Leave Make a Difference?" *Journal of Labor Economics* 16(3): 505–45.

Waldfogel, Jane, Yoshio Higuchi, and Masahiro Abe. 1999. "Family Leave Policies and Women's Retention after Childbirth: Evidence from the United States, Britain, and Japan." *Journal of Population Economics* 12(4): 523–45.

Yimyam, Susanha, and Martha Morrow. 2003. "Maternal Labor, Breast-Feeding and Infant Health." In *Global Inequalities at Work: Work's Impact on the Health of Individuals, Families and Societies*, edited by Jody Heymann. New York: Oxford University Press.

PART II

THE NEW REALITIES OF DELIVERING SAFETY-NET PROGRAMS

CHAPTER 7

Nonprofit Helping Hands for the Working Poor: New Realities and Challenges for Today's Safety Net

Scott W. Allard

A new type of safety net has emerged in recent decades to assist low-income Americans, far different from the safety net in place during the War on Poverty of the 1960s.[1] Contrary to old notions and assumptions that view cash assistance as the dominant approach to antipoverty assistance, the twenty-first-century safety net depends heavily upon social service programs that offer helping hands to working poor populations. Government agencies and nonprofit organizations today spend more than $150 billion annually on social services such as job training, adult education, child care, substance abuse and mental health counseling, and emergency assistance that support work activity, meet basic needs, and promote greater personal well-being—more than double real-dollar spending on such services in 1975 (Allard 2009a). By comparison, federal and state government spending for Temporary Assistance for Needy Families (TANF), welfare cash assistance, the Supplemental Nutrition Assistance Program (SNAP, formerly the Food Stamp Program), and the Earned Income Tax Credit (EITC) reached about $130 billion in 2009 (Center on Budget and Policy Priorities 2010; Kneebone 2009; U.S. Department of Health and Human Services 2009).

Shifts in the composition of our safety net lead to a number of new realities for the ways society seeks to help the poor. Social service programs have become critical sources of safety net support for working poor families today, as they address a wide range of material and nonmaterial needs for millions of low-income persons who may not be eligible for cash assistance. Of particular significance is the central role that community-based nonprofit service organizations, both secular and faith-based, play in the modern safety net. Whereas government and nonprofit organizations largely occupied separate spheres of the safety net prior to the War on Poverty, expansion of public funding for social service programs in the last four decades has led to growing interdependency between government and nonprofit service organizations within the modern American welfare state (Allard 2009a; Smith and Lipsky 1993). Today, government programs fund most social services available in our communities through contracts and grants with nonprofit service organizations. Charitable foundations and private philanthropy complement this public commitment by directing tens of billions of dollars in support to nonprofit service organizations each year. Consequently, local safety nets take on a particularly important role in the delivery of antipoverty assistance, as the ability of communities to connect working poor families to many types of safety net help rests on the capacity of local service organizations.

Along with changes in the composition of safety net assistance, the relationship between place and the delivery of safety net assistance has changed. Whereas cash assistance program benefits can be delivered directly to recipients, most social services cannot be brought directly to an individual at home. Clients typically visit a social service provider, often several times, to receive assistance or complete a program. Evidence indicates, however, that social service programs are not always equitably distributed in or accessible to poor neighborhoods (Allard 2008, 2009a, 2009c; Allard and Cigna 2008; Allard and Roth 2010). Poor persons who do not live in proximity to relevant service providers will find it difficult to receive needed help because of the complexity and cost of commutes between home, work, child care, and a service organization, particularly if they are reliant on public transportation. Moreover, we should expect individuals to be more likely to know about providers located in the immediate community and to have greater trust in community-based organizations than in providers located farther away. Lack of access to social service providers should be expected to reduce program participation, increase rates of program attrition, be related to lower work activity, and dampen program efficacy (Allard 2009a; Kissane 2010; Zuberi, forthcoming).

Matters of access are complicated by the fact that social service program funding can be volatile from one year to the next. Public and private funding for social services is cyclical, falling and rising with ebbs and flows in the economy. Nonprofit service organizations must cope with lost or shifting revenue streams right when the demands placed upon them increase. Shifting public policy priorities and changes in the focus of private philanthropy shapes the availability of program funding from one year to the next. Competitiveness for public funding and private support changes as crises emerge or perceptions about pressing societal needs shift. Changes in funding also may be driven by impressions about program quality and efficacy. To the extent that social service funding is cyclical, unstable, and insufficient, therefore, we should expect there to be volatility in program delivery that compromises the structural integrity of the contemporary safety net.

Just as the Great Depression highlighted the patchwork and insufficient nature of the safety net in place in the early 1930s, the Great Recession that began in 2007 highlights the fragility of today's safety net. Historically high rates of unemployment, prolonged periods of joblessness, and real dollar declines in household income have increased demand for emergency cash or food assistance, housing assistance, and employment services. Individuals and families with no previous interaction with antipoverty programs—many of them working at least part-time—have sought aid in unprecedented numbers. Need has far outpaced the capacity of government or nonprofit agencies to provide help (Allard and Roth 2010; Mabli et al., 2010). At the same time the recession has affected every major revenue source for nonprofit service providers: government grants and contracts, charitable giving, foundation and corporate support, as well as commercial and earned revenue (Allard and Roth 2010; Nonprofit Finance Fund 2010). Just when working poor families need help most, it appears the capacity of the safety net to offer a helping hand is at its weakest.

This chapter examines these new realities and challenges facing the contemporary safety net. Throughout the chapter I cite research findings from my analyses of the Multi-City Survey of Social Service Providers (MSSSP) and the Rural Survey of Social Service Providers (RSSSP), which I completed with executives of government and nonprofit social service agencies in three metropolitan areas (Chicago, Los Angeles, and Washington, D.C.) and four multicounty rural sites (southeastern Kentucky, south-central Georgia, southeastern New Mexico, and the border counties between Oregon and California) between November 2004 and June 2006. For additional detail on these survey data and to access cited articles, papers, or reports, please visit www.scottwallard.com.[2]

NEW REALITIES IN TODAY'S ANTIPOVERTY SAFETY NET

The American antipoverty safety net comprises a bundle of governmental and nongovernmental programs targeting assistance to low-income populations who lack adequate income, food, housing, or access to health care. Government cash assistance intended to reduce material poverty is the most visible component of the contemporary safety net (Blank 1997; Coll 1995; Scholz and Levine 2001). Prominent cash assistance programs—TANF, SNAP, and the EITC—provided roughly $130 billion in federal assistance to tens of millions of working poor households in 2009 (Center on Budget and Policy Priorities 2010; Kneebone 2009; U.S. Department of Health and Human Services 2009). Many states administer their own general assistance, earned income tax credit, and welfare programs that complement these federal cash assistance programs (Pennucci, Nunlist, and Mayfield 2009; Williams, Johnson, and Shure 2009).

Political and scholarly discussion so often focuses on cash assistance programs that we fail to notice the social service programs that constitute a growing share of antipoverty assistance. The most familiar social service programs address basic material needs through emergency cash assistance grants, food pantries, home-delivered meals, soup kitchens, temporary shelters, utility assistance, and provision of clothing or necessary household items. Since passage of welfare reform in 1996, social service programs that help adults find work or become work-ready also have become more salient. Such programs can range from employment services focusing on job search and interviewing, to vocational training and skill development, to basic adult education and literacy courses. Many social service programs help low-income job seekers overcome common barriers to employment by providing child care, transportation assistance, and health services. Other common social service programs focus on family counseling and child welfare issues, or assist individuals with a variety of physical health problems, disabilities, mental health issues, and substance abuse problems, often in residential or in-patient treatment settings (Smith 2010).

Once a modest component of the safety net, the number and size of social service programs have more than doubled since 1975. Social service programs now constitute a larger portion of the safety net than ever before and receive more government funding than most major cash assistance programs combined. The Congressional Research Service (2003) estimates that federal and state government spending for a limited set of means-tested social service, job training, housing, adult education, and energy assistance programs in the early 2000s reached at least $120 billion

each year.[3] Examining a wider range of programs for low-income populations, Scott W. Allard (2009a) estimates that federal, state, and local government social service program expenditures exceed $150 billion annually.
It is important to note that despite these aggregate trends in total national
expenditures, Thomas Gais, Lucy Dadayan, and Suho Bae (2009) find evidence that state governments' social service spending per poor person flat-
tened in the mid-2000s and began to decline slightly in the years immediately
prior to the Great Recession of 2007.

A common reaction to the shifting mix of safety net assistance is to ask
whether the current arrangement makes sense. Yet, expansion of social
service programs in the past forty years has not occurred with significant
public debate or through a single policy initiative or reform. It is not the
product of a coordinated federal, state, or local effort. Instead, growth of the
social service sector has occurred piecemeal, driven by hundreds of policy
changes and emerging revenue streams across the many levels of American
government (Allard 2009a; Smith 2010; Smith and Lipsky 1993). As a
result, the politics and decisions surrounding social service programs delivery or funding rarely become salient, simultaneously favoring private interests that provide helping hands to the poor and placing program funding in
a tenuous position because many policymakers do not fully understand the
role of social service programs within the safety net.

We also might ask whether social service programs are more effective
than cash assistance programs and whether the current mix of assistance is
optimal for addressing poverty. Unfortunately, such questions are difficult
to answer. Social service programs provide help to a wider range of households than do cash assistance programs, often helping families cope with
temporary periods of job loss or lost income. Many households receiving
cash assistance also receive assistance from social service programs, which
makes it difficult to identify program effects, particularly when very little
data track social service utilization, cash assistance receipt, and relevant
household outcomes with adequate temporal precision. Finally, many of the
new institutional, organizational, and political realities of the safety net
detailed in this chapter also make it difficult to provide clear answers to
questions about program efficacy and impact.

A first step toward understanding how the shifting mix of antipoverty
assistance matters in the lives of low-income families and how we might
craft better policy or programs should be to understand the new realities
of an increasingly service-oriented safety net. More thorough understanding of the new realities that define the contemporary safety net should help
improve the way we deliver social assistance to working poor families, as

well as guide new empirical research strategies that might identify the impact of the changing nature of the safety net.

THE CRITICAL ROLE PLAYED BY NONPROFIT ORGANIZATIONS

In contrast to the safety net in place for several decades immediately following the New Deal, in which local nonprofit service organizations played a more modest role in the delivery of antipoverty assistance, the contemporary antipoverty safety net is highly dependent upon local community-based nonprofits to deliver social service programs to low-income populations.[*] As federal and state government agencies began to increase funding for social services in the late 1960s, they often turned to local nonprofit service organizations to provide the service delivery capacity necessary to connect tens of millions of Americans with expanding programs of assistance (Salamon 2003; Smith 2010; Smith and Lipsky 1993). Such institutional arrangements are more efficient and cost-effective than direct government provision of social services, allowing public dollars to stretch and provide more assistance to working poor families.

Precipitous growth in the nonprofit service sector has followed in the ensuing decades. Total employment in the nonprofit social service sector increased by nearly 400 percent from 1977 to 2002 (Smith 2010). Revenues for the nonprofit social service sector more than doubled from 1977 to 1997 (Salamon 2003). Growth continued into the 2000s, as the number of social service and employment-related nonprofits increased by 65 percent from 1990 to 2003 (Allard 2009a) and revenues reported by nonprofit individual, family, and emergency relief service providers increased by more than 50 percent between 1999 and 2006 (Smith 2010). To a greater extent than is often assumed by scholars and experts, nonprofits in almost every urban, rural, and suburban community have become primary providers of publicly funded social service programs for the poor.

Some nonprofit providers are very small, relying upon a limited number of volunteers to provide emergency assistance to a few families each month. Modest- to mid-sized nonprofits often retain a small number of full-time staff, but draw upon part-time staff, interns, and volunteers to administer programs to several hundred clients per year. At the other end of the spectrum are large nonprofit organizations that provide dozens of services to thousands of clients each year through a highly bureaucratized administrative apparatus. Some nonprofits focus programming exclusively on low-income populations; others maintain caseloads that are a mix of poor and non-poor individuals. Many nonprofits focus their efforts on particular communities or client populations. For instance, some providers only serve women, individuals of a specific race or ethnic group, or residents of a defined neighborhood or community. Others may choose to work exclusively with HIV-AIDS populations, victims of domestic violence, or formerly incarcerated individuals.

Scholars often make distinctions between secular nonprofit organizations and faith-based organizations (FBOs), or religious nonprofits. In contrast to secular nonprofit service organizations, faith-based service organizations maintain some type of connection to a religious community or congregation. The strength of these connections is shaped by how closely a faith-based service provider couples resources, authority structures, and cultural elements from religious organizations (Smith and Sosin 2001). Some faith-based service organizations may have their origins in a religious community, but do not currently incorporate religious values or elements into service provision. At the other end of the spectrum are FBOs where the spiritual and social missions are more fully integrated, particularly among congregation-based programs. A host of faith-based service organizations fall in between, finding unique ways to blend funding, structure, and cultural elements from both religious and secular sources.

FBOs are thought to be more likely to operate in high-poverty neighborhoods than secular nonprofits, making them more responsive to the needs of the most disadvantaged persons and distressed communities (Allard 2008; Chaves and Tsitsos 2001). Faith-based providers are perceived to be more trusted community-based institutions, which may increase the likelihood that poor persons will seek and receive support services. In addition, some clients may prefer to be served, or may be better served, by an FBO that shares their spiritual or religious orientation (Campbell 2002; Graddy 2006; Greenberg 2000; Owens and Smith 2005; Smith 2007). FBOs are also thought to be more effective than secular organizations because they provide more holistic services that address clients' spiritual as well as physical and material needs, yet there is little empirical evidence to support such assertions (Carlson-Thies 2004; Smith 2007).

Although it is difficult to get precise estimates from existing data sources, Allard (2009a, 2009b) estimates that about two thirds of local nonprofit social service organizations are secular. It is important to recognize, however, that FBOs and secular nonprofits often occupy specific niches within local safety nets. Faith-based nonprofits in urban and rural areas are most likely to offer services to meet immediate material needs, such as emergency food or cash assistance. For example, Allard (2008) finds that nearly 90 percent of faith-based nonprofits operating in urban and rural areas offer emergency assistance of some kind, compared to less than 60 percent of urban and rural secular nonprofits. Many religious congregations and churches provide emergency assistance or counseling programs for low-income households through informal programs supported through in-kind donations and limited external revenue (Smith 2010).

In contrast, FBOs are less likely than secular nonprofits to offer services requiring trained professional staff, such as outpatient mental health treatment, substance abuse programs, or employment-related services. Allard (2009a) finds that roughly half of all urban secular nonprofit organizations offer employment services, compared to about one third of FBOs operating in urban areas. Similarly, 51 percent of urban secular nonprofit social service organizations and 36 percent of rural secular nonprofit social service organizations provide mental health or substance abuse programs (Allard 2008). Only about one third of urban and rural FBOs offer outpatient mental health or substance abuse services. These differences in service mission also shape organizational structure. Thus, secular nonprofits on average tend to maintain much larger operating budgets and staffing levels than FBOs operating in similar communities (Allard 2009b).

The prominent role played by secular and faith-based nonprofits poses many challenges for local safety nets as well. Government cannot require nonprofits to operate programs or mandate that nonprofits pursue programs to reach the hardest-to-serve populations. Nonprofit organizations choose which services to provide, funding streams to seek, and populations to target. Even when receiving public funding, nonprofits maintain substantial discretion over everyday implementation of programs at the street-level. Such discretion makes it difficult for government to hold private nonprofits publicly accountable, which can be problematic if the priorities of nonprofit organizations do not fit with public policy agendas or if nonprofit service organizations fail to meet performance benchmarks. Reliance upon nonprofit organizations to deliver safety net assistance, therefore, can be accompanied by trade-offs among achieving greater efficiency in the provision of assistance, ensuring equitable provision of assistance, and promoting program effectiveness.

PRIMACY OF LOCAL SAFETY NETS

Changes in how we provide antipoverty assistance also create important new institutional realities for the safety net. Rather than a single safety net administered top-down by the federal government, the American safety net comprises tens of thousands of unique local safety nets. Local safety nets administer federal cash assistance programs, such as TANF or SNAP, along with a wide array of social service and health service programs for low-income populations that receive federal, state, and local funding. Counties are the primary geographic unit of local safety nets because most federal and state government programs are administered through county-level agencies and offices, but municipalities fund additional programs and services to low-income residents. Even though funding may originate at higher levels of government, capacity to deliver social services and antipoverty assistance is provided by local organizations.

Social service programs often do not carry entitlement status, making them discretionary components of local safety nets. To a greater extent than is the case for cash assistance programs, the content and availability of social service programs vary widely by county, city, town, and neighborhood (Allard 2009a; Allard and Roth 2010). Local priorities, public and private, determine the types of social service programs that will be available. County and municipal government administrative agencies structure publicly funded program grants and contracts, shaping how services are delivered, which areas are served, and how outcomes will be assessed. The characteristics of a community's nonprofit social service sector reflect local political culture, presence of private philanthropy, and civic leadership (Allard and Cigna 2008; Allard 2009c). Nonprofit social service organizations and charitable foundations focus their work locally, often specifying service provision or funding within a discrete set of counties, municipalities, or neighborhoods. Community-based nonprofit service organizations also work closely with local government officials and administrative agencies to shape program structure and implementation.

The localness of social service provision leads those components of the safety net to be more varied from place to place than most cash assistance programs, despite the fact that policy prescriptions often assume consistency in provision of social services from one place to another. Availability of services differs from one county or municipality to the next within a given state, region, or metropolitan area. Eligibility for social service programs often is tied to one's county or municipality of residence. Where working poor families live, therefore, determines the bundle of social services available to help cope with job loss, deal with barriers to employment, and provide basic material needs. Complicating matters further, there is reason to believe that commuting patterns and unstable living arrangements common among working poor households make it difficult for needy individuals to receive assistance in their place of residence (Allard 2009a).

Primacy of local agencies and organizations in the delivery of social service programs also creates a fragmented institutional structure with which the contemporary American safety net must wrestle. The multitude of actors engaged in social service financing and delivery make it difficult to coordinate programs and reduce duplicated programmatic efforts. A myriad of competing priorities and goals exist that make it difficult for local safety nets to develop comprehensive and timely responses to changes in need and poverty. (See Sandfort, this volume, chapter 8, for further discussion of these issues.) Moreover, the safety net creates intergovernmental competitive pressures that may discourage local places, particularly those where poverty rates historically have been low, from providing social services so as to avoid becoming a destination for low-income populations (Peterson 1981). So even though scholarly attention often focuses upon social welfare policymaking activity at the national or state level, much of the important action shaping whether working poor families have access to safety net assistance today takes place at the local level.

PUBLIC FUNDING FOR PRIVATE HELPING HANDS

Nonprofit social service providers operating in a decentralized safety net draw upon a large number of funding sources to support programs. Government grants and contracts are by far the most important sources of funding for the nonprofit social service sector. Today, most of the nearly $90 billion in revenues reported to the Internal Revenue Service (IRS) by nonprofit social service organizations come from federal, state, and local government agencies (Allard 2009a).[5] As government funding has become more readily available in the past few decades, nonprofit service organizations have become adept at finding public revenue streams to support their varied missions and client needs. Quite often, nonprofit providers receive program funding from more than one public agency and in more than one program area to serve several different client populations, with funding commonly drawn from agencies across the different levels of government.

Nearly all secular nonprofit organizations receive at least some government funding. Allard (2009a) finds that almost 85 percent of urban secular nonprofit organizations reported receiving government grants or contracts of some kind to support operations in the previous three years. Secular nonprofit organizations receiving government grants or contracts are likely to be dependent on those sources of revenue. Close to 60 percent of secular nonprofits in urban and rural areas receiving government funds are dependent on those funds for at least half of their budget (Allard 2008).

Interviews with a small sample of social service providers in the suburban areas of metropolitan Chicago, Los Angeles, and Washington, D.C., suggest similar dependency of secular nonprofits on public revenue streams (Allard and Roth 2010). Such findings reinforce the notion that secular nonprofit service organizations and government agencies have strong reciprocal relationships. Without public funding, many secular nonprofits would struggle to maintain operations; without secular nonprofit organizations, many government programs could not be delivered at the street level.

Counter to popular perception, a sizable share of FBOs also receive public funds. More than half of faith-based nonprofits interviewed in the MSSSP and RSSSP that did not incorporate religious elements into service provision reported receiving government funding (Allard 2008, 2009a). More striking perhaps, nearly one third of faith-based agencies in urban areas that integrate religious principles and practice into service provision reported receiving support from government sources (Allard 2008). It is important to note that FBOs are not permitted by law to use public funds to support worship or proselytizing activities, nor can they incorporate faith elements into programs. Even though it may be surprising that a substantial portion of FBOs receive public support, it is likely that faith-based providers comply with the law by funding programs with religious content through nongovernmental revenue sources and using governmental funds for programs without religious content. In addition, government funds do not constitute a substantial share of operating revenues for most faith-based organizations. Only 26 percent of FBOs that receive public funding are dependent on those funds for more than half their revenues (Allard 2009b).

Nearly all nonprofit service providers, particularly those not reliant on government funding, also receive support through grants from charitable organizations and giving from private individuals (Allard 2009a). Roughly two thirds of nonprofit service providers draw upon revenues from other nonprofit organizations, and more than 70 percent receive support through private individual giving (Allard 2009b). Neither source of funding, however, is the source of a significant share of nonprofit service organization operating revenues. The lone exception is smaller faith-based service organizations, particularly those in rural areas, which are more likely to depend on private giving for most of their operating budget (Allard 2008).

Medicaid has become a more prominent source of revenue for nonprofit service providers in the past few decades. Today, Medicaid funds support a wide range of nonprofit services, including child welfare services, programs for the developmentally disabled, and mental health and substance abuse treatment (Smith 2010). About one quarter of urban nonprofit service organizations and 20 percent of rural nonprofit service organizations report receiving Medicaid funds (Allard and Smith 2009). Growth in Medicaid funding is due in part to expansion of Medicaid-eligible populations and procedures, which has allowed qualifying safety net providers to receive Medicaid funding for certain types of services. Moreover, Medicaid reimbursement rates can be much higher than those from other social service grants or contracts, making such funds attractive to providers.

Suggestive that Medicaid can be a particularly important revenue source for rural safety nets, Scott Allard and Steven Rathgeb Smith (2009) find 51 percent of rural nonprofits receiving Medicaid funds drew more than half of their operating budget from those funds, compared to 27 percent of urban nonprofits receiving Medicaid. It should be noted, however, that reliance on Medicaid exposes nonprofit service providers to a set of pressures that may not be present in other revenue streams. Not only must providers maintain Medicaid-eligible client caseloads and maintain cost structures that fit within Medicaid reimbursement rates, but decisions about which services and populations are eligible for Medicaid are made at the federal and state—as opposed to the local—level (Allard and Smith 2009). Higher rates of dependency upon Medicaid funding among rural nonprofits, therefore, suggest that future changes to Medicaid regulations, eligibility, and reimbursement rates will have a more acute impact on rural than on urban safety nets.

Earned revenues through fee-for-services paid directly by clients or private insurance, or through commercial enterprises, have become another important emerging source of revenue for nonprofit social service providers. As is the case for Medicaid, private sources of earned revenues can reimburse nonprofits at a more generous rate than other types of grant or contract arrangements. Running commercial enterprises such as childcare centers, restaurants or cafés, and cleaning or maintenance services has become an increasingly popular way for nonprofits to create sustainable revenue streams and at the same time promote the mission of the organization (Community Wealth Ventures 2008). As of 2010, roughly one third of urban and rural nonprofit service providers report earned revenue. These remain relatively new sources of funding for most service organizations—for only a small percentage of nonprofits do earned revenues make up more than half of all revenues (Allard 2009a, 2009c).

Despite steady expansion of public and private support for social service programs in the past thirty years, social services program funding can be highly unstable. Instability in program funding in large part reflects the discretionary nature of social service programs. Because there is no legal obligation for state, county, or municipal government to provide or maintain a particular social service program in a specific community, programs are vulnerable to shifts in revenues and community priorities. This is particularly true during economic downturns, when government expenditures, grants from charitable foundations, and private donations from individuals contract. The pro-cyclical responsiveness of social service program funding means that resources available to low-income populations decrease right at the time when need for assistance increases (Allard 2009a; Grønbjerg 2001; Johnson, Lav, and Ribeiro 2003; Salamon 1999).

Social service program funding can shift even during relatively stable economic times. Public policy and philanthropic priorities change as new social problems and crises emerge, which in turn shapes how government and private funding is dispersed to safety net providers. A nonprofit service organization's ability to compete for government grants and the attention of private donors fluctuates as perceptions about pressing societal needs shift. Program outcomes also can dictate changes in funding, as government agencies and charities may take past program effectiveness, quality, and efficiency into account when allocating resources for the future.

Instability or unpredictability of funding may lead nonprofits to be cautious about expanding staffing, locating to more preferred office space, or trying to reach more clients. Agencies and organizations that cannot achieve a consistent flow of revenue will be forced to cut staff, reduce available services, or limit the number of people served. In extreme cases, agencies or organizations may be forced to temporarily close or even permanently shut their doors because of insufficient or inconsistent funding. The realities of social service financing force nonprofit organizations to devote substantial energy to maintaining program funding, seeking new or more diversified sources of funds, and finding replacement revenues. Volatility in program funding streams makes assistance less available to those in need and also destabilizes the agencies and organizations that provide the safety net's foundation.

Analyses of MSSSP and RSSSP data demonstrate how funding cuts set off dramatic ripples throughout local safety nets. Forty-five percent of nonprofit and for-profit service organizations interviewed in urban and rural areas reported a decrease in revenue in recent years (Allard 2009b). Seven of ten urban social service providers and nearly eight of ten rural social service providers experiencing a funding cut reduced service provision by cutting programs, staff, and client caseloads, or closing temporarily (Allard 2009a, 2009c). Of significant concern, there is evidence that nonprofit service providers located in high-poverty areas are more likely to reduce service provision due to decreases in funding than in low-poverty areas (Allard 2009a). Strategies for coping with funding cuts also vary by the type of service provider. Secular nonprofit organizations, because they generally are larger organizations and carry larger staffs than FBOs, are more likely to reduce staff in response to funding cuts. About 60 percent of secular nonprofit organizations in both surveys indicated staffing reductions in the wake of funding losses (Allard 2008), compared to less than one third of religious nonprofits (Allard 2009b). Reflecting the vulnerability associated with being a small and modestly funded organization, faith-based service providers appear more likely than secular nonprofit organizations to close temporarily because of funding cuts (Allard 2008). Although different nonprofit organizations draw on different combinations of funding, it appears that issues of volatility and instability in service delivery arrangements are more the rule than the exception across urban and rural nonprofit service sectors.

PLACE MATTERS

Place matters differently to the social service elements of the safety net than to cash programs. Unlike cash assistance programs, most social service programs cannot be delivered directly to clients' homes. This means that living nearby service providers should be a critical determinant of receiving help from a service-based safety net (Allard 2009a; Kissane 2010). Information about the services available is likely to be a function of proximity to providers because an individual is more likely to know about or receive referrals for agencies located in the immediate neighborhood than in neighborhoods farther away. As noted, service providers in the immediate neighborhood may be more trusted than providers located further away (Kissane 2010; Owens and Smith 2005). Living in closer proximity to providers reduces commuting burdens, especially if office visits must be coordinated with already complex trips between home, a child-care provider, and work. Further, the limitations of public transportation in many communities and low rates of automobile ownership among low-income households make it even more critical that providers be located near poor populations. Inadequate access to social service agencies can be thought of as equivalent to failing to provide assistance altogether. If programs are not well matched to communities where need is highest and most persistent, we might expect social service programs to have little impact on poverty or the well-being of working poor families.

A number of factors shape the location decisions of community-based social service organizations. First, a number of organizational characteristics or imperatives favor certain types of neighborhoods or locations over others. An organization's mission often specifies a neighborhood or population to serve. Such priorities endure over time, even as demographic patterns and need in the surrounding community shifts. Organizations working with particularly vulnerable or at-risk populations may choose locations that prioritize protecting anonymity and confidentiality over shorter commutes. In certain settings a program's theory of change may dictate working with clients within a particular environment or away from an environment containing perceived negative influences. The manner in which service providers prioritize key organizational stakeholders also will shape location decisions. Service providers may prefer to locate within low-income neighborhoods to be proximate to clients and key community partners. Others may choose a location that seeks to strike a balance between many different stakeholders apart from clients. For example, service providers may locate near communities where pools of available trained professional workers or potential board members reside.

Fiscal considerations and overhead costs also shape location decisions. The primacy of public funding often dictates that nonprofit organizations locate in counties or municipalities where program grants and contracts are available. Likewise, the need to access private giving, charitable philanthropy, and earned revenue may provide incentives for organizations to locate closer to donors and individuals capable of paying fees for services. The cost of leasing office space can be an important determinant of program location, particularly in urban areas where rental rates for commercial space can be quite high. Even if affordable space can be found in low-income communities, it may not be well suited for service provision. Modest-sized nonprofit service organizations may be limited to office space that can be obtained for low or no cost through unique community partnerships or places of worship. Finally, some providers may choose to locate closer to concentrations of low-income individuals to achieve economies of scale for service delivery.

Given the importance of place and access, it is not surprising that two thirds of nonprofits in urban areas draw a majority of their clients from within three miles (Allard 2009a). Nevertheless, several studies provide evidence that high-poverty neighborhoods have less access to social service programs than low-poverty neighborhoods (Allard 2008, 2009a, 2009c, 2009d; Grønbjerg and Paarlberg 2001; Mosley et al. 2003; Peck 2008). For example, Allard (2009a) finds that urban census tracts with poverty rates over 20 percent have access to about 30 percent fewer social service slots than the average urban tract when controlling for supply and potential demand for services. Such mismatches persist when looking specifically at access to employment services, outpatient mental health, or emergency food assistance.

Access to social service components of the safety net varies by the racial composition of neighborhoods as well. High-poverty, predominately black tracts have about half as much access to employment services, emergency cash and food assistance programs, and outpatient mental health or substance abuse services as low-poverty, predominately white tracts. Similar patterns are evident for high-poverty, predominately Hispanic tracts, although the magnitude of mismatch between Hispanic and white neighborhoods is slightly smaller than that between black and white neighborhoods (Allard 2009d). Neighborhoods with higher poverty rates, however, have greater access to faith-based organizations that incorporate religious elements into service delivery than do lower poverty neighborhoods (Allard 2008). Such findings are consistent with expectations that places of worship and religious congregations located in high-poverty communities play a particularly active role in providing assistance to the poor in surrounding communities.

NEW CHALLENGES FACING TODAY'S SAFETY NET

The Great Recession has posed the most serious test to the American safety net since social service program expenditures became a key complement to cash assistance programs, exposing many of the safety net's vulnerabilities. Poverty and need have increased substantially since the recession began in 2007. Job loss and decreases in household income have forced many families to seek assistance from social service agencies for assistance with household bills, food, and job search (Allard and Roth 2010; Mabli et al. 2010). The impact of the recession has been felt as powerfully in suburban communities as in central city and rural areas (Kneebone and Garr 2010). Suburban social service providers in metropolitan Chicago, Los Angeles, and Washington, D.C., report the types of clients seeking help are changing as a result of the recession. Client caseloads have become increasingly composed of two-parent households, families with no previous connection to the safety net, and households where at least one adult is working (Allard and Roth 2010).

With long-term unemployment having reached historically high levels (U.S. Department of Labor, Bureau of Labor Statistics 2010c), there remains concern whether economic recovery will improve the job prospects for many working poor families, particularly for low-skilled job seekers at the lower end of the labor market. Seasonally adjusted unemployment rates for adults twenty-five years or older without a high school diploma peaked near 16 percent in early 2010, with unemployment rates exceeding 30 percent for youths age sixteen to twenty-four without a high school diploma and not in school. For those with a high school diploma and some college, unemployment rates in the current recession are on par with unemployment rates for those without a high school diploma in the recession of 2001 (U.S. Department of Labor, Bureau of Labor Statistics 2010a, 2010b). If previous recessions and current labor market trends are any guide, it should take at least four or five years for unemployment rates among those without a college degree to return to prerecession levels.

Such expectations suggest employment and adult education service agencies will be particularly important to improving the job prospects for low-skilled workers, even after the recession has officially ended. In chapter 3 of this volume Michael Stoll proposes employment service programs that promote timely skill development and learning relevant to demands of employers, while also providing supportive post-employment services to ensure job retention and advancement among low-skilled workers. Similarly, Paul Osterman (this volume, chapter 4) proposes a number of program models implemented through collaboration among government, employers, and social service providers that can improve skill acquisition and advancement into good jobs.

These are extremely promising visions for how we might improve employment trajectories among those at the bottom of the income ladder, yet there is evidence that employment services and adult education programs are weakly accessible to high-poverty communities. Instead, employment and adult education programs appear to locate nearer concentrations of job opportunities in downtown areas and inner-ring suburbs (Allard 2009a). Such location choices may help programs connect to employers and labor-market opportunities, but this spatial arrangement also may make it difficult for many low-income residents of isolated urban neighborhoods and rural communities to access these types of programs. Compounding the problem further, Scott Allard and Benjamin Roth (2010) find there are relatively few employment service providers in outer suburban areas, where unemployment rates have risen significantly since 2007.

Consistent with trends documented by Stoll in chapter 3, the Great Recession has had a disproportionately large impact on men's labor-force participation, and gender gaps in unemployment have widened in the last few years. Rates of unemployment for white male adults over 20 increased from 3.9 percent in December 2007 to 9.0 percent in February 2010, yet unemployment rates for white women increased from 4.0 to only 7.3 percent. Gender differences in unemployment during the Great Recession are particularly striking for blacks, as the unemployment rate among black males over twenty years old increased from 8.4 percent in December 2007 to 17.0 percent in February 2010. Rates for black women increased during that same period, from 7.1 percent to 12.1 percent (U.S. Department of Labor, Bureau of Labor Statistics 2010a).

Apart from their implications for the changing nature of the labor market, the fact that men have been displaced from the workforce at much higher rates than women has implications for the safety net. Data from the MSSSP and RSSSP suggest that many nonprofit social service providers target resources toward women, who are more likely to be the primary caregivers in poor and non-poor families and are most likely to retain custody of children. About two thirds of all providers—urban and rural, secular and faith-based—report caseloads to be majority female; almost 20 percent serve women nearly exclusively. The disconnect between jobless men and social service elements of the safety net likely compounds barriers to employment and exacerbates isolation from labor-market opportunities that many experience. It also likely undermines the ability of social service programs to engage fathers in building stronger and healthier families.

The Great Recession has had an equally dramatic impact on public expenditures for social welfare programs, particularly social service programs. Most states are struggling with severe budget deficits and many are forecast to remain in significant deficit position even after the economy recovers. A recent study estimated that states will have to resolve about $375 billion in budget gaps during 2010 and 2011 (McNichol and Johnson 2010). Social service programs become prominent targets for budget cutting in part because they are not entitlements and in part because many policymakers do not understand how central social service programs are to today's safety net. Although some of the hardest budget cuts remain to be made, many states are cutting social service programs, laying off state agency employees, or imposing furloughs to reduce spending (Johnson, Oliff, and Williams 2010). Social service providers are not only being asked to help rising numbers of low-income families cope with job loss and need during the recession, but many are asked to do it with fewer revenues and little guarantee of support moving forward.

Making matters worse, we might expect the Great Recession to continue to weaken the fabric of the modern safety net for years to come. Instability in program funding and philanthropy has led many nonprofits to cease or reduce operations. Other providers are running out of options and are likely to close soon. Consolidation and mergers, particularly among financially troubled service organizations, may not be viable options for many providers. Public expenditures for social service programs, which may have leveled off or declined in many states following the recession of 2001, are likely to remain well below pre-2007 levels (Gais, Dadayan, and Bae 2009). These fiscal realities will force nonprofits to compete even harder for public and private resources than has been the case in the past. We should expect the ripple effect of these conditions to persist even after recovery occurs, destabilizing the nonprofit service sector and limiting the assistance that local safety nets will be able to provide in the future.

IMPLICATIONS FOR FUTURE POLICY AND RESEARCH

The antipoverty safety net in the United States has undergone a significant, but often overlooked, transformation in the past several decades. Social service programs have emerged as a primary mode for delivering assistance to families near and below the poverty line. Today's safety net relies upon tens of thousands of local social service organizations, many of them nonprofits, to provide helping hands to low-income populations. Successful delivery of social service programs hinges on a community's ability to ensure that providers—particularly the nonprofit service providers upon which the safety net largely depends—are accessible to the poor and operate in a reliable fashion. Disparities in access to service components of the safety net heighten the obstacles that low-income, low-skilled workers already face when seeking work and trying to achieve greater well-being. Mismatch and volatility within the service-based nonprofit safety net will compound existing political, economic, and social inequalities, dampening service program effects even if interventions are otherwise well designed.

Findings here suggest that our contemporary service-based safety net may not be as responsive to the Great Recession and changing labor-market conditions as we might believe. Not only are service providers challenged to provide help to low-income populations amid a volatile funding environment that contracts when need rises, but the safety net's reliance upon local government and nonprofit organizations for the delivery of aid makes it difficult to coordinate activity and target resources efficiently. Consequently, it will be difficult for our local safety nets to develop immediate or comprehensive responses to sudden shifts in need. The recent recession also underscores the fragility of the contemporary safety net, as government funding and private support for programs have shrunk even as demand for help reaches historic levels.

The new realities of the contemporary safety net discussed here have profound implications for future antipoverty and economic security policy. The ability of communities to translate antipoverty policy into successful programs on the ground depends on the presence of stable and accessible service providers. For example, consider the implications of place and access for some of the prominent components of the Obama administration's antipoverty strategy. Efforts to create transitional jobs for displaced workers or to train low-skilled workers will be dependent upon the presence of relevant service providers near concentrations of job seekers. Effects of social service programs intended to strengthen parenting and engage noncustodial fathers will likely vary according to the availability of such programs in neighborhoods where needs are greatest. Accomplishments of the White House Office of Faith-Based and Neighborhood Partnerships will rest on the strength and sustainability of local faith-based and secular nonprofit service organizations. Likewise, neighborhood investment through programs such as the Promise Neighborhoods initiative will yield results only if there is adequate nonprofit service delivery infrastructure in place (White House 2009).

Fewer resources and rising need suggest that policymakers and community leaders will be looking for innovative solutions that produce tangible returns on social service programs and investment. Such returns are measured not only by changes in individual or household earnings, or other behavioral transformations associated with participation in a particular safety net program, but also by reduced public safety net expenditures moving forward as families achieve greater well-being. A growing understanding of successful new nonprofit organizational forms, joint public-private ventures, and social enterprise may help local actors adopt solutions that help the working poor by means of more diversified and sustainable revenue streams.

In chapter 8, Jodi R. Sandfort outlines a vision for how states and communities may redesign programs, utilize intermediary organizations, and rethink service delivery relationships to build stronger community networks and tap into the knowledge of frontline social service organization staff. However difficult it may be to improve coordination and collaboration within our highly decentralized and fragmented local safety nets, improving how we provide helping hands to working poor families in the future will depend on how well we find new ways to organize and administer social service and cash assistance programs today. Fortunately, examples of innovation abound in our local safety nets, and chapters in this volume highlight many promising possibilities currently being implemented in our communities.

In light of the issues outlined in this chapter, it is important to consider innovative antipoverty solutions that help connect people in need to critical social service assistance in their communities. Increasingly, there are examples of state health and human service agencies partnering with community-based organizations to connect low-income families with assistance. In suburban Chicago, for example, the State of Illinois Department of Human Services has been working with food banks and pantries to implement an experimental "Express Stamps" program designed to connect food pantry clients eligible for SNAP with immediate temporary food assistance benefits until they can formally apply for SNAP at a government office (Illinois Department of Human Services 2009). ACCESS Florida, an award-winning online application system implemented by the State of Florida Department of Children and Family, allows individuals to apply for Medicaid, food stamps, welfare, and refugee assistance through Web portals in more than 2,600 community-based organizations (Florida Department of Children and Family 2010). Social enterprises connected to employment service programs offer promising pathways for connecting the hardest-to-employ populations with work opportunities. For instance, the Cara Program and its social enterprise, Cleanslate Chicago, provide skill development, job training, job placement, and post-employment support services to low-income job seekers, posting 72 percent job retention for placed students after one year (Cara Program 2008). Others have proposed expanding the successful New Hope demonstration project in Milwaukee, which offered low-income adults who are working at least thirty hours per week a bundle of support services through community-based agencies: earnings supplements, subsidized child care and health insurance, access to temporary community-service jobs, and caseworker referrals to other needed services (Bos et al. 2007). Key to New Hope's success was delivering consistent, guaranteed, and easily accessible social services and earnings supplements through neighborhood-based professional caseworkers.

Even when programs are funded and delivered, the structural, fiscal, institutional, and organizational realities of the contemporary safety net make it difficult to assess their efficacy. The impact of social service programs is difficult to compare to income maintenance programs. First, the proliferation and variety of local social service organizations makes it very difficult to track program expenditures and offerings, let alone outcomes. Stoll (this volume, chapter 3) provides an example of the challenges facing evaluation of social service programs when he describes the difficulty of assessing the impact of Workforce Investment Act (WIA) funds. Data are not readily available that permit accurate tracking of social service program use across individuals and time. Nor do most local service organizations track program or client outcomes in a manner that would permit empirical research to pinpoint specific service program effects. Data limitations are further complicated by the fact that many low-income individuals likely receive help from many different programs at any point in time and there is significant self-selection into programs of assistance. We also should not lose sight of the other goals and values embedded within safety net programs. For example, given the share of safety net resources dedicated to social services, we should consider issues of equity in access and responsiveness to need to be paramount.

Finally, the new realities of the safety net suggest the research agenda surrounding poverty and the safety net should be recast to reflect the contours of antipoverty assistance today. Scholars are only beginning to understand the institutional and organizational consequences of recent transformations in the safety net. Although this chapter highlights many recent research findings about the organizational context for social service delivery, many unanswered questions remain. Understanding the politics of local safety nets and the factors shaping decisions by nonprofit providers about service delivery will be important for explaining the evolution of antipoverty policy in the coming years. Similarly, it is important to develop empirical strategies and data that enable us to assess the impact of social service programs, as well as the factors that shape help-seeking behavior and program participation in the first place. Commonly identified barriers to employment such as lack of information, low levels of trust, low literacy, poor health, and inadequate access to transportation should also function as obstacles to receiving assistance through a service-based safety net (Allard 2009c). Better insight into how service utilization affects individual outcomes is needed to assess the contributions made by the social service components of the safety net and to improve the provision of services that promote self-sufficiency among hard-to-serve populations. By coherently integrating the social service elements of the safety net into ongoing research regarding poverty and inequality, scholarship can generate more complete answers to many of the most pressing poverty policy research questions that will emerge in the coming years and decades.

NOTES

1. This project was supported by research grants from the Metropolitan Policy Program at the Brookings Institution, Brown University, the Center for Policy Research at Syracuse University, the Department of Housing and

Urban Development, the RUPRI Rural Poverty Center, and the West Coast Poverty Center at the University of Washington. Additional support came from the Institute for Research on Poverty at the University of Wisconsin–Madison, the Institute for Policy Research at Northwestern University, and the National Poverty Center at the University of Michigan.

2. Organizations were invited to participate in the MSSSP and RSSSP if they offered basic material assistance (emergency cash or food assistance), out-patient mental health or substance abuse services, or employment-related services (job training, job search, adult education) on-site at no or low cost to adults near or below the poverty line. Surveys collected more detailed information about location, services provided, clients served, funding, and organizational characteristics. With response rates that exceed 60 percent in each site, these surveys are the most comprehensive and geographically sensitive data about social service provision currently available. Nevertheless it is important to note that these survey data reflect a very specific subset of the nonprofit social service sector. Excluded are nonprofit agencies that serve children only or a specific adult client population exclusively (for example, adults with disabilities, ex-offenders). Nonprofits offering only in-patient or residential programs were also excluded from the surveys. Because survey respondents were identified through existing community directories and phonebook listings that primarily identify more formalized nonprofit service agencies within a community, these surveys risk missing very small or less formal nonprofit organizations that often operate in poor communities. In addition, these data do not include information about churches unless they are listed in directories as offering formal programs of assistance.

3. Expenditures are reported in 2008 dollars.

4. Nonprofit organizations must register with the Internal Revenue Service as tax-exempt charitable organizations under section 501(c)(3) of the Internal Revenue Code; thus they are often referred to as 501(c)(3) organizations. Exempt status requires that nonprofit organizations subject themselves to government regulation of their finances and political lobbying activity; private donations are tax deductible (see Berry and Arons 2003).

5. Reported estimates of nonprofit social service organization revenues are based on 2003 data from the National Center for Charitable Statistics. These figures include human and employment service nonprofits filing tax-exempt nonprofit status with the Internal Revenue Service, but exclude nonprofits unlikely to serve low-income working-age adults.

REFERENCES

Allard, Scott W. 2008. "Accessibility and Stability of Nonprofit Service Providers: Faith-Based and Community-Based Organizations in Urban and Rural America." In *Innovations in Effective Compassion: Compendium of Research*

Papers, edited by Pamela Joshi, Stephanie Hawkins, and Jeffrey Novey. Washington: U.S. Department of Health and Human Services Office of the Assistant Secretary for Planning and Evaluation, The Center for Faith-Based and Community Initiatives. Available at: http://aspe.hhs.gov/fbci/comp08; accessed July 10, 2010.

———. 2009a. *Out of Reach: Place, Poverty, and the New American Welfare State.* New Haven, Conn.: Yale University Press.

———. 2009b. "State Dollars, Nonstate Support: The Complexity of Local Nonprofit Welfare Provision in the United States." Paper presented at the Politics of Non-State Social Welfare Provision conference. Harvard Academy for International and Area Studies, Harvard University (May 8–9).

———. 2009c. "Mismatches and Unmet Needs: Access to Social Services in Urban and Rural America." In *Welfare Reform and Its Long-Term Consequence for America's Poor,* edited by James P. Ziliak. Cambridge: Cambridge University Press.

———. 2009d. "Place, Race, and Access to the Safety Net." In *Colors of Poverty,* edited by Ann Chih Lin and David Harris. New York: Russell Sage Foundation.

Allard, Scott W., and Jessica Cigna. 2008. "Access to Social Services in Rural America: The Geography of the Safety Net in the Rural West." Rural Poverty Research Center working paper no. 08-01. Available at: www.rupri.org/Forms/WP08-01.pdf; accessed July 11, 2010.

Allard, Scott W. and Benjamin Roth. 2010. "Suburbs in Need: Rising Suburban Poverty and Challenges for the Safety Net." Brookings Institution, Metropolitan Policy Program working paper.

Allard, Scott W., and Steven Rathgeb Smith. 2009. "Medicaid and the Funding of Nonprofit Service Organizations." Paper presented at the American Political Science Association Meetings. Toronto (September 3–6).

Berry, Jeffrey M., and David F. Arons. 2003. *A Voice for Nonprofits.* Washington, D.C.: Brookings Institution Press.

Blank, Rebecca. 1997. *It Takes a Nation.* Princeton, N.J.: Princeton University Press.

Bos, Hans, Greg J. Duncan, Lisa A. Gennetian, Heather D. Hill. 2007. "New Hope: Fulfilling America's Promise to 'Make Work Pay'." Discussion paper 2007-16. Washington, D.C.: Brookings Institution, Hamilton Project.

Campbell, David. 2002. "Beyond Charitable Choice: The Diverse Service Delivery Approaches of Local Faith-Related Organizations." *Nonprofit and Voluntary Sector Quarterly* 31(2): 207–30.

Cara Program. 2008. "Our Community: Annual Report." Available at: www.the caraprogram.org/annualreport/TCP_Annual%20Report%202008.pdf; accessed July 11, 2010.

Carlson-Thies, Stanley. 2004. "Implementing the Faith-Based Initiative." *Public Interest* 155(spring): 57–74.

Center on Budget and Policy Priorities. 2010. "Policy Basics: Introduction to the Food Stamp Program." Available at: www.cbpp.org/files/policybasics-foodstamps.pdf; accessed July 11, 2010.

Chaves, Mark, and William Tsitsos, 2001. "Congregations and Social Services: What They Do, How They Do It, and With Whom." *Nonprofit and Voluntary Sector Quarterly* 30(4): 660–83.

Coll, Blanche D. 1995. *The Safety Net*. New Brunswick, N.J.: Rutgers University Press.

Community Wealth Ventures. 2008. "Social Enterprise: A Portrait of the Field." Available at: www.communitywealth.com/pdf-doc/Field%20Study%20 FINAL.pdf; accessed July 11, 2010.

Congressional Research Service. 2003. *Cash and Noncash Benefits for Persons with Limited Income: Eligibility Rules, Recipient and Expenditure Data, FY2000–FY2002*. Report no. RL32233.

Florida Department of Children and Family. 2010. "ACCESS Florida Food, Medical Assistance and Cash." Washington, D.C.: Congressional Research Service. Available at: www.dcf.state.fl.us/programs/access; accessed July 11, 2010.

Gais, Thomas, Lucy Dadayan, and Suho Bae. 2009. "The Decline of States in Financing the U.S. Safety Net: Retrenchment in State and Local Social Welfare Spending, 1977–2007." Albany, N.Y.: Nelson A. Rockefeller Institute of Government.

Graddy, Elizabeth A. 2006. "How Do They Fit? Assessing the Role of Faith-Based Organizations in Social Service Provision." *Journal of Religion and Spirituality in Social Work* 25(3–4): 129–50.

Greenberg, Anna. 2000. "Doing Whose Work? Faith-Based Organizations and Government Partnerships." In *Who Will Provide? The Changing Role of Religion in American Social Welfare*, edited by Mary Jo Bane, Brent Coffin, and Ronald Thiemann. Boulder, Colo.: Westview Press.

Grønbjerg, Kirsten A. 2001. "The U.S. Nonprofit Human Service Sector: A Creeping Revolution." *Nonprofit and Voluntary Sector Quarterly* 30(2): 276–97.

Grønbjerg, Kirsten A., and Laurie Paarlberg. 2001. "Community Variations in the Size and Scope of the Nonprofit Sector: Theory and Preliminary Findings." *Nonprofit and Voluntary Sector Quarterly* 30(4): 684–706.

Illinois Department of Human Services. 2009. "Express Stamps Demonstration Project Expansion." Available at: www.dhs.state.il.us/page.aspx?item= 26333#a_toc3; accessed on July 11, 2010.

Johnson, Nicholas, Iris J. Lav, and Rose Ribeiro. 2003. "States Are Making Deep Budget Cuts in Response to the Fiscal Crisis." Center on Budget and Policy Priorities. Available at: www.cbpp.org/3–19–03sfp.htm; accessed on July 11, 2010.

Johnson, Nicholas, Phil Oliff, and Erica Williams. 2010. "An Update on State Budget Cuts." Washington, D.C.: Center on Budget and Policy Priorities.

Kissane, Rebecca Joyce. 2010. " 'We Call It the Badlands': How Social-Spatial Geographies Influence Social Service Use." *Social Service Review* 84(1): 3–28.

Kneebone, Elizabeth. 2009. "Economic Recovery and the EITC: Expanding the Earned Income Tax Credit to Benefit Families and Places." Washington, D.C.: Brookings Institution, Metropolitan Policy Program.

Kneebone, Elizabeth, and Emily Garr. 2010. "The Suburbanization of Poverty: Trends in Metropolitan America, 2000 to 2008." Washington, D.C.: Brookings Institution, Metropolitan Policy Program.

Mabli, James, Rhoda Cohen, Frank Potter, and Zhanyun Zhao. 2010. "Hunger in America 2010: National Report Prepared for Feeding America." Washington, D.C.: Mathematica Policy Research, Inc.

McNichol, Elizabeth, and Nicholas Johnson. 2010. "Recession Continues to Batter State Budgets; State Responses Could Slow Recovery." Washington, D.C.: Center on Budget and Policy Priorities.

Mosley, Jennifer E., Hagai Katz, Yeheskel Hasenfeld, and Helmut A. Anheier. 2003. "The Challenge of Meeting Social Needs in Los Angeles: Nonprofit Human Service Organizations in a Diverse Community." Los Angeles: UCLA, School of Public Policy and Social Research, Center for Civil Society. Available at: www.spa.ucla.edu/ccs/docs/challenge.pdf; accessed July 11, 2010.

Nonprofit Finance Fund. 2010. "2010 State of the Sector Survey." Available at: www.nonprofitfinancefund.org/docs/2010/2010SurveyResults.pdf; accessed July 11, 2010.

Owens, Michael Leo, and R. Drew Smith. 2005. "Congregations in Low-Income Neighborhoods and the Implications for Social Welfare Policy Research." *Nonprofit and Voluntary Sector Quarterly* 34(3): 316–39.

Peck, Laura R. 2008. "Do Anti-Poverty Nonprofits Locate Where People Need Them? Evidence from a Spatial Analysis of Phoenix." *Nonprofit and Voluntary Sector Quarterly.* 37(1): 138–51.

Pennucci, Annie, Corey Nunlist, and Jim Mayfield. 2009. "General Assistance Programs for Unemployable Adults." Olympia: Washington State Institute for Public Policy.

Peterson, Paul E. 1981. *City Limits.* Chicago: University of Chicago Press.

Salamon, Lester M. 1999. *America's Nonprofit Sector.* New York: Foundation Center.

———. 2003. "The Resilient Sector: The State of Nonprofit AMERICA." In *The State of Nonprofit America*, edited by Lester M. Salamon. Washington, D.C.: Brookings Institution Press.

Scholz, John Karl, and Kara Levine. 2001. "The Evolution of Income Support Policy in Recent Decades." In *Understanding Poverty*, edited by Sheldon H. Danziger and Robert H. Haveman. New York: Russell Sage Foundation.

Smith, Steven Rathgeb. 2007. "Comparative Case Studies of Faith-Based and Secular Service Agencies: An Overview and Synthesis of Key Findings."

In *A Comparative View of the Role and Effect of Faith in Social Services*, edited by Steven Rathgeb Smith, John P. Bartkowski, and Susan Grettenberger. New York: Rockefeller Institute of Government, Roundtable on Religion and Social Welfare Policy.

———. 2010. "Social Services." In *The State of Nonprofit America*, edited by Lester M. Salamon. 2d edition. Washington, D.C.: Brookings Institution Press.

Smith, Steven Rathgeb, and Michael Lipsky. 1993. *Nonprofits for Hire.* Cambridge, Mass.: Harvard University Press.

Smith, Steven Rathgeb, and Michael R. Sosin. 2001. "The Varieties of Faith-Related Agencies." *Public Administration Review* 61(6): 651–70.

U.S. Department of Health and Human Services. 2009. "TANF Financial Data." Available at: www.acf.hhs.gov/programs/ofs/data/index.html, see link for FY 2009; accessed July 11, 2010.

U.S. Department of Labor, Bureau of Labor Statistics. 2010a. "Employment Status of the Civilian Population 25 Years and Over by Educational Attainment." Available at: www.bls.gov/news.release/empsit.t04.htm; accessed July 27, 2010.

———. 2010b. "College Enrollment and Work Activity of 2009 High School Graduates." Available at: www.bls.gov/news.release/hsgec.nr0.htm; accessed July 27, 2010.

———. 2010c. "The Employment Situation—April 2010." Available at: www.bls.gov/news.release/archives/empsit_05072010.htm; accessed July 27, 2010.

White House. 2009. "Poverty: Progress." Available at: www.whitehouse.gov/agenda/poverty; accessed July 11, 2010.

Williams, Erica, Nicholas Johnson, and Jon Shure. 2009. "State Earned Income Tax Credits: 2009 Legislative Update." Washington, D.C.: Center on Budget and Policy Priorities.

Zuberi, Anita. Forthcoming. "Limited Exposure: Children's Activities and Neighborhood Effects in the Gautreaux Two Housing Mobility Program." *Journal of Urban Affairs.*

CHAPTER 8

RECONSTITUTING THE SAFETY NET:
NEW PRINCIPLES AND DESIGN ELEMENTS
TO BETTER SUPPORT LOW-INCOME WORKERS

JODI R. SANDFORT

As the introductory chapter of this volume describes, the current social welfare system of the United States evolved incrementally, as policymakers built upon the foundation of the Social Security Act. While public social benefits such as Medicaid and Supplemental Security Income developed because of changing economic and demographic conditions, fundamental issues in the social welfare arena were not reconsidered. Other chapters in this volume discuss why new policy options, such as asset development or labor-market enhancements, are now necessary, and they explore how to accomplish more deep-seated change. In this chapter, I take a different course. I hold constant the policy options and instead focus on the actual operation of the social welfare system. How could a system be designed that actually aligns with the new policy goals of "making work pay" for low-income citizens?

In the mid-1990s, when the United States eliminated an entitlement to public assistance, public policy goals shifted from "income support" to "work support." Current service delivery arrangements remain largely untouched. Cash and near cash benefits, such as tax credits or food support, employment services, and other social services, continue to be delivered through systems built for another era. As Scott W. Allard (this volume, chapter 7) notes, nonprofit organizations play a critically important role in the safety net. Yet public management approaches do not capitalize on their resources. There are new ideas and approaches that could be applied to redesign these systems and work more effectively with networks of public and private organizations (Goldsmith and Eggers 2004; Sandfort and Milward 2008). In this chapter, I consider how such an approach, if carried out purposively, could actually reconstitute the safety net for low-income workers.

I begin by describing current service delivery structures used for implementing cash assistance, work support and other social services for the poor, paying particular attention to the assumptions underpinning these administrative arrangements. As Scott Allard (this volume) describes, these arrangements do not constitute a true system at all. Rather, they are fragmented gestures that actually place additional burdens upon low-income citizens rather than ameliorating them. To develop new principles that guide design, I rely upon backwards mapping analysis. This approach considers how systems can be oriented to maximize the impact of policy where frontline staff and citizens interact. It differs markedly from the assumptions of performance contracting that have shaped much administrative reform in the last fifteen years (Fredrickson and Fredrickson 2007; Heinrich and Choi 2007; Moynihan 2008). Rather than seeing government as merely an issuer of contracts for service, this analysis highlights that government can play an essential role improving the capacities of private organizations and public-private partnerships. Purposive public investment can both create and leverage network-wide resources that are currently underused. Certainly it is neither feasible nor desirable to "wipe the slate clean" and begin anew, but it is necessary to explore options for systems redesign.

The current economic environment and long-term fiscal constraints facing the United States increase the urgency of this task. Public resources are even more limited than in the past. The needs of citizens are considerable. System inefficiencies arising from outdated assumptions and administrative practices are inexcusable. System ineffectiveness because of narrow conceptions of what is scalable cannot be allowed. We must think carefully about system design to help reform our social-welfare system to thrive in the new realities of the twenty-first century. This chapter begins such a discussion.

CURRENT SERVICE STRUCTURES

Scholars and social-welfare advocates within the United States often draw upon the "safety net" as a metaphor for public policies and service delivery arrangement supporting the poor. While scholars decry the holes in this "net" (Albelda and Withorn 2002; Cloward and Piven 1971; Ehrenreich 2002), the metaphor itself conjures up images of a coherent set of policies and aligned services designed to catch disadvantaged citizens during a crisis. It implies elements that operate as an integrated whole. Yet we are far from that reality. Though Jacob S. Hacker (this volume, chapter 2) describes what he calls the Great Risk Shift in the balance of risk over the last thirty years, it is fair to say that in terms of daily operations, no coherent social-welfare system—no real safety net—has ever really existed in the United States.

As the introductory essay of this volume points out, the 1935 Social Security Act established a foundation for social-welfare system policy and service provision that was incrementally modified throughout the twentieth century. Some changes enhanced the initial premise of the act, such as bringing income support to disabled adults or extending benefits to needy parents. Others tried to deal with emerging issues, such as changes in family structure, increased volatility of labor markets, and the severing of social benefits such as health care from employment. Fundamentally, though, these policies were shaped by a deep ambivalence about the role of government in ameliorating poverty and income inequality (Gordon 1994; Katz 1986; Lemann 1988; Patterson 2000; Soss 2002; Stone 2008). Historians point to a distinction made between the "deserving" and "undeserving" poor (Gordon 1994; Gordon 2002; Katz 1986; Patterson 1986; Skocpol 1992) that became deeply embedded in both policy and its administration. Old Age, Survivors, and Disabilities Insurance—the official name for Social Security—was available for those worthy of support, poor through no fault of their own. The federal government assumed administrative responsibility and crafted program rules and procedures to assure accessibility and efficiency. In contrast, cash welfare for single mothers or transient men was shaped in relation to a presumption of unworthiness. States and counties assumed administrative responsibility for these programs, with considerable variation in policy and practice resulting.

While some federal and state public organizations were involved, other policies depended heavily on nonprofit agencies for implementation (Smith and Lipsky 1993; Allard 2009). Over the last century, social-welfare system policy created a maze of administrative systems. As Allard (this volume, chapter 7) reports, tens of thousands of unique local "safety nets" now exist, created by the incremental adoption of policies, each responding to particular problems, depending upon new institutions and different administrative tools (Salamon 2002). Some policy arenas are governed by public entities. In others, policy created boards of public, nonprofit, and business elites to govern. In some cases, public bureaucracies are the main service delivery infrastructure, whereas in others the public sector benefited from nonprofit expertise. Each policy created its own implementation structure (Hjern and Porter 1981), often guided by the administrative assumption of the need to curb citizen demand in light of inadequate resources. To understand fully the resulting complexity and how it inhibits our abilities to create a vibrant social-welfare system that can meet the challenge of new social realities, let us consider the current implementation structures being used in various programs for low-income citizens.

Variation Among Implementation Structures

When thinking of the safety net, many people conventionally focus on a set of policies that provide cash or near-cash support to low-income citizens. Some of these policies, such as Temporary Assistance for Needy Families (TANF), provide direct cash transfers on a time-limited basis. Others provide subsidies for particular goods, such as food, medical care, or child care. In these sets of policies, public bureaucracies are the main institutions administering public benefit. For a few programs, such as Medicaid and Supplemental Nutrition Assistance Program (formerly the Food Stamp Program), federal rules shape much of program administration. Significant administrative authority rests with state governments for distributing cash assistance and child-care subsidies. In some instances states devolve such responsibility to county governments. Thus, even though these programs are implemented by public organizations, there is considerable variation in policy and practice between the states (Adams, Snyder, and Sandfort 2002; Ewalt and Jennings 2004; Soss et al. 2001). Throughout, the dominant administrative assumption is of top-down control and written rules, focused on assuring fair eligibility assessment (Brodkin 1986; Meyers, Glaser, and MacDonald 1998; Sandfort 2000). Benefits are targeted to those in extreme destitution. As a result, eligibility determination for many programs occurs through face-to-face interviews, where citizens must provide documentation of their conditions to access support. Although policy changes have encouraged people to work and to see cash and other assistance as work-supports, administrative practice of these programs still often necessitates that clients take time from their jobs or family responsibilities to secure and maintain benefits.

Many other public policies targeted to low-income citizens are implemented through other partnerships forged between government and nonprofit service providers. For example, a national network of nonprofit Community Action agencies operates many federal programs, such as Head Start (which provides early education enrichment and family support to very low-income children), Low Income Home Energy Assistance, and Weatherization Assistance. State governments work with this network to implement different initiatives for low-income citizens, such as surplus food distribution, Individual Development Accounts, and volunteer mobilization. These nonprofits were established during the 1960s' federal War on Poverty and as a result operate in both remote rural and urban regions designated by the government (Clark 2000). Although many respond to local needs and in many rural areas have become the largest nonprofit human service agency, federal and state governments are their dominant funders. Like the public bureaucracy, their administration is guided by top-down rules within government-defined service areas.

A second, parallel service delivery infrastructure in which government and nonprofits partner is in workforce development. Michael A. Stoll (this volume, chapter 3) discusses the federal and state public policies that fund training, job placement, on-the-job training, and work retention. The incremental nature of policy adoption in this field has created a dizzying array of programs and administrative authorities. Six federal agencies, as well as many state-level departments (Rubinstein and Mayo 2007), administer these public programs. For example, a Minnesota inventory identifies seventy-one public programs, each administered by sixteen state and federal agencies.[1] These public agencies in turn work through community or technical colleges, private for-profit firms, and nonprofit agencies to deliver actual training and workforce development services. The federal Workforce Development Act of 1998 attempted to increase coordination, emphasizing one-stop service provision, state-level governance bodies, and local governing Workforce Investment Boards (WIBs). Like Community Action, local WIBs operate within officially designated geographic areas where they are responsible for providing an access point for all federal programs (Herranz 2008). Yet because of more robust state funding and private-sector workforce initiatives in this field, federal mandates have limited consequences in some states.

In addition to financial subsidies and employment, federal and state governments increasingly use tax expenditures to reward work (Dickert-Conlin,

Fitzpatrick, and Hanson 2005; Garfinkel 1990). Significant expansion has come in the last fifteen years through the Earned Income Tax Credit (EITC) and similar state-level benefits. An appealing aspect of this government tool is its seeming lack of administrative apparatus because eligibility is assessed through annual income tax preparation (McDaniel 2002). Because the process of tax filing can be daunting, particularly for low-income people with limited English or education, private nonprofits leverage volunteers to assist in tax preparation through grants from the federal Internal Revenue Service (and, in some instances, state governments).

In many of these examples, nonprofits were created because of the adoption of top-down public policies (Smith and Lipsky 1993). Yet settlement houses, mutual aid associations, and other community-based organizations also long have served low-income citizens. These organizations use charitable contributions to offer clothing, child care, and emergency shelter. They run food banks and English classes (Cordes and Henig 2001; Hasenfeld and Powell 2004; Fabricant and Fisher 2002). As Allard (this volume, chapter 7) describes, these organizations have become significant forces in the public social-welfare system infrastructure. State and local government departments contract with them for culturally specific programs, chemical dependency treatment, mental health, and enhanced case management for multiproblem clients. Other nonprofit specialist organizations also compete for such contracts and all are evaluated according to specific terms of performance. Administratively, it is assumed that competition among such private agencies leads to great efficiencies and higher-quality services, although this assumption is not backed up with much empirical evidence (Bickers 2007; Heinrich and Choi 2007; Van Slyke 2003). This belief often limits consideration of ways in which public investment could help improve how such agencies work with low-income citizens.

These various implementation structures emerged as institutions and networks were asked to carry out the policies adopted incrementally over the last century. Through various small and large public management decisions, society has created a mass of administrative systems ostensibly focused on supporting low-income workers. Many assumptions underpinning these arrangements align with federal or state policymakers' perspectives. From that vantage point there is a substantive distinction between cash assistance, Medicaid, Energy Assistance, Head Start, employment training, and tax assistance. Considerable technical details must be adhered to regarding eligibility and program access; mastery of such details requires specialization. Yet, as this brief overview highlights, the specialization can create a maze of programs, each with different entry points and accountabilities. There is no coherent system but rather an amalgam of policy gestures, each focused on slightly different ends.

Consequences of Administrative Complexity at the Frontlines

The top-down categorical orientation of many of these arrangements creates significant consequences: at the public-sector frontline, in nonprofit agencies, and for citizens. Many of these consequences are hidden from common view. Privatization has stripped many previous functions from public agencies. From the vantage point of public workers, a daunting maze of nonprofit organizations exists, some with contracts for employment services, others for housing, still others that provide transitional housing, fuel assistance, emergency food, early-childhood services, or ethnically based services. Frontline staff's knowledge of these agencies often emerges from experience, making phone calls, and perusing available brochures (Sandfort 1999).

Nonprofit service organizations experience the complexity in a different way. Many receive funding from state, county, and city governments, and from more than one department within each level. Each funder has its own grant and contracting application, proposal or bidding processes, negotiation terms, and accountability requirements (Grønbjerg 1993; Smith 2005). Because payment processes also vary, nonprofits develop funding strategies contingent upon the practices of their public funders. Staff working directly with clients must know the range of available community resources. Like the public welfare workers, the ability to locate the resources requires very specific, technical knowledge because of the particularity of local arrangements.

In day-to-day operations, staff in public organizations and private agencies must deal with these consequences as they interact with low-income citizens. The lack of systematic design often serves to create the tasks that are their daily work. They complete and process applications, make service referrals, and document results for categorical funding sources. What can get lost amid this activity is a focus on the ultimate goals of public policy. It is not that organizations are not well versed in tracking various program outputs; most grants or contracts from funders carry requirements to document performance. However, the very structure of service arrangements obscures the real goal: the cumulative effect of these many investments. Are low-income Americans able to navigate the labor market and adequately support their families?

The consequences of current arrangements naturally are felt most acutely by low-income citizens (Soss 2002; Rank 1994). Think for a moment of a low-income mother. She might be working two jobs to make ends meet, shuttling a toddler back and forth to day care on a city bus, sharing an apartment with a friend. How does she navigate the current service arrangements? Or consider a middle-aged couple whose grown children repeatedly come to stay with them when experiencing transitions in their own lives. The couple's history of retail work doesn't provide them a solid asset base or any access to health insurance, which, as they age, is increasingly important. What type of safety net can they access?

When either family seeks assistance from the public bureaucracy, it currently confronts distinct applications for health insurance, nutrition assistance, and child-care subsidies. The same is true if it inquires about employment training opportunities, assistance with energy costs, or transitional housing in local nonprofits. Each program has unique eligibility criteria and documentation requirements. Oftentimes they must be accessed through different agencies. Dealing with the daily operations of these systems actually make it difficult to maintain a job. To find applications for "work supports" and attend eligibility interviews and benefit redetermination meetings, citizens must take time from work and family. Time spent navigating the local service bureaucracy is time not focused on building employment skills or caring for family issues.

To support low-income citizens so that they can work and improve their circumstances, we need to redesign these current arrangements. We need to realize the essential role private nonprofits play at various levels of government as partners in public service provision (Salamon 1995). We need to invest in structures that capitalize on technical expertise, embrace a new public-sector role, and use new information technology resources. In short, we need to reconstitute the safety net so that it supports low-income, working Americans with the tools of the twenty-first century. To do so, we must first articulate principles to guide investment in the redesign of such a system.

USING BACKWARD MAPPING TO GENERATE DESIGN PRINCIPLES

To guide such a redesign, it is helpful to articulate new principles to focus our reconstruction of the system. An analytical tool called "backward mapping," developed many years ago by Richard Elmore (1979), is helpful. Backward mapping involves focusing not on the incremental adoption of work-support policies and programs and the top-down administrative logic that supports them, but on the interactions of frontline workers and citizens to provide beacons to orient system redesign. Considerable research stresses the significance of such frontline interactions in cash assistance and social-welfare system provision (Brodkin 1986; Cooney 2007; Hasenfeld 1992; Meyers, Glaser and MacDonald 1998; Sandfort 2000).

Our analysis starts by examining the specific behavior that generates the need for policy intervention. In this case, citizens earning at or near the minimum wage face considerable job instability. Conditions are challenging; job cycling and lay-offs are common (Blank, Danziger, and Schoeni 2006; Cancian et al. 2002; Ehrenreich 2002). Without intervention, former welfare recipients and other low-income workers' earnings remain low over the long term (Cancian et al. 2002; Zedlewski, Chaudry, and Simms 2008). Few low-income jobs provide benefits—neither health nor dental, nor retirement savings. Yet these workers struggle with a high incidence of physical and mental health problems, as well as challenging health issues within their families that often inhibit their ability to retain work (Powers 2003; Siefert et al. 2004). Many struggle with the high costs of dependent care for their children and aging parents. Employment alone does not address these challenges. While public policies and programming do exist to help with some of these issues, significant percentages of eligible families do not access public programs (Zedlewski, Chaudry, and Simms 2008).

These realities generate the need for public policy intervention. Backward mapping analysis begins by considering the desired qualities at the frontline of a system. What interactions should citizens experience from publicly funded agencies so that their employment efforts are supported and they are able to manage their family issues? What interactions would enable them to pursue other opportunities? Think about our single mother working two jobs with a toddler, the middle-aged couple who for years have worked at retail jobs that don't provide benefits, even though they are increasingly a base of support for their extended family. What interactions would support their work efforts and allow them to access public resources for which they are eligible?

In thinking through these questions, four reasonable design principles emerge, which meet both the objective of public systems and citizens' needs.

1. *Fair application of policy.* Work-support benefits need to be targeted to individual circumstances as delineated in public policy. Eligibility criteria need to be met and benefits distributed in a fair manner so that they reach groups for which they are targeted.

2. *Accessible services.* At the margins of the labor market, job hours rarely adhere to the conventional nine-to-five schedule. Consequently, pub-

licly funded programs must be accessible at various times of the day and have a range of access points. Information about public benefits should be communicated clearly for citizens with a wide range of abilities and languages. Application processes should be user-friendly.

3. *Appropriate matching of need to support and services.* The specifics of people's lives vary, and the need for work supports differs. When people are asked to reveal personal information to public systems, the process can be eased significantly if frontline staff and citizens speak the same language and share cultural references. It might be difficult in some locations to accommodate the diversity of all client populations, yet attention to small details often can ease relations tremendously.

4. *Reliable information to aid decisionmaking.* In the new economy, information is plentiful, even overwhelming. Sources that provide consistent information and resources that help people answer the most pressing and persistent problems they face are priceless. Such resources allow people to develop options when they must respond to the unexpected.

Such principles are logical. Consistent implementation of them would assist, rather than hinder, citizens' efforts to navigate the dynamics of the low-wage labor market. They are, in Elmore's notion, characteristics of frontline interaction inadequately supported by current administrative assumptions and arrangements in social-welfare system delivery. Because analysis based on backward mapping starts from frontline conditions, it challenges system designers to move out of a top-down analytical framework. Instead, the analytical challenge becomes to design systems that support interactions between frontline staff and citizens and embody these principles. They also act as dimensions of performance measurement that help to define implementation effectiveness. Given the inherent limitation of public resources, our design also must consider how to use the tools of the twenty-first century such as networks, information infrastructures, and new approaches to public governance.

ELEMENTS IN NEW SYSTEM DESIGN

Current social-welfare system administration was designed top-down: static structures were developed incrementally from policy parameters. Backward mapping pushes us in the opposite direction. Analytically applying this tool focuses our attention on considering how, at each level of the bureaucracy or service network, managers could create incentives to achieve the desired frontline interactions.

It is more feasible to envision state-level administrative reform than a national-level design, yet because of state variation, it is not possible to definitively identify policy programs to include in system redesign. Some states might be poised to include the full range of cash and near-cash benefits, such as Temporary Assistance for Needy Families, Supplemental Nutrition Assistance, Low-Income Home Energy Assistance, Individual Development Accounts, various employment and training programs, early-childhood education efforts, and emergency food support. Others might focus on a narrower programmatic band. Yet each state faces some choices of how to proceed. In all situations, there are specific design elements that can be defined. If the focus is on elements rather than particular structures, networks that take advantage of particular local and state resources can be developed. Such network systems can evolve to respond to future conditions (Goldsmith and Eggers 2004).

The specific institutions involved in a reconstituted safety net also will likely take different forms. In some states there are rich networks of neighborhood organizations with deep historical roots that will be important elements in the system redesign. In others, Community Action agencies, established originally by government, might be the main direct service providers. Intermediary agencies with sophisticated technical skills that package public and private resources already exist in some places. Their expertise would need to be applied more broadly or gaps filled in other states. New statewide systems will need strong public governance to assure accountability to citizens. Depending upon the context, governance authority could rest within a state agency, in a governor's office, or a quasi-public entity that is a public-private partnership. In any particular state, all of the elements must be held together through formal networks and clearly defined responsibilities.

Table 8.1 summarizes the system design elements of direct service providers, intermediaries, and public governance. Direct service providers work directly with families. They are the ones whose practice must align most closely with our backward mapping principles, and their work is crucial to a high-functioning system. However, they can only provide that level of service if they have adequate technical and information resources from elsewhere in the network.

Intermediary organizations, public or private, can provide such support. Their role is packaging concrete resources and essential technical knowledge for the network: financial, program, organizational resources, network capital, and policy awareness. These "implementation resources" (Hill 2003) can improve effectiveness and efficiency within the whole system.

TABLE 8.1   Design Elements Needed to Reconstitute the Safety Net

Design Element	Roles	Promising Examples
Direct service providers	Work to ensure that basic principles of service delivery are achieved: • Fair application of policy • Accessible services • Appropriate matching of service to need • Reliable information	• Multiservice organizations • "Centers for Working Families" • Enhanced case management through information systems
Intermediary agencies	Work to increase the efficient sharing of resources within the network around the following: • Financial resources • Program capacity • Organizational capacity • Network capital • Policy understanding	• Joint fund development for public and private sources • Tools and technical assistance for direct service • Facilitated peer learning • Advocacy training; fiscal and social analysis
Public governance	Work as systemwide guardian to achieve public intent (enable workers to navigate and thrive in low-wage labor market): • Fair eligibility determination • Design and integrate network • Guard against private-interest capture • Monitor systemwide results	• Electronic application and eligibility verification

Source: Author's compilation.

Finally, public governance must act as a neutral guardian to ensure that the system remains focused on public rather than private goals. Public agencies must ensure that eligibility for public programs is assessed fairly and assume responsibility for systemwide design and integration. Each system element has unique roles and core competencies upon which the others depend. Let's examine each in turn, and consider promising current examples being used throughout the country to support low-income workers that also are consistent with our system design principles.

Direct Service Providers

Direct service organizations provide assistance and support to low-income citizens. They are essential because of their particular knowledge of community resources, client circumstances, and local labor-market dynamics. With this knowledge, staff can work to embody the backward mapping principles, providing services that are fair, accessible, appropriate, and reliable for their clients. Trusted resources can be invaluable to low-income citizens, who can make use of help in strategizing how to navigate the inevitable challenges that arise when one is trying to balance competing demands among work, life, and family responsibilities. Seasoned staff recognize the morality inherent in direct service work (Hasenfeld 2010) and know that trust must be earned through quality relationships. Oftentimes service effectiveness hinges on frontline staffs' ability to work with clients to achieve small wins that over the longer term add up to something more significant (Herr, Halpern, and Wagner 1995). To be supported in such activities, staff and supervisors need organizational reinforcement that enables access to resources, tools, and information that can be customized to respond to particular needs. They also must be managed in ways that incentivize and reward responsive practice. Without this intentionality, frontline staff respond to the dissonance between what the needs of the people and the design of policy with actions inconsistent with policy intent (Maynard-Moody and Musheno 2003; Sandfort 2000).

Many organizational settings could support effective practice. Some nonprofit organizations operate in service niches, such as employment training or early-childhood education, that provide such client-centered programming. Faith-based organizations may bring in unique values that might be particularly important to families struggling at the edge of the economy. Long-standing organizations, such as settlement houses and mutual assistance associations, try to work holistically with low-income families by offering many services in one place. In spite of these strengths, too often such organizations do not feel that client-centered practice is reinforced by systems dynamics; pressures pull them in other directions, such as those mandated by private funders or public authorities (Fabricant and Fisher 2002; Jennings 2002).

There are exceptional leaders at the frontlines of current social-welfare system delivery who try to overcome strictures that currently accompany the categorical nature of funding, narrow eligibility requirements, and pressures to document outputs rather than more large-scale results. A few current experiments are worth highlighting because they operate more in keeping with our desired frontline conditions. A national foundation is investing in "Centers for Working Families" in thirteen metropolitan areas, with others under development. Controlled social experiments also are happening in three local "Work Advancement and Support Centers."[2] At all these sites a broad range of employment, financial services, and income supports are combined, sequenced, and delivered to clients. Staff members help low-income workers stabilize income, access public work-support programs, and obtain fairly priced financial services by resolving credit problems. Eventually, they turn to building assets through matched savings accounts and other products.

Another model operates in rural North Carolina. Connect Inc. uses enhanced information systems to improve how staff members work directly with low-income citizens making the transition from public cash assistance to work.[3] Because it operates in rural areas and across large geographic areas, Connect Inc. developed computer software to enrich, automate, and track clients in ways not typical with traditional case management. By drawing on comprehensive databases and client management software, staff members access information about employment, transportation, child care, and other services across the region. They regularly participate in three-way calls with the client to facilitate access to work-support resources and to role-model how to effectively navigate complex situations.

Flexible philanthropic dollars and, increasingly, public funds support these direct service efforts. They are bolstered with information systems that integrate across the silos of current service arrangements. They build upon the unique role that community-based organizations can play in helping single parents who are confronted with unstable employment and limited social support. Because of their unique contextual knowledge of places, direct service organizations can tap and build upon local resources. Although program evaluation of these specific innovations is ongoing, their promise is that they can deliver more accessible, appropriate, and reliable information and service to low-income citizens. Such improvements, though, require new types of investments: intermediary organizations that help facilitate these changes and support them at the frontlines.

Intermediary Organizations

Intermediary organizations are a second design element in a more coherent system geared to the new realities of low-income workers.[4] Intermediaries operate in many substantive areas. They garner information and resources to decrease transaction costs between two parties—in this case, direct service providers and the state—thereby increasing operational efficiencies and program effectiveness. Intermediaries "build capacity" of service agencies by buffering them from environmental turbulence, providing access to new sources of financing, offering program tools, bolstering management support, creating networks among similar organizations, and cultivating policy knowledge (see table 8.1). They also provide information to public decisionmakers about the successes and challenges of policy implementation visible from frontline agencies. Intermediaries are one administrative tool for enhancing systems' capacity in a context where neither pure markets nor public provision operate effectively.

Although not yet widely used for safety-net programs, intermediaries play important roles in fields such as mental health, community economic development, and affordable housing. (See Paul Osterman, this volume, chapter 4, for a discussion of their roles in workforce development.) Much like social welfare, these three fields have all experienced significant policy changes in the thirty years since 1980. As a result, they needed to redesign service systems. Each depends upon various forms of government funding, including grants-in-aid, tax credits, contracts, and vouchers. Keith Provan and H. Brint Milward's (1994) research in Arizona highlights intermediary organizations that began managing networks of mental health providers after deinstitutionalization to create a continuum of care, which led to more positive outcomes for vulnerable citizens (Milward et al. 2010). In community economic development and housing, nonprofit community development corporations' work is bolstered by various intermediaries that package resources at a magnitude not possible by individual direct service agencies (Glickman and Servon 1999; Smith 2008; Walker 1993; Walker and Foster-Bey 2004). Initially, national philanthropic funders such as the Ford Foundation, Local Initiatives Support Corporation, and Enterprise Foundation seeded intermediaries' formation; now the public sector has come to depend upon them as essential partners in urban redevelopment and affordable housing construction.

Since welfare reform, some private foundations—most notably the Annie E. Casey Foundation—have funded intermediaries to bring new resources to direct service providers assisting low-income families. Their efforts reflect the new reality that in a decentralized social-welfare system, some parts of the system must focus on research, development, and improving implementation conditions to assure and improve service effectiveness. Many of these efforts currently are being evaluated, so no definitive conclusions can be drawn, but they offer some promising practices to consider. For example, Seedco, a national intermediary organization, developed an on-line benefits tool called *Earn*Benefits that allows frontline staff to help workers assess their eligibility for work-support benefits such as food support, health insurance, tax credits, and energy assistance.[5] Citizens can ascertain what the application process requires, get information about local access points, and manage administrative requirements so they can maintain benefits once they are secured. The intermediary works with local partners to customize the tool since public program eligibility, application processes, and community resources vary by state and locality. Intermediaries bring a level of technical expertise that enables the development of such tools, which can provide invaluable support to direct service providers.

Intermediaries also build program capacity by disseminating field-specific technical knowledge. In current service arrangements, many policies require staff to master significant technical details in order to implement them. For example, helping low-income citizens access tax credits requires technical knowledge about tax preparation, distinctions between state and federal rules, and electronic filing processes. Even though the Internal Revenue Service provides funding for nonprofits to run voluntary tax preparation sites, many multiservice agencies feel unable to take on this task because of the technical complexity. Intermediaries such as the Center for Economic Progress and Accountability Minnesota help such organizations recruit volunteers, offer certified training, and monitor results.[6] They also develop alternative financial products that can be offered to customers to help them experience mainstream financial services. In these ways the intermediaries provide technical assistance and strategic partnerships to bolster direct service providers' ability to offer services consistent with the principles of backward mapping. Many categorical public programs are quite technical; intermediary organizations can specialize in particular arenas and share this expertise with direct service organizations.

Intermediaries also can build networks and policy awareness among direct service organizations. This can occur in various ways, but all focus on convening people from different vantage points so they can share information and grapple with finding solutions to problems they have in common. For example, Seedco in New York City works through a subsidiary, the Nonprofit Assistance Corporation, which regularly convenes an alliance of sixteen direct service organizations that provide training and employment support. Through peer learning and formal training, valuable explicit and tacit knowledge is developed and shared across the network (Agranoff 2008; Argyris and Schon 1974). Such meetings also serve as learning venues for those operating at the system level, offering insight into how policy ideals manifest near the ground. Important "lessons from the field" and more nuanced understanding of the importance of cultural competence and neighborhoods improves the learning of the whole network. Such learning builds adaptive capacity of the whole system.

Another model is the Economic Analysis and Research Network, which operates at a more macro level. This network brings together statewide intermediaries in forty states who conduct and highlight policy analysis about issues disproportionately affecting low-income working families.[7] This information, accompanied by the state-level budget analysis conducted by many of these same organizations, is an important resource that local service providers can draw on to inform planning and to understand their own work within a larger policy context.

These examples point to potential roles intermediary organizations can play. Intermediaries can bolster financial resources, program capacity, organizational and management capacity, network capital, and policy awareness (see table 8.1 for a summary). Such activities allow decentralized networks to align around common aims. In the new reality, where government and nonprofits work together to implement and refine social-welfare system policies, such activities are essential to enabling the whole to operate as a coherent system.

Public Governance

To support practices consistent with the design principles, the reconstituted safety net must have an entity that serves as a neutral administrator, system designer, and monitor. These are the new key competencies of public governance. Unlike any other institutions, governments allow society to develop collective responses to "wicked problems" (Agranoff 2007; Milward et al. 2010). Public management has gone beyond old administrative assumptions grounded in bureaucratic authority and rules, and increasingly reflects the new reality that public and private organizations must sometimes work together in loosely coupled yet centrally governed networks. In other words, the role of the public sector can change from one being a service-providing *government* to one of providing *governance* within social welfare.

Many technical details would need to be worked out and many empirical tests of various models conducted if this vision of social-welfare system redesign is to be realized. Conceptually, public governance is the only mechanism that can viably walk states down such a path. Without public-sector intervention, neither current institutions nor market forces will create change. Public governance possesses unique authority to assure adherence to policy mandates, design and integrate implementation networks, and define and monitor system-level performance. Let's consider the possibilities of each and some examples of current experiments.

Public policy defines particular eligibility criteria for cash assistance, supplemental nutrition assistance, child-care subsidies, earned-income tax programs, and other social-welfare system programs. It would not be rational to pass responsibility for eligibility determination to intermediaries or private providers. Yet current administrative practices could be improved. In many states, state or county staff determine eligibility for cash and near-cash programs. Interacting with staff in local offices can create barriers for low-income citizens because conventional office hours require people to take time off from work, first come, first serve practices create long waits in reception areas, and frequent recertification paperwork is easily misplaced. Eligibility determination should be not only fair but also accessible, and the process should ensure that clients receive appropriate services. Some states—Utah is one—are centralizing eligibility determination and utilizing information technology systems to streamline processes. Applications are taken on-line for some programs, and application materials are electronically accessible in others. Staff use electronic information now readily available in other state agencies rather than requiring paper documentation of an applicant's wages, assets, and address. Many states use such approaches in other work-support programs, such as unemployment insurance. Making use of existing data can streamline service provision and decouple eligibility determination from face-to-face interactions.

Under public governance, managers are seeing their roles differently than they did under traditional public bureaucracies. Making progress on large public goals requires collaborative management through partnership with other organizations (Agranoff 2007; Klijn 2005; Milward et al. 2010; O'Toole, Meier, and Nicholson-Crotty 2005). In other fields, public managers are playing new roles, such as facilitators and system designers, to make this vision a reality (Blomgren and O'Leary 2008; Kickert, Klijn, and Koppenjan 1997; Crosby and Bryson 2005). Given the interests entrenched in current institutional arrangements, such public governance in social-welfare system provision will require real leadership. In light of the range of institutions and fields currently involved in income- and work-support programs, the purposive design of networks is essential (Agranoff 2007; Agranoff and McGuire 2003; Klijn 2005).

In this context, design involves rising above the details of the original legislative mandates, unique implementing institutions, and professional relationships that have become de facto state-level service arrangements. It requires thinking carefully about how to arrange design elements into a coherent system focused on buffering low-wage workers from the dynamics of the labor market. It requires taking risks—because no empirical evidence currently exists to guide design options. What are the most effective sites of direct services that support low-income workers in a particular state? Is a co-location or call center model more effective in reaching families in particular regions of the state? What intermediary organizations can provide resources to enhance the program, organizational, and network capacity of direct service organizations? How can these various nodes be linked through information systems to facilitate efficient and effective communication about benefits, community resources, or program innovations? How can linkages change as new situations arise? Although the specific answers to these design questions will vary by state, developing them is fundamental to effective public network operation.

Figure 8.1 offers a visual representation of a network design option incorporating all of the elements I have discussed.[8] This visual assumes that, like markets, public service delivery systems have a shared infrastructure of rules, institutions, and knowledge provided by an array of public and private organizations. Public leaders must recognize, hone, and further refine this infrastructure. The United Way, private foundations, and corporations already invest in infrastructure that serves low-income citizens, yet the critical linkages between them and other system components are often not made. Frontline service organizations have important knowledge that they have gained from their service delivery practice, knowledge that is often lost in the top-down and contracted-out administrative systems built in the last century. Systems that capitalize on frontline knowledge of local conditions will be able to operate more effectively to realize our backward mapping principles of citizen services. But systems also need to invest in that knowledge development through the purposive use of intermediaries and the establishment of robust information systems.

FIGURE 8.1   State-Level Network of Funding and
Other Implementation Resources

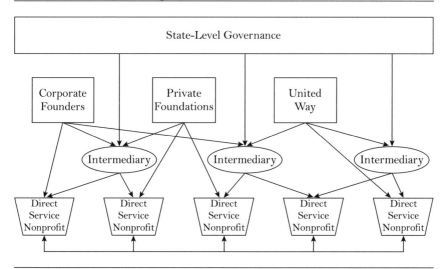

Source: Author's illustration.

A final role of public governance in a system reflecting the new realities is to ensure that citizens can access information about public investments and results. To do so, public leaders must help articulate enterprise-level outcomes or larger systemwide standards of performance. Current policy reflects multiple, and sometimes competing, goals: enhancing earnings from low-wage work, providing early-childhood education so parents can work, limiting access to cash assistance, limiting family size, providing emergency services, and mandating participation in the low-wage labor market. Even more minute performance measures structure the reporting requirements of the actual service providers. The contested nature of poverty reduction and incremental adoption of policies over time created this diversity. Political realities make it likely that such dynamics will continue, but public governance can guarantee that minute measures are not what drive the operation of the entire work-support system. Instead, governance can involve a public process toward clear, systemwide results that are articulated, measured, and used to make adjustments throughout the system.

These new roles for the public sector in social welfare are consistent with new realities. The public sector is no longer the hierarchical bureaucracy of twentieth-century government; it is using new decisionmaking processes, and its representatives are assuming new roles as integrators in many fields. Leadership is essential to reconstitute the system so that it focuses more clearly on helping low-wage workers navigate the dynamics of the labor market. Leaders will need to discover new ways to communicate and work with the private nonprofit, philanthropic, and business entities already involved in current service delivery arrangements. They will need to focus on designing, integrating, and assessing the performance of the actual networks used for policy implementation.

CONCLUDING THOUGHTS

Since the mid-nineties, the goals of the American welfare state have dramatically shifted. Although temporary assistance is available to very needy citizens, the focus of government intervention is on supplementing earnings from employment and providing employment and social services. Unfortunately, the infrastructure of public service delivery has not shifted to account for this new emphasis on supporting people as workers.

This chapter has described how current arrangements prevent low-income workers from efficiently accessing publicly funded programs designed to help them navigate the low-wage labor market, make ends meet for their families, or create opportunities for advancement. Yet these structures are outcomes of the decisions of our government. They are based on assumptions of the old era that distinguished between the deserving and undeserving poor, tried to limit citizen demand for public services, and embraced top-down approaches to public management. Twenty-first-century realities require us to consider how advances in systems design can realign the public welfare system so that it can more effectively achieve policy goals.

Backward mapping focuses our attention on the frontline experiences of citizens. From this vantage point, characteristics of high-quality service delivery become clear. Agencies must fairly assess eligibility for services. Services must be accessible to workers with inflexible work schedules and must be matched to particular family circumstances. Agencies should help people sift through the mass of information they encounter about work supports. Direct service organizations play an essential role in carrying out these visions, but their work must be supported by a network of resources. Intermediary organizations can provide some essential elements of support with their unique ability to package resources in ways not accessible to many direct service agencies. And public governance is needed to ensure proper design, alignment, and performance of the whole network.

The direction taken by many public systems' reform efforts seemed to suggest that the path to creating more effective services for citizen "customers" involved merely moving to performance contracting. This approach holds private non-profit and for-profit organizations accountable for particular results. I argue here that the nature of the problem at hand—responding to the challenges created for citizens by the realities of contemporary low-wage labor markets—requires more thoroughgoing change, particularly in the public funding of intermediaries and the development of stronger public governance. Crafting an effective social welfare system requires working in partnership with private service and intermediary organizations. Much of the redundancy, complex relationships, and categorical program silos that exist in current service arrangements were results of a lack of such system oversight. Although no state is currently operating a complete system as envisioned here, the examples provided throughout this chapter suggest that private funders and organizations are not waiting for the public to act; they are taking the initiative in making small experiments to reconstitute a safety net geared to the new reality of actual social needs. The government has a social imperative to promote opportunity and economic security for low-income citizens and to ensure the efficient operation of a social-welfare system that actually supports low-income workers so they are able to survive, thrive, and have opportunities for advancement.

NOTES

1. For more information on Minnesota's public programs for job seekers, see www.positivelyminnesota.com (accessed July 11, 2010), the website of the Minnesota Department of Employment and Economic Development.

2. Evaluation of the first initiative, sponsored by the Annie E. Casey Foundation, is being conducted by Abt Associates; preliminary assessment is due in late 2010. The second experiment is being done by Manpower Development Research Corporation. For more information see www.aecf.org/MajorInitiatives/FamilyEconomicSuccess/CentersforWorking Families.aspx; accessed July 12, 2010.

3. Northern Connections operates a similar model in west central Minnesota. For more information, see www.connectinc.org (North Carolina) and www.northernconnections.org/ (Minnesota).

4. In theories of the state, nonprofit organizations are sometimes conceptualized as "intermediary" institutions interfacing between citizens and government. The term also is used in various literatures to represent organizations carrying out dramatically different roles (Brown and Kalegaonkar 2002; Honig 2004). For conceptual clarity, I modify a framework developed by

Norman J. Glickman and Lisa J. Servon (1999, 2003) describing the roles of community economic development intermediaries that focus on building capacity in programs, organizations, networks, finances, and policy.

5. For more information about the initial learning of *Earn*Benefits see www.aecf.org/upload/PublicationFiles/FES3622H5026.pdf; accessed July 12, 2010. See Seedco's website: www.earnbenefits.org; accessed July 12, 2010. The Minnesota office of the Children's Defense Fund has developed a similar on-line tool, Bridges to Benefits, for use throughout Minnesota, the Dakotas, and Montana, at www.bridgetobenefits.org; accessed July 12, 2010.

6. Center for Economic Progress is the convener of the National Community Tax Coalition, www.centerforprogress.org, which also provides national training on free tax preparation. Accountability Minnesota is a statewide free tax preparation intermediary, www.accountabilitymn.org; both accessed July 12, 2010.

7. The Economic Analysis and Research Network is coordinated by the Economic Policy Institute; see www.earncentral.org; accessed July 12, 2010.

8. This model sees government as network integrator. For other design options, with government playing different roles, see Stephen Goldsmith and William D. Eggers (2004, chapter 4).

REFERENCES

Adams, Gina, Kathleen Snyder, and Jodi R. Sandfort. 2002. "Getting and Retaining Child Care Assistance: How Policy and Practice Influence Parents' Experiences." Occasional paper no. 55. Washington, D.C.: Urban Institute.

Agranoff, Robert. 2007. *Managing Within Networks: Adding Value to Public Organizations.* Washington, D.C.: Georgetown University Press.

———. 2008. "Collaborating for Knowledge: Learning from Public Management Networks." In *Big Ideas in Collaborative Public Management,* edited by L. B. Bingham and Robert O'Leary. Armonk, N.Y.: M. E. Sharpe: 162–94.

Agranoff, Robert, and Michael McGuire. 2003. *Collaborative Public Management: New Strategies for Local Governments.* Washington, D.C.: Georgetown University Press.

Albelda, Randy, and Ann Withorn, eds. 2002. *Lost Ground: Welfare Reform, Poverty and Beyond.* Cambridge, Mass.: South End Press.

Allard, Scott W. 2009. *Out of Place: Poverty, Place and the New American Welfare State.* New Haven, Conn.: Yale University Press.

Argyris, Chris, and Donald A. Schon. 1974. *Theory in Practice: Increasing Professional Effectiveness.* San Francisco: Jossey Bass.

Bickers, Kenneth N. 2007. "Service-Contracting, Co-Production, and Coalitions in the Delivery of Employment-Related Services." *Public Administration Quarterly* 31(2): 159–91.

Blank, Rebecca, Sheldon Danziger, and Robert Schoeni, eds. 2006. *Working and Poor: How Economic and Policy Changes Are Affecting Low-Wage Workers.* New York: Russell Sage Foundation.

Blomgren, Lisa B., and Rosemary O'Leary, eds. 2008. *Big Ideas in Collaborative Public Management.* Armonk, N.Y.: M. E. Sharpe.

Brodkin, Evelyn. 1986. *The False Promise of Administrative Reform: Implementing Quality Control in Welfare.* Philadelphia: Temple University Press.

Brown, L. David, and Archana Kalegaonkar. 2002. "Support Organizations and the Evolution of the NGO Sector." *Nonprofit and Voluntary Sector Quarterly* 31(2): 231–58.

Cancian, Maria, Robert Haveman, Daniel Meyer, and Barbara Wolfe. 2002. "Before and After TANF: The Economic Well-Being of Women Leaving Welfare." *Social Service Review* 76(4): 603–41.

Clark, Robert F. 2000. *Maximum Feasible Success: A History of the Community Action Program.* Washington, D.C.: National Association of Community Action Agencies.

Cloward, Richard, and Frances Fox Piven. 1971. *Regulating the Poor: The Functions of Public Welfare.* New York: Random House.

Cooney, Kate. 2007. "Fields, Organizations and Agency: Toward a Multilevel Theory of Institutionalization in Action." *Administration and Society* 39(6): 687–718.

Cordes, Joseph, and Jeffrey R. Henig. 2001. "Nonprofit Human Service Providers in an Era of Privatization: Toward a Theory of Economic and Political Response." *Policy Studies Review* 18(4): 91–110.

Crosby, Barbara C., and John M. Bryson. 2005. *Leadership for the Common Good: Tackling Public Problems in a Shared-Power World.* San Francisco: Jossey-Bass.

Dickert-Conlin, Stacy, Katie Fitzpatrick, and Andrew Hanson. 2005. "Utilization of Income Tax Credits by Low-Income Individuals." *National Tax Journal* 58(4): 743–85.

Ehrenreich, Barbara. 2002. *Nickel and Dimed: On (Not) Getting By in America.* New York: Henry Holt.

Elmore, Richard. 1979. "Backward Mapping: Implementation Research and Policy Decisions." *Political Science Quarterly* 94(425): 601–16.

Ewalt, Jo Ann, and Edward T. Jennings, Jr. 2004. "Administration, Governance, and Policy Tools in Welfare Policy Implementation." *Public Administration Review* 64(4): 449–62.

Fabricant, Michael, and Robert Fisher. 2002. *Settlement Houses Under Siege: The Struggle to Sustain Communication Organizations.* New York: Columbia University Press.

Fredrickson, David G., and H. George Fredrickson. 2007. *Measuring the Performance of the Hollow State.* Washington, D.C.: Georgetown University Press.

Garfinkel, Irwin. 1990. "The Potential of Child Care Tax Credits to Reduce Poverty and Welfare Dependency." *Population Research and Policy Review* 9(1224): 45–63.

Glickman, Norman J., and Lisa J. Servon. 1999. "More than Bricks and Sticks: What Is Community Development Capacity?" *Housing Policy Debate* 9(3): 497.

————. 2003. "By the Numbers: Measuring Community Development Corporations' Capacity." *Journal of Planning Education and Research* 22(3): 240–56.

Goldsmith, Stephen, and William D. Eggers. 2004. *Governing by Network: The New Shape of the Public Sector.* Washington, D.C.: Brookings Institution.

Gordon, Linda. 1994. *Pitied but Not Entitled: Single Mothers and the History of Welfare.* New York: Free Press.

Gordon, Teresa P. 2002. "Who Deserves Help? Who Must Provide?" In *Lost Ground: Welfare Reform, Poverty and Beyond,* edited by Ron Albelda and Anne Withorn. Cambridge, Mass.: South End Press.

Grønbjerg, Kirsten. 1993. *Understanding Nonprofit Funding: Managing Revenue in Social Service and Community Development Organizations.* San Francisco: Jossey Bass.

Hasenfeld, Yeheskel. 1992. *Human Services as Complex Organizations.* Newbury Park, Calif.: Sage Publications.

————. 2010. "The Attributes of Human Service Organizations." In *Human Services as Complex Organizations,* 2d ed. Los Angeles: Sage Publications.

Hasenfeld, Yeheskel, and Lisa E. Powell. 2004. "The Role of Non-Profit Agencies in the Provision of Welfare-to-Work Services." In *Organizational and Structural Dilemmas in Nonprofit Human Service Organizations,* edited by Hillel Schmid. Binghamton, N.Y.: Haworth Press.

Heinrich, Carolyn J., and Youseok Choi. 2007. "Performance-Based Contracting in Social Welfare Programs." *The American Review of Public Administration* 37(4): 409–35.

Herr, Toby, Robert Halpern, and Suzzane Wagner. 1995. *Something Old, Something New: A Case Study of the Post-Employment Services Demonstration in Oregon.* Chicago: Project Match/Erikson Institute.

Herranz, Joaquin. 2008. "The Multisectoral Trilemma of Network Management." *Journal of Public Administration Research and Theory* 18(1): 1–31.

Hill, Heather C. 2003. "Understanding Implementation: Street-Level Bureaucrats' Resources for Reform." *Journal of Public Administration Research and Theory* 13(3): 265–82.

Hjern, Benni, and D. O. Porter. 1981. "Implementation Structures: A New Unit of Administrative Analysis." *Organizational Studies* 2(3964): 211–27.

Honig, Meredith I. 2004. "The New Middle Management: Intermediary Organizations in Education Policy Implementation." *Educational Evaluation and Policy Analysis* 26(1): 65–87.

Jennings, James. 2002. "Welfare Reform and Neighborhoods: Race and Civic Participation." In *Lost Ground: Welfare Reform, Poverty and Beyond*, edited by Ron Albelda and Anne Withorn. Cambridge, Mass: South End Press.

Katz, Michael. 1986. *In the Shadow of the Poorhouse: A Social History of Welfare in America*. New York: Basic Books.

Kickert, Walter, Eric-Hans Klijn, and Joop F. M. Koppenjan, eds. 1997. *Managing Complex Networks: Strategies for the Public Sector*. London: Sage.

Klijn, Erik-Hans. 2005. "Networks and Inter-Organizational Management: Challenging, Steering, Evaluation and the Role of Public Actors in Public Management." *The Oxford Handbook of Public Management*, edited by Ewan Ferlie, Laurence Lynn, and Christopher Pollitt. Oxford: Oxford University Press.

Lemann, Nicholas. 1988. "The Unfinished War." *Atlantic Monthly*, December. Available at: www.theatlantic.com/past/politics/poverty/lemunf1.htm; accessed July 11, 2010.

Maynard-Moody, Steven, and Michael Musheno. 2003. *Cops, Teachers, Counselors: Stories from the Frontlines of Public Service*. Ann Arbor: University of Michigan Press.

McDaniel, Paul. 2002. "Tax Expenditures as Tools of Government Action." In *The Tools of Government Action: Guide to the New Governance*. New York: Oxford University Press.

Meyers, Marcia, Bonnie Glaser, and Karin MacDonald. 1998. "On the Front Lines of Welfare Delivery: Are Workers Implementing Policy Reforms?" *Journal of Policy Analysis and Management* 17(1): 1–22.

Milward, H. Brint, Keith Provan, Amy Fish, Kimberly R. Isett, and Kun Huang. 2010. "Governance and Collaboration: An Evolutionary Study of Two Mental Health Networks." *Journal of Public Administration and Research Theory* 2(supp 1): 125–41.

Moynihan, Donald P. 2008. *The Dynamics of Performance Management: Constructing Information and Reform*. Washington, D.C.: Georgetown University Press.

O'Toole, Jr., Laurence J., Kenneth J. Meier, and Sean Nicholson-Crotty. 2005. "Managing Upward, Downward and Outward." *Public Management Review* 7(1): 45–68.

Patterson, James T. 2000. *America's Struggle Against Poverty in the Twentieth Century*. 4th ed. Cambridge, Mass.: Harvard University Press.

Powers, Elizabeth T. 2003. "Children's Health and Maternal Work Activity: Static and Dynamics Estimates under Alternative Disability Definitions." *Journal of Human Resources* 38(3): 213–43.

Provan, Keith, and H. Brint Milward. 1994. "Integration of Community-Based Services for the Severely Mentally Ill and the Structure of Public Funding: A

Comparison of Flow Systems." *Journal of Health Politics, Policy and Law* 19(4901): 865–94.

Rank, Mark. 1994. *Living On the Edge: The Realities of Welfare in America*. New York: Columbia University Press.

Rubinstein, Gwen, and Andrea Mayo. 2007. "Training Policy in Brief: An Overview of Federal Workforce Development Policies." Report. Washington, D.C.: Workforce Alliance.

Salamon, Lester. 1995. *Partners in Public Service: Government-Nonprofit Relations in the Modern Welfare State*. Baltimore: Johns Hopkins University Press.

———. 2002. *The Tools of Government Action: A Guide to the New Governance*. New York: Oxford University Press.

Sandfort, Jodi R. 1999. "The Structural Impediments to Human Service Collaboration: The Case of Frontline Welfare Reform Implementation." *Social Service Review* 73(3): 314–39.

———. 2000. "Moving Beyond Discretion and Outcomes: Examining Public Management from the Frontlines of the Welfare System." *Journal of Public Administration Research and Theory* 10(4): 729–56.

Sandfort, Jodi R., and H. Brint Milward. 2008. "Collaborative Service Provision in the Public Sector." In *Handbook of Inter-Organizational Relations*, edited by Steve Cropper, Marke Ebers, Chris Huxham, and Peter Smith Ring. Oxford: Oxford University Press.

Siefert, Kristine, Colleen Helflin, Mary Corcoran, and David Williams. 2004. "Food Insufficiency and Physical and Mental Health in a Longitudinal Survey of Welfare Recipients." *Journal of Health and Social Behavior* 45(2): 171–86.

Skocpol, Theda. 1992. *Protecting Soldiers and Mothers: The Political Origins of Social Policy in the United States*. Cambridge, Mass.: Harvard University Press.

Smith, Brent C. 2008. "The Sources and Uses of Funds for Community Development Financial Institutions: The Role of the Nonprofit Intermediary." *Nonprofit and Voluntary Sector Quarterly* 37(1): 19.

Smith, Steven R. 2005. "Managing the Challenges of Government Contracts." In *The Jossey-Bass Handbook of Nonprofit Leadership and Management*, edited by Robert Herman and Associates. San Francisco: Jossey-Bass.

Smith, Steven R., and Michael Lipsky. 1993. *Nonprofits for Hire: The Welfare State in the Age of Contracting*. Cambridge, Mass.: Harvard University Press.

Soss, Joe. 2002. *Unwanted Claims: The Politics of Participation in the U.S. Welfare System*. Ann Arbor: University of Michigan Press.

Soss, Joe, Sanford F. Schram, Thomas P. Vartanian, and Erin O'Brien. 2001. "Setting the Terms of Relief: Explaining State Policy Choices in the Devolution Revolution." *American Journal of Political Science* 45(2): 378–95.

Stone, Deborah. 2008. *The Samaritan's Dilemma: Should Government Help Your Neighbor?* New York: Nations Books.

Van Slyke, David M. 2003. "The Mythology of Privatization in Contracting for Social Services." *Public Administration Review* 63(3): 296–315.

Walker, Christopher. 1993. "Nonprofit Housing Development: Status, Trends and Prospects." *Housing Policy Debate* 4(3): 369.

Walker, Christopher, and John Foster-Bey. 2004. "Community Development Intermediation and Its Lessons for the Workforce Field." In *Workforce Intermediaries for the Twenty-First Century*, edited by Robert P. Giloth. Philadelphia: Temple University Press.

Zedlewski, Sheila, Ajay Chaudry, and Margaret Simms. 2008. A *New Safety Net for Low-Income Families*. Low-Income Working Families Project. Washington, D.C.: Urban Institute (July).

INDEX

Boldface numbers refer to figures and tables.

243